The Green IT Guide

How to Make Your IT Systems and Business Sustainable and Carbon Neutral

Second Edition

Mike Halsey

Apress®

The Green IT Guide: How to Make Your IT Systems and Business Sustainable and Carbon Neutral, Second Edition

Mike Halsey
Charente, France

ISBN-13 (pbk): 979-8-8688-1232-3   ISBN-13 (electronic): 979-8-8688-1233-0
https://doi.org/10.1007/979-8-8688-1233-0

Managing Director, Apress Media LLC: Welmoed Spahr
Acquisitions Editor: Ryan Byrnes
Development Editor: Laura Berendson
Coordinating Editor: Gryffin Winkler

Cover designed by eStudioCalamar

Distributed to the book trade worldwide by Apress Media, LLC, 1 New York Plaza, New York, NY 10004, U.S.A. Phone 1-800-SPRINGER, fax (201) 348-4505, e-mail orders-ny@springer-sbm.com, or visit www.springeronline.com. Apress Media, LLC is a California LLC and the sole member (owner) is Springer Science + Business Media Finance Inc (SSBM Finance Inc). SSBM Finance Inc is a **Delaware** corporation.

For information on translations, please e-mail booktranslations@springernature.com; for reprint, paperback, or audio rights, please e-mail bookpermissions@springernature.com.

Apress titles may be purchased in bulk for academic, corporate, or promotional use. eBook versions and licenses are also available for most titles. For more information, reference our Print and eBook Bulk Sales web page at http://www.apress.com/bulk-sales.

Any source code or other supplementary material referenced by the author in this book is available to readers on GitHub (https://github.com/Apress). For more detailed information, please visit https://www.apress.com/gp/services/source-code.

If disposing of this product, please recycle the paper

*It's amazing to me to even consider this,
but this is my 25th book (frankly I never thought
I'd get past one). My great thanks must go
to my late mother, who gave me the help, support,
and the vital push I needed to start this amazing career.*

*My sincere thanks must also go to all the people
at Apress whom I've worked with now for more than a
decade, with special mention in no particular order
for Jonathan Hassell, Mark Powers, Steve Weiss,
Gwenan Spearing, James T. DeWolf, and Jonathan
Gennick. You have all given me so much support
and encouragement over the years, and I have
learned a great deal from you all. Thank you.*

Table of Contents

About the Author

Mike Halsey is the author of 25 books on IT systems, Microsoft Windows, productivity, and accessibility. He has been a Microsoft Most Valuable Professional (MVP) awardee since 2011 and is a recognized technical expert. He is known for being the author of the popular *Windows Troubleshooting* books (Apress) and video courses for Pluralsight and has also written *The IT Support Handbook* (Apress), now in its second edition.

Mike is well versed in the problems and issues that PC users, IT pros, and system administrators face when supporting and maintaining all aspects of a PC ecosystem. He spent many years as a teacher and built skills in helping people understand sometimes intimidating subjects in easy-to-understand ways and put these skills to great effect in his books and training videos. Mike lives in the south of France with his border collies, Evan, Robbie, and Téo, and tries to live as sustainable a life as possible. You can contact him on Twitter, Mastodon.social, and Bluesky, all @MikeHalsey.

About the Technical Reviewer

 **Laurent Gébeau** lives close to Paris, France. He is a Microsoft Certified Professional (MCP) and has been troubleshooting Windows, network, and computer problems since 1994. In January 2004, Laurent was awarded the Most Valuable Professional (MVP) status by Microsoft, renewed every year since. After more than 30 years of managing IT in small and medium companies, Laurent is now the co-owner of a company, giving IT services to other companies: computers, servers, security, cloud services. See `https://www.axeperf.com` for more information. He has also created `https://www.toutwindows.com` (25 years) and `https://www.cloud-pour-tous.fr/`. Laurent is passionate about IT, networks, Internet, and photography.

Acknowledgments

With thanks for Ed Waldron and Chris Anthony

CHAPTER 1

Understanding Your Place on Planet Earth

There have been a great many major issues that have troubled the world and humanity over the centuries, and on all of these issues there have been advocates and deriders – subjects such as democracy vs. communism, the treatment of animals, one religion vs. another, borders, equality and gender identity, where people settle and why, and more besides.

This isn't anything new and in fact is something that we should embrace and be proud of. I want to get this point out of the way from the very start. I am not here to be all preachy and holier-than-thou. I am not here to even claim that climate change exists (though the Earth is definitely not flat and man *has* been to the Moon).

Difference of opinion is a great thing. As a species, humanity is extraordinarily varied. This doesn't make us any different from plants, animals, birds, and fish, where we can find so much variety that it's not even all been discovered yet. I'm not talking about how people look, their gender or none, where they're from, or what they like to do behind the closed door of their own home. I'm talking about people having a difference of opinion.

Within the scientific community, there is difference of opinion about climate change. This covers every aspect of the subject from whether it exists at all to whether it's been instigated by humanity, to what the effects of a changing climate will be anyway.

M. Halsey, *The Green IT Guide*, https://doi.org/10.1007/979-8-8688-1233-0_1

It's this difference of opinion that spurs scientific and philosophical achievement and helps the human race learn and progress. I'm fairly certain, though obviously there is no evidence for this, that early mankind might have been split for a while over the use of bones to hit animals over the head to knock them out or of the bow and arrow to hunt at medium to long range.

It's not a stretch to imagine this might be the case, with the "old guard" grunting there was nothing wrong with just spearing a fish and trying to kill an antelope at long range was a waste of time. In this circumstance there would have been some debate, some watching, probably some mild laughter when it all went wrong, and finally a mutual understanding that perhaps this bow and arrow contraption might not be such a bad idea after all.

So it is with climate change. Some people say it doesn't exist; some people say it does. Some people say we've caused it, and other people say it would have happened anyway. Both sides of this create a debate, and it is from debate that we learn, both from each other and also by using this as a launchpad to undertake research so we can better understand what is *really* going on.

What isn't in question though is that the Earth has been going through a fairly turbulent time in recent years, and flooding, rising temperatures, melting ice caps, and other things we term "natural disasters" are more frequent and much worse than they used to be.

When you add into this that the cost of living around the world is getting more expensive and the cost of doing business is getting more and more expensive with regulation, energy costs, and more pushing up the price of everything, it's clear we should be doing something about it, if only to drive the bills back down again.

So this brings me to the point of this book. It's not to say, "You're at fault. You're doing it wrong," but rather to look at the way we conduct business in the twenty-first century from a more philosophical viewpoint and to see if there's anything we can do to improve things for ourselves, our stakeholders, our customers, our suppliers, and our communities.

This is the approach I take in this book, one of inclusivity and corporate responsibility; after all, you wouldn't be doing the right thing if you deliberately pushed up the running costs for your business, would you?

One thing is for certain though, that the science and the debate is changing regularly and rapidly, so I also won't be addressing many specific technologies that I know will change and be upgraded over the coming years, though there have been innovations in the last few years. I'll talk about such subjects in more general terms to keep this book as relevant into the future as it is on the day I began writing it. I hope you find it helpful.

What Is Climate Change and Why Does It Matter?

Climate change, also known as global warming, climate variability, and a multitude of other terms, is something that first came to mainstream attention in the late 1970s when scientists noticed that the ozone layer, the part of the Earth's stratosphere that absorbs solar radiation, was thinning. It took about 20 years, however, before the public and political debate really began to start about what was causing it, what the knock-on and other effects might be, and what else might be going on that we hadn't noticed yet, thus resulting in the Rio summit in 1992 deciding – at least – to stop chlorofluorocarbons (CFCs) responsible for the troubles.

The political establishment has now broadly accepted the case for climate change, and there have been treaties and initiatives such as the Paris Climate Accords of 2016, to try and do something about it.

There are some in the scientific community who say we must act immediately to prevent a global catastrophe, some who say we can act more slowly, and others that claim it's likely already too late to do anything at all and that we should instead pack up and just go down the pub (I might have exaggerated that last part).

What is crystal clear, at least to this observer, is that governments aren't acting anywhere near as quickly as business is. Let's take vehicles as an example. I'm originally from the UK and now live in the south of France. I drive a small, completely electric vehicle (EV) to ferry me around, and shortly after first getting this vehicle, I had to go to the city of Angouleme for my French residency permit meeting. Upon arrival, I discovered the town's electric car charging points had been completely removed.

It is this that I term as "squeaky bum time," that highlights just how far behind governments are. Europe is set to ban the sale of all new cars that run on gasoline (petrol) or diesel from 2035. The UK has an even more ambitious target of banning sales by 2035 at the latest. France has a reasonably good network of electric car charging infrastructure, and since I wrote the first edition of this book, it's been greatly expanded. But it can still be spotty, patchy, and unreliable in places, especially outside of the major metropolitan towns and city regions. There are now a lot of free applications to know if an electric charging point will be free and available for you at your destination, but also there's no way to know if it'll be working at all or, as in my own example, even exist in the first place.

Some apps and services exist to help us all make sense of this, but they're spotty and patchy as well, being only as good as the information they're fed. In the opinion of this observer, if governments pulled their collective fingers out, things might not be so bad, but at the rate they're all progressing in the deployment of electric charging points, there will likely never even remotely be enough to meet demand by the time all new cars on the road have to be electric.

The Benefits to Business

Corporations on the other hand have picked up this ball and rolled with it. Many of them are seeing the benefits in adopting more environmentally friendly policies and practices, and it is these initiatives, from the Gates' foundation machine that can make clean drinking water from poo to the creation of planes that fly purely from electricity or hydrogen and container ships that can potentially capture 95% of the carbon they emit, that we tend to hear about on the news.

The benefits to these businesses are very clear: they make the business more popular, raise its profile, and hopefully result in that business becoming much more profitable and competitive. This should be a no-brainer to anybody running a business from a small enterprise to a global corporation.

I would argue that *this* is why climate change matters to business. To bring it down to its simplest and crudest point, it's good PR. Nobody is going to stop using your products and services because you're seen as helping the environment or at least having targets for when you will be helping the environment.

On the contrary in fact, word quickly gets around that company A is reducing the power consumption and dissipated heat from its data centers and that company B has switched all of its paper supplies, from letterheads to loo roll, to bamboo.

If the end result of driving down costs and driving up efficiency also means one less ice cap will melt or that a village on the coast won't be hit by a flood, that's just the icing on the cake. A cynical view you might say, and I'd agree, but if it helps make the medicine easier to swallow, it's probably worth it.

The Benefits to Individuals

So while the benefits to business are pretty much summed up by profits and money, what are the benefits to individuals? I'm a self-employed person sitting in my home office. I have no employees to inspire, no stakeholders to keep on side, and no customers to impress. You might be unsurprised to hear that this too comes down to money.

I don't want you to think at this point that I'm entirely motivated by greed because I'm not. There are real and very tangible benefits to reducing our carbon emissions and using and creating technologies that are more environmentally sustainable.

Money, however, is just as important to individual people as it is to corporations. If you can remember the last time your energy bills were reduced by your supplier, then you're very probably luckier than most. Just as with business, the cost of living just keeps rising, and with two major events at the beginning of the twenty-first century, the 2008 economic downturn and the Covid pandemic, still to pay for, it's not going to be going down for a considerable time yet.

If, however, we use more energy-efficient IT and other devices in our homes, the very first we'll notice is that our bills go down, and I can't see anybody complaining about that.

Setting an Example

I'll give you an example here of how changing behaviors for individuals can help with climate change as since I wrote the first edition of this book, I've changed my own behaviors considerably and absolutely for the better.

This begins with the products I buy for my home and the food I eat. I made the decision to stop buying from the supermarkets, which are all large corporations that screw over small producers and especially farmers (this is all well documented) and ship and transport products all around countries, continents, and the planet in the name of giving the consumer "choice."

Then the supermarket says they're driving down prices to help the consumer, which of course is utter rubbish. Do you ever see the profits for the big supermarkets drop? Because I don't. They're only dropping prices because they have other big supermarkets to compete with, and they're all still making big profits and paying huge salaries to their boards and CEOs and huge dividends to their shareholders.

When these companies say they're "driving down prices," what they really mean is they're squeezing and screwing over their suppliers. For the last few years, I've lived in the middle of farmland, and it's really brought home to me just how hard these people work for the food and other goods they produce. I have *never* seen these people take a day off work and certainly never seen them take a vacation. Even on Christmas morning, they need to be out feeding the cattle and performing essential and routine maintenance and other jobs around their farms.

So I stopped buying from the supermarkets anything that I could buy either from a local supplier or from a small business elsewhere within France. By my calculation this would eliminate the need for many of the products and foods I buy to be transported by road and eliminate almost entirely the need for goods to be transported by sea or air.

It's been hugely successful for me, too, and the research into what's available and where I can get it was kind of fun. The list of products I now source locally or from small, independent French companies includes bread (obviously, I live in France after all), meat, fish, eggs, vegetables, fruit, milk, cheese, coffee, ice cream, all my dog food including kibble (which is now insect-based and thus far higher in protein than regular biscuits), and tinned meat. Hand and body soap, washing liquid for clothes and dishes, dishwasher tablets, and floor, surface, and toilet cleaners also come from small French businesses along with bamboo-based toilet, kitchen roll, clothes fabric softener and shower gel. Additionally my drinking water comes fresh from a local spring.

There are also potato chips (crisps to the rest of the world) available locally I've not tried yet and regional vineyards from whom I can purchase wine. Other products I purchase occasionally include jam, honey, soup, lasagna, quiche, and pies, and other meals can be purchased from local businesses or markets.

I know that not everybody will have a local spring they can get water from, but most places, even in a town or city, will have a market where traders are selling vegetables, fruit, and meat. It's well worth exploring your options as I've found with many people that the usual reasons for not doing so, such as "We're very busy and don't have time," don't hold water very well. Not only is exploring local markets fun, but if families have time to watch Netflix, they probably have time to pop to a market at lunchtime or on their way home from work.

You might ask why I do this and what the advantages are, beyond having access to very fresh fruits and vegetables. From my own point of view, I'm either keeping money within my local community, which benefits the local community and ultimately benefits me, too, because reinvestment is made in my own community, or I'm helping support small businesses, which create jobs in their local communities and keep that money in those communities too. This is not to mention the benefits that come from products not being shipped, flown, and transported unnecessarily.

Lastly I have built my own vegetable garden, called a potager here in France, which is doing extremely well growing a selection of fruits and vegetables from potatoes to strawberries (see Figure 1-1). I'll be purchasing some pots for the terrace in the next couple of weeks in which I intend to grow my own herbs.

Figure 1-1. *My home potager is doing extremely well*

Then of course there are the other things I can do and am doing including the installation of solar panels and new double glazing and generally trying to be more conscious of the goods I buy and where in the world they come from. Let's face it, buying less crap that we don't need can only be a good thing from whichever way you look at it.

In the process of trying to decarbonize my own life, I've discovered several things that have surprised me. I've already mentioned that some of it I've found fun, such as attending local markets (especially in good weather) and finding small French businesses online that can provide goods I would otherwise purchase at the supermarkets.

Other things have surprised me though, chief among which is the high quality of the goods on offer from smaller businesses. These companies have sprung up because there was a niche they could fill. This might have been to provide higher-quality products than were available elsewhere, or it could be to put a different spin on a product.

Let me take the dog food as an example. The biscuits (kibble) I said were insect-based. They also include other nutrients such as vegetables, but an insect-based diet is much higher in protein than regular food and is becoming more popular not just for our furry friends but also for ourselves. One of the reasons is that it's very sustainable. It takes a long time to breed a cow, but you can have a room full of insects in a couple of weeks. It's the same logic behind using bamboo as a paper substitute.

B2C

Two other benefits of purchasing products from small businesses rather than major supermarkets are the perks that supermarkets simply cannot offer you. For me the biggest benefit is a subscription-based model. You might have already seen Amazon doing this, offering to automatically send you product X or Y every few weeks or months when you're likely to need more.

Both the dog biscuits and the tinned meat come on a subscription model. The number of dogs doesn't change week to week, the amount they eat doesn't change, and so I know exactly how much food I need and when I'm likely to need it. The same can be said for other products including coffee (I'd need to get a coffee delivery every few days then – Ed). This means that I no longer need to think about shopping for dog food; it just arrives at the door when I need it.

The other benefit is that when you buy products on a subscription basis, companies will often offer you a rolling discount. I get discounts of up to 15% on both the dog biscuits and the tinned meat, and this can only be a good thing, especially when the postage is also included.

This is all part of a move by smaller and even some major companies to ship directly to the consumer instead of to major chain stores. It's called B2C (business to consumer), sometimes BTC. There are a huge number of companies doing this successfully. You might be familiar with Harry's, who deliver shaving products for men, or perhaps HelloFresh, who deliver most of the ingredients you need to cook meals, and in exactly the right quantities for your household, to you on a regular basis.

A few bigger companies also follow the B2C model. Tesla is probably the largest and best known example. They don't provide their cars to independent dealers; you can only purchase a Tesla online or from one of their own showrooms.

I can only see B2C becoming more popular, not receding, and in the UK where I used to live, the effects of this are already beginning to be seen with the largest supermarket chains, including Tesco and Sainsbury's, closing some of their huge mega-out-of-town sites, to focus more on smaller stores in more central locations, and I've heard rumblings about US retailers including Walmart considering the same.

Not all companies in the B2C model will succeed though. All the mattresses in my home come from a B2C company called Hypnia (and they're all super-comfy), but perhaps their better known rival firm,

Casper, has struggled in recent years. Many other B2C companies have either folded completely or pivoted to selling to resellers instead (B2B, or business to business). So there are risks involved, especially when getting food on subscription. The dog biscuit company sent me an email a few months ago saying they were stopping the sale of kibble for cats due to low demand. Then the customer has to find a different supplier, and sometimes quickly.

Out with the Old?

There is a long-used phrase where I hail from, "Out with the old, in with the new," and it's widely accepted that a shiny new computer, tablet, or smartphone will be faster, more efficient, and better in every way than one that's even a few years old, let along something that is ten years or perhaps even several decades old, such as the transistor radio that has sat on the kitchen windowsill in your grandmother's house since you were small.

This approach to technology is a double-edged sword, and there are two very important threads here that must be considered. The first is energy efficiency, and the second is security and privacy.

I'll talk much more about this in Chapter 3, but the short version is that crime on the Internet, both criminal and state-sponsored, doesn't stand still, and older IT equipment can be highly vulnerable to hacking and malware, which is the real reason Microsoft, Google, and Apple keep updating their operating systems (OSs) and you get near-constant updates to the software and apps you use.

To the first point, however, it's not necessarily true that newer technology is more power-efficient than older tech. Again something I'll detail in full in Chapter 2, while new processors and circuitry contain smaller and smaller components, each of which consumes less power than their predecessors, they're also far more powerful than the technology they replace.

These smaller circuits in modern devices can result in excess heat dissipation (and any excess heat given off by a device is energy that's not being used by the system and that is just being wasted instead by throwing it off into the air) and needing more powerful and energy-consuming chargers and power supplies to get it all working in the first place.

As an example of this, in late 2020 Apple released its M1 processor line. This was a new series of chips that would power the coming generations of iPads and iMac desktops and MacBook laptops and that were a powerful match for their rivals from Intel and AMD. These chips evolved from, and were built on, foundations Apple laid several years earlier in the processors they were making for the iPhone, and it speaks as to just how powerful those iPhone processors had become over time.

The iPhone 12, released around the same time, needed a charger that consumed a minimum of 20 W (watts) of electricity, and we use wattage to measure power draw, while the iPhone 6, released seven years prior but still receiving operating system updates after the launch of the iPhone 12, only needed a 5 W charger, which might be small in itself, but across a population that can scale to a significant change in overall energy consumption. Last, Samsung and Xiaomi now need up to 30 W to charge efficiently.

But, I hear you cry, the iPhone 12 is a much better phone than the iPhone 6, with a better, brighter, larger screen, a far superior camera, and more besides. I use the iPhone as an example because everybody reading this book will know what it is and how it has evolved as a product. It's safe to say though that not everybody needs the features or power of a new phone, just as not everybody needs the features or power of a new laptop or desktop computer.

There are people in the world who just want to do some fairly straightforward things with their phone, such as messaging, maps, and perhaps even making the odd phone call (do people still do this? – Ed). This is just as there are some people who on their home or work PCs just need to use Microsoft Office or maybe only a web browser.

At the time of writing this, Microsoft state on their website that the minimum requirements to install and run Microsoft Office are a dual-core processor running at 1.6 GHz or faster, 4 GB of RAM (memory) or just 2 GB for the 32-bit version that does almost all the same things, 4 GB of available disk space, a screen resolution of 1280 by 768 pixels, and DirectX 9 to power the graphics.

DirectX is significant because it means we can gauge what hardware we can run Office on. DirectX 9 was first released back in 2002 for Windows XP, and the rest of the specification, such as the minimum 2 GB memory requirement and 4 GB storage, fit well with PCs from the time.

Now it's very easy to argue that if you install any software or operating system on a device that just meets the absolute minimum required specifications, then you'll have a truly horrible experience, and having hardware that's newer and faster will give you a much better time.

But this would still give us PC hardware released for Windows Vista in 2006, which (I'm writing this book in 2024) is 18-year-old hardware. The minimum specifications for Windows 11, released in 2021, state an eighth-generation Intel Core processor or newer. These processors, codenamed "Coffee Lake," "Amber Lake," and "Whiskey Lake," were first released in 2017, meaning when Windows 11 was released, a four-year-old computer would not only be considered perfectly adequate for running the operating system at its launch, but it would also be supported for a maximum of another ten years, potentially making the PC 14 years old when it's no longer receiving updates. Windows 7 as an example received updates in extended support to the end of 2022, 13 years after it launched.

Going back to that Windows Vista PC, there's no reason why it couldn't still be in use today as support for Windows 10 doesn't end until October 2025, and then Microsoft are offering an optional three years of paid-for updates, potentially making that simple Office PC 22 years old when its finally retired. This ought to be some kind of record, but you can be reasonably certain that for specific repetitive tasks in business, such as payroll, many of these computers will still be in use today.

The upshot of this is that we can reasonably expect not to have to retire a PC for 12 years from the date of purchase. This fits well with consumers especially who, and I've never been able to figure this out, are more than happy to drop $1,000 on a new smartphone every year, but are usually very reluctant to replace the PC on which they actually get work done. But more on all this later in the book.

When I was getting started writing my book *Troubleshooting and Supporting Windows 11* (Apress, 2022), a close friend and his colleague who worked as the IT managers for a UK school discovered an old Windows XP laptop that was in excellent physical condition and that still happily booted to the desktop (see Figure 1-2). This PC would potentially have been between 16 and 21 years old (XP was released in 2001 and Vista was released in 2006).

Figure 1-2. *Even older laptops can be in use years later*

So where do we sit with how power-efficient computers are? I'll cover this in much more depth in Chapter 2, but the short version is that this will vary considerably between phones, tablets, and laptops on the one side and desktop PCs on the other. With the former it's quite straightforward to gauge the power consumption as the wattage of the power supply will be printed on a label on the unit, and you'll know how long it takes to charge from an empty battery to a full one. Desktop PCs, especially older ones, will be less energy-efficient as they get older – this is for several reasons. The power supplies in them work rather like car engines in that as they get older the amount of power they produce reduces and they have to work harder to output a high level of energy. While a PC running customer relationship software isn't analogous to driving a classic car up a very steep hill, it's still true that more energy will be needed to achieve the same tasks.

In addition to the power output of the power supply (PSU) being reduced, we then have to factor in other components on the motherboard, from the processor to the hard disk, that will use older fabrication technologies, 12 nm (nanometers), 15 nm, and so on, rather than the 7 nm or 3 nm tech of more modern chips.

If you've ever been in science class at school and tried to run an electrical signal down a thick piece of wire, you'll have discovered that the amount of power you get at the other end is actually more than if you put the same amount of power down a much thinner piece of wire.

This might seem incorrect but it's how resistance works. The thinner the wire, the greater its resistance as thinner wires drop more volts, and the less volts a component gets, the harder it has to work; thus, it draws more power than a thicker wire would. This in theory makes older computers much more energy-efficient, and so there's a trade-off to be made, but it begins to get really complicated when you factor in the increasing power and power usage requirements of newer components and processors, the need for security, the desire to get people working as quickly as possible, and the power wasted waiting for an older PC to start compared with the few seconds of a new one.

When you then scale this up to data center workloads and the amount of data and processing they are tasked with doing, the newest, fastest technology will turn out to be much more efficient in the long run.

All of this I'll help you understand in detail throughout this book. This extends not just to the devices on our desks and in our pockets, but to the services we buy into and use – while we're on the subject of older hardware and its power efficiency though ...

A Brief History of Computers and the Climate

The computer boom that came out of the 1970s and 1980s was actually quite late in the development of computers. It's arguable that calculating machines, dating all the way back to ancient Greece, can be considered "computational devices" though the first real computer in the world, at least by the standards we judge computers today, was the Colossus machine at Bletchley Park in the UK (see Figure 1-3).

Figure 1-3. *Colossus was designed to decode Nazi communications*

Colossus and Enigma

Colossus, which I've been lucky enough to visit myself, was designed and built during the Second World War in 1943 to help the British decode Nazi communications.

These communications, dubbed radio teleprinter messages, had been encrypted using a device that was at the time unknown to the allies and was later discovered to be the Lorenz SZ42 cipher.

In use by 1944, the Colossus machines (there were ten of them in total) with the help of expert code-breakers from the UK such as Alan Turing, and especially from Poland who remain largely uncredited to this day, were able to decipher the messages after German operators made a mistake in 1941 that led to two different messages being transmitted using the same cipher.

Additionally on May 9, 1941, the British Royal Navy captured a German U-Boat, U-110, in the North Atlantic. On board was an Enigma cipher machine that was used in the field by the German military to decode messages encrypted using the Lorenz machines. The destroyers HMS Bulldog, HMS Broadway, and HMS Aubrietia attacked U-110 whose crew surrendered after the submarine was seriously damaged. The device was taken to Bletchley Park in Buckinghamshire, 53 miles (85 km) from London, where researchers from Poland, who had been working to decipher messages from the machine as early as 1932, were consulted. The Lorenz machines had already been in use in Germany as a business tool since the early 1920s.

By 1942 the allies were regularly able to read messages sent by the Nazis although the decryption process was slow and handled by operators using pencil and paper, though in February 1942, the Germans, realizing messages were being intercepted, introduced more complexity to the cipher, scuppering most further attempts to decipher the codes until the summer of 1943.

By the time of D-Day on the sixth of June, 1944 (80 years ago almost to the day I'm writing this – it's the fourth of June, 2024, now), and with the help of the Colossus machines, the German ciphers were broken and military communications could be read in near real time. This was taken advantage of by the allies, who kept the knowledge that they had broken the cipher completely secret.

Misinformation was fed to the Nazis about the D-Day landings, and the decrypted messages were able to be used to confirm the Germans had fallen for the ploy. Because of Colossus, German naval messages were being intercepted, decrypted, translated, and sent to allied commanders within just 2.5 hours, giving the allies a huge tactical advantage that won them the war.

ENIAC and ARPANET

It is safe to say that many of the computing advances that followed in later years were also funded and implemented by the military. ENIAC, the Electronic Numerical Integrator and Computer, went live at the US Army's

Ballistic Research Laboratory in December 1945 and was used to study the feasibility of nuclear weapons.

The Internet itself came out of ARPA, the Advanced Research Projects Agency of the US Department of Defense. ARPANET (Advanced Research Projects Agency Network) as it was called began development in 1966 to enable connections to remote computers, and in 1969 those first connections took place. By 1975 the project had been considered a success, and control was passed to the Defense Communications Agency.

It's not all bad news with the militarism of early computing though as both ENIAC and ARPANET were later handed over to academia, ENIAC being given to the University of Pennsylvania in 1946 and ARPANET being expanded to universities in 1981.

ARPANET was formally decommissioned in 1990 after the creation of what we now know to be the Internet, and the US National Science Foundation and the US Computer Science Network permitted worldwide proliferation of their new TCP/IP-based system. Sadly all the Colossus machines were dismantled by the British government and their existence kept secret for several decades afterward.

Birth of the IBM PC

It was the Americans again who pushed forth with what we call modern computing, and IBM (International Business Machines) who made popular typewriters at the time wanted to create an affordable computer to be sold to businesses.

This affordability criteria resulted in IBM's engineers buying almost all the parts off the shelf for what would become the IBM 5150 Personal Computer when it was released in August 1981.

Rival US company Compaq saw an opportunity with this off-the-shelf approach to release their own PCs, but IBM had copyrighted the BIOS, programming on a chip on the motherboard that told the hardware and software how they should communicate with one another.

Undeterred, Compaq circumvented IBM's copyright by setting up two small teams of engineers. The first of these teams disassembled the IBM BIOS, detailing what it did and how it worked. The second team, not having any contact with the IBM BIOS at all, used the notes from the first team to build a completely new BIOS that did all of the same things.

Phoenix Technologies (known as Phoenix Software at the time) used a similar approach to create their own IBM-compatible BIOS, and the explosion in growth of the IBM-compatible PC market quickly followed. Phoenix's BIOS and UEFI (Unified Extensible Firmware Interface) technologies are still used on modern PCs today.

The First Data Centers and Supercomputers

Data centers are everywhere in the modern world as computing and business has moved inexorably to the cloud. They're not a new concept, however, with the first data centers being based around the ENIAC computers in the 1940s. As computers became smaller and more useful to both academia and business, they were able to fit in a single room within a premises where data and computing for the organization took place, usually by departments having to book time on the machines a few weeks in advance.

It wasn't until 1997 that the modern data center started to appear, enabling companies and individuals around the world to take advantage of fast Internet connectivity (well, fast at the time anyway).

The first supercomputer appeared in 1960 at the US Navy Research and Development Center. LARC (Livermore Advanced Research Computer) had significantly more processing power than everyday computers and spawned an industry that included the IBM 7030 Stretch, which was 100 times as powerful as a modern computer at the time of its launch. Perhaps the most famous supercomputer was the Cray-1, launched in 1975; it was known for its circular shape around which was a small seating area covering the power supplies and cooling systems.

Watt About Efficiency?

As you might imagine with the earliest computers and servers, power efficiency wasn't really the aim. Of course these machines could give off a tremendous amount of heat, with dissipating heat being energy that's not being used for computational tasks and is therefore expended as wasted energy.

You might wonder where this history of servers, data centers, and supercomputers fits with the modern story of climate change. This is where we hit a conundrum as we have modern data centers and supercomputers pumping out huge amounts of heat and using huge volumes of electricity that's generated by power stations that also pollute the environment, doing all the computational work for scientists and governments on what climate change is and how we can combat it. It's perhaps one of the most dysfunctional and co-dependent relationships in history.

This means we have to look at the history of computers in an open-ended fashion. This is because the original IBM 5150 PC only came with 63 W (watt) power supply, compared with the typical 500 W or larger power supply for a desktop PC 40 years later, but those early power supplies were horribly inefficient and wasted huge amounts of electricity by turning it into heat.

In 1992, the Environmental Protection Agency (EPA) created an eco-certification for electronic devices, called Energy Star.

In 2004 a new initiative was launched in the computer industry called 80 Plus. This was a certification program aimed at informing purchasers how efficient the power supplies in their computers were. This program allowed makers of power supplies that were 80% or more efficient in turning electricity into useful power to more easily promote the fact, and they had different categories (see Table 1-1).

Table 1-1. Efficiencies for the 80 Plus certification program

80 Plus Test Type	115 V Internal Non-redundant				230 V Internal Redundant				230 V Internal Non-redundant			
Percentage of Rated Load	10%	20%	50%	100%	10%	20%	50%	100%	10%	20%	50%	100%
80 Plus		80%	80%	80%						82%	85%	82%
80 Plus Bronze		82%	85%	82%		81%	85%	81%		85%	88%	85%
80 Plus Silver		85%	88%	85%		85%	89%	85%		87%	90%	87%
80 Plus Gold		87%	90%	87%		88%	92%	88%		90%	92%	89%
80 Plus Platinum		90%	92%	89%		90%	94%	91%		92%	94%	90%
80 Plus Titanium	90%	92%	94%	90%	90%	94%	96%	91%	90%	94%	96%	94%

By contrast, the power supply in the IBM 5150 was 60– 70% efficient, meaning up to 40% of the electricity consumed was wasted, and this is a lot.

Now there are billions of computers in the world today on desktops and in data centers compared with the thousands of the early to mid-1980s. This low power efficiency of older computers wasn't deliberate, as there were limitations to the technology available at the time, and there simply wasn't the emphasis on power efficiency that we have today.

Another major change that has occurred during this period is a far greater emphasis on the longevity of components. You might remember, if you're as old as I am (I'm embarrassingly old – Ed), that electronics could reasonably be expected to conk out after five or six years and that you would look to replace a desktop PC every three or four years – this is possibly what prompted the three-year cycle for the releases of new Windows versions. We've already been looking in this chapter at 10–14 years using a PC before purchasing a new one, and that's only because of the end of support for the desktop operating system.

It's entirely possible now for a modern computer to be running for 20 years if properly maintained and kept free of dust, which brings me neatly on to ...

Cleaning Up, Saving Money

Dust is a nightmare, as is pet hair. They are both an insulator and a conductor. This means that at best they'll clog up the air vents on a desktop or laptop PC and cause it to heat up, which in turn will cause the fans to spin more quickly, the components inside to operate more slowly, and the whole shebang to become much less efficient.

If dust and hair get onto the motherboard and into the components of a PC, there is the potential for electrical shorts, though most modern components are relatively impervious to these.

It's important with any PC, be it a desktop or a laptop, to give it a clean occasionally. You should be careful how you do this, however, as just sticking the hose of a vacuum cleaner inside the case risks causing physical damage to any components you knock against.

You should use a vacuum cleaner on a low setting against the air vents on a laptop or inside and outside the case of a desktop. Use a brush attachment if you have one, but always be gentle. Before vacuuming a PC or laptop, the careful use of an unused paint brush can release collected dust and hair in hard-to-reach areas. Also be careful with fans: making them turn with vacuum will produce electricity (re)injected to the motherboard, so turn them carefully.

Just doing this occasionally will help save you money and help your PC to stay efficient. Additionally you can raise your desktop PC off flooring that can conduct static electricity and therefore attract more dust, like nylon carpet tiles in an office. A good, sturdy, wooden, or metal case holder is recommended here, preferably one on wheels to make it simple to pull the PC out and clean behind and underneath it.

Putting More RISC into PCs

Back in the late 1980s, a British computer company called Acorn, which made the famous Electron and BBC Micro home computers, dipped their toe into processor design. They wanted to break into the business computer market and so developed a new processor architecture called RISC (Reduced Instruction Set Computing). This helped the processor become more efficient, thus faster, but it wasn't enough to help the company crack a market that IBM compatibles, with chips and software by Intel and Microsoft, were by that time already dominating.

Acorn didn't rest on their laurels though, and you might now know the company as ARM (Advanced RISC Machines). ARM decided not to produce their own chips, but to license their designs to other companies to produce. By the time we reached the late 2010s, practically every single smartphone and tablet on the planet was powered by an ARM-designed processor, and by 2020 we were seeing desktop PCs and laptops both from Apple and running Microsoft Windows also based on ARM processor designs.

The companies licensing chip designs from ARM included giants such as Apple, Samsung, and Huawei, with each then taking reference designs from ARM and building on them to produce their own variants, such as the Apple M line, which launched in 2020.

big.LITTLE

One of the clever things that ARM did was to introduce a technology that is known as *big.LITTLE*. This places different cores, each running at different clock speeds and sometimes even made using different fabrication processes, on the same die. The result is that you will have a slower clock speed core that will be used when the computer is performing less demanding, everyday tasks and faster more complex cores that only come into use when more demanding workloads require them.

This design was implemented with the aim of helping smartphone batteries last longer on a single charge, by reducing the power consumed by processing light tasks. As the power of ARM chips increased, however, it was felt this could be scaled upward to larger and larger PCs. As I write this, big.LITTLE desktop chips are in their early stages for Intel with two generations of processors released thus far, but ARM processors are now being used in data centers to help reduce power consumption and make the whole operation much more processor- and energy-efficient.

Looking to the Future

big.LITTLE is just one example of how the landscape of desktop and server computing is changing to help make the computers we use more energy-efficient and climate-friendly.

We do need to plan ahead with our infrastructure, so it's useful to keep one eye on the present and the other eye on the future. This helps us maintain compatibility between the equipment we purchase now and the components we can use to upgrade that equipment tomorrow.

Right to Repair

It is always going to be preferable to upgrade our existing technology if we can, rather than just buy something completely new, and there has been a movement ongoing for a few years now called *Right to Repair*. The people supporting this movement are concerned about the sheer volume of electronic devices containing scary chemicals, which I will come to in the next section, from smartphones to laptops that are ending up in landfill.

Many companies have already signed up to the principles of Right to Repair and are beginning to make their technology much more serviceable, rather than some technology, particularly smartphones, which are glued together and cannot be repaired at all.

You can find the repairability policies for companies on their websites, but iFixit has repairability scores for a great many laptops, tablets, and smartphones, which you can find online at `www.ifixit.com/Right-to-Repair/Repairable-Products`. Additionally the website has useful guides, both in text and with helpful diagrams, and videos to help you repair your own equipment.

European regulation and legislation has created a repairability index, which should now be labeled on electronic devices (see `https://www.economie.gouv.fr/particuliers/tout-savoir-indice-reparabilite`).

What a Waste

I will talk about e-waste and recycling our technology in detail in Chapter 6. This subject is very important because of a little thing called e-waste (electronic waste). We might think of computer chips as being made from silicon, which is just sand, but it's much more complex than that.

Cadmium is used in rechargeable batteries, contacts, and switches. Mercury can be found in LCDs (liquid crystal displays), switches and batteries. Lead is common in TV and computer screens. Chromium can be found in the metal housings of phones, tablets, and laptops. Nickel is a common component of circuit boards, and cadmium is commonly used in everything from batteries to game consoles.

None of these materials are good for the environment when left in a PC on a landfill site. It gets worse, too, with all manner of scary-sounding and impossible-to-pronounce materials you may never have heard of acting as pollutants for our environment. Phthalates are plasticizers used to make PVC plastic. Brominated flame retardants can be found in computer cases and are known to cause brain development problems and to kill fish. Alkylphenols can cause significant damage to fish and the environment, as can organic compounds known as tributyltin and triphenyltin.

Computers also contain copper, aluminum, phosphorus, tin, iron, silver, gold, and one you've likely never even heard of, tantalum (wasn't that a character in *Star Trek*? – Ed). If all of these chemicals and minerals sound kind of scary when it comes to our smartphones, computers, and the environment, you'd likely be right. We might not see too much problem with gold or copper being dumped, but everybody knows the danger posed to both the environment and our own lives by mercury and lead.

Let's Go WEEE

It's not all bad news though, and in Chapter 6 I'll talk more about WEEE, which, rather than being the sound our children make when going down a waterslide, actually stands for the Waste Electrical and Electronic Equipment Directive. It's one of several such regulatory frameworks around the world governing the disposal and recycling of e-waste. France's name for this is DEEE, which includes taxes and the collection and recycling process of electronic wastes.

Indeed recycling e-waste is big business, and companies exist that make a healthy profit from carefully stripping and separating the gold, cadmium, and other precious and recyclable metals and chemicals from everything from laptops to cars. This again is something I'll discuss in Chapter 6.

big.LITTLE isn't the only environmentally friendly product we can look forward to using, however, and in Chapter 13 I'll examine some of the other technologies coming our way or that already exist and that you might never have even heard of from office flooring that generates electricity as we walk to data centers in space.

I'd like to slip in an aside at this point as there's one technology that I myself am particularly excited about, the carbon-capture artificial tree. This is something that can be placed in a company car park, around the offices, or anywhere in gardens, towns, and cities and that is capable of extracting carbon dioxide from the atmosphere 1,000 times more efficiently than a regular tree. It's a fascinating product, and I'd rather like to have one of my own. There is a great article about this technology you can find online at `https://pcs.tv/3kTOdTp` if you have time for a read.

Banning Powerful Computers

Another movement that's gaining traction is simply banning computers over a certain power, and we can certainly see more countries adopting this policy as the years roll on. In July 2021, six US states placed a complete sales ban on high-end, pre-built gaming PCs.

California, Colorado, Hawaii, Oregon, Vermont, and Washington all banned the sale of PCs that consume more than a maximum amount of kWh/yr (kilowatt hours per year) of electricity. What's more, the regulations are changing, adapting with the times and becoming more stringent.

This will affect businesses where PCs are needed for power-hungry tasks such as CAD (computer-aided design), graphics, and video rendering and obviously high-end gaming and virtual-reality rigs.

It's something to keep a close eye on, and I'll talk more about government environmental initiatives that can affect your IT equipment and services in Chapter 11.

Summary

You probably know by this point that the world of making and keeping your IT equipment and services environmentally friendly is fairly complex and highly regulated. Long gone are the days when you just walked into a showroom and bought any old PC off the shelf. There are many considerations to make now when purchasing new equipment and many important questions to ask when buying in cloud and Internet services.

So in the next chapter, we'll look at how you check and gauge how much power your IT systems are actually using and how you can discover the power usage of the cloud services you buy. We'll then look at what is and isn't considered acceptable for power usage and what it is you can do about it.

Lastly we'll look at the differences that can be faced dependent on where you live or work in the world, as your carbon footprint might be significantly higher in some countries than in others – this will vary on things like the uptake of renewable energy; the use of nuclear-, coal-, and gas-powered power stations; and the general climate of the country in question.

I hope this chapter has given you a good introduction to and a broad understanding of the subjects we'll be covering in this book, but I'm not going to baffle you with figures and regulations (we'd be well over 1,000 pages if I tried that and you'd only use this book for helping you get a good night's sleep). Using broad strokes though, we can work together to reduce our impact on the planet because, let's face it, it's the one thing we can guarantee we all have in common.

CHAPTER 2

Knowing the Impact Your IT Systems Have

It's one thing to say that we need to do something about the amount of electricity consumed by our computers and devices, but another thing altogether to figure out if what you're using is actually power-efficient in the first instance or how power-efficient any new equipment might be.

The Energy-Efficient House Refit

When I wrote the first edition of this book, I used this section to explain the process I went through obtaining energy-efficient appliances for the upgrade of two kitchens at my home in France, one in the house and the other in the gîte, which is an outhouse common to French countryside properties. For this I could use the European energy efficiency rating, which labels appliances from G to A to give a quick indication of how much energy the appliance will use (see Figure 2-1). This is a very handy guide, even if the purchaser only looks at the A-to-G rating. It goes slightly further than the *EnergyGuide* information provided in the USA, which just states the yearly operating cost.

© Mike Halsey 2025
M. Halsey, *The Green IT Guide*, https://doi.org/10.1007/979-8-8688-1233-0_2

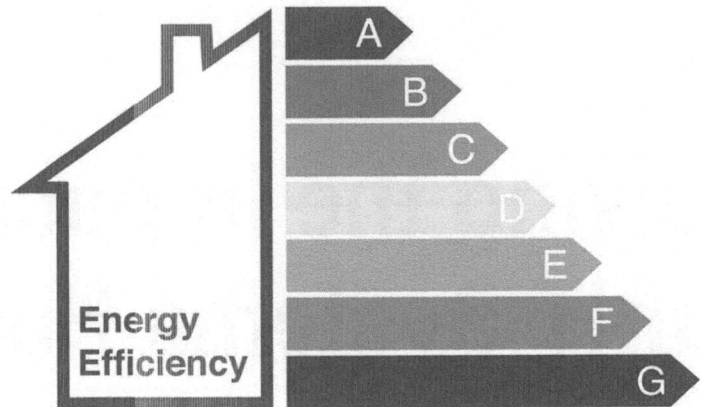

Figure 2-1. *Energy efficiency ratings in Europe are labeled from A to G*

The most recent purchase was just last month when I bought a chest freezer to go in my shed. This is to store vegetables and fruit grown in my potager (vegetable beds; see Chapter 1 for more on this) so that I have a regular and plentiful supply during the winter months. I purchased a Whirlpool chest freezer in the end that was actually quite a bit larger than I had intended to get, and this was purely on the basis that it was rated C for efficiency, when all the other chest freezers I found were rated F or G.

Additionally since writing the first edition of this book, I have installed monoblock air conditioners. Occasionally in the summer months, here it can reach as high as 45 °C (113 °F) or even 50 °C (122 °F), which makes being even indoors enormously difficult for me, but especially for my three dogs (you know your friends in Arizona are laughing at you right now – Ed). Anybody who has to endure these temperatures will know that it's no fun having to close all the curtains and sit in the dark all day just to try and keep the bulk of the heat out.

I went with the monoblock air conditioners partly because everything is built into the one unit, eliminating the need for pipework and additional boxes on the outside of the house. You drill two large and one small hole through the wall for air in, air out, and water out (I'll come to this) and then hang the unit on the wall – it's all very quick and tidy. The other reason to choose monoblock units is that they also function as fans, drawing in air from outside, heaters, and dehumidifiers, which is especially useful in the gîte, as – as anybody that lives in a tiny or very small home will attest – even something as simple as turning on the kettle will quickly cause a buildup of humidity, which in turn will lead to mold throughout the winter.

When it came to purchasing these monoblock units, I struggled to find any that were energy-efficient as the available choice is limited, and everybody that sells them, certainly here in France, all rebadge and resell exactly the same model. It would appear there's one big manufacturer, one model and that's your lot.

So the trick was going to come with programming them in such a way as to make them energy-efficient instead. They're controlled through a universal smart home app, which supports multiple timers. This enables me to have the dehumidifier turn on for half an hour or more a day through the winter, but not in the summer, and for the heater to be used in the winter evenings if it's especially cold, to help supplement the radiators.

For the air conditioning, I've programmed them to watch the local weather forecast. Obviously I can turn them on and off manually as I need to, but I've set them to come on automatically when the forecast says the temperature will reach 28 °C (82 °F). This is just about the only way I could use them in any kind of energy-efficient way.

The overall aim of all of this was to reduce my energy consumption, and this has extended to all of the other appliances in the house from refrigerators to washing machines, before I go further and fit battery-backed solar panels.

Where I hit another problem though with the kitchens was when I wanted to purchase a couple of wine and beer fridges, something so innocuous you'd think it wouldn't throw up a challenge. Looking online (by far the best place to find energy-efficient products as the cheaper ones in stores are very commonly the most inefficient), all of the wine fridges I could find were F and G rated. These are hardly efficient at all, and I searched through somewhere in the region of 400 wine fridges before finally discovering one, but only one, that had an A energy efficiency rating.

Then there's my car. I live in the middle of nowhere, and they don't let me out much anyway, so I decided I'd try and do my bit for the planet by purchasing and driving only a very small all-electric vehicle. Originally I had a Citroën Ami, which was new at the time I purchased it (see Figure 2-2 on the right), but have now switched to a much larger and considerably more comfortable Aixam eCoupe. Both of these are "sans-permis" vehicles, meaning you don't need a license to drive one in France as it's essentially a quadricycle. This was perfect for me as, always having lived in cities before in the UK, I'd never wanted to take my driving test as I hadn't felt I'd needed to with good public transport always being available (okay, so maybe your friends in Arizona aren't laughing at you now – Ed). This time, with the nearest supermarket being 7.5 km away (I know that people in the USA and Canada think this is a walk to the corner shop), I had to get a vehicle.

Figure 2-2. *The Citroen Ami seemed like a good idea at the time*

This all seemed like a good idea at the time, but I have since come to realize that I shall have to take my driving test at some point after all and purchase a more appropriate electric vehicle as the 100 km (62-mile) maximum range of the Aixam is very limiting, especially when followed by a 4-hour recharge time as, though I have fitted a Type-2 electric car charger to my house to future-proof the property, the Aixam will only charge slowly from a two-pin domestic plug.

Clearly then while progress is being made by manufacturers, there's still a long way to go. And so it is with the equipment we use for work, from desktop computers to printers. As an example of this, in the previous chapter I mentioned that some states in the USA have already begun banning the sale of pre-built powerful computers. This is a trend that is certain to continue both across the USA and Canada and also with the European Union (EU) who began some years back by banning the sale of powerful vacuum cleaners and kettles.[1]

As I write this, there's also talk in the US presidential election of a ban on cheap electric vehicles from China, on the grounds they are hurting US motor manufacturing. This of course is a manufacturing industry that's still very much wedded to the internal combustion engine, with Tesla being the only major manufacturer of electric vehicles in the country.

There's a double-edged sword to this, and it would be a great idea if it spurred US vehicle manufacturers to build more electric vehicles, which sadly I doubt it will, as while China makes great electric cars, they still have to be shipped around the world on massive container ships, which comes with its own carbon footprint.

Anyway, back to technology. While the ban on the sale of powerful gaming PCs in some states is perfectly fine for the average PC user and even the average business when rolling out new PCs to their workforce, it's terrible news for whole other groups of people: people working in computer-aided design (CAD) and engineering; those involved in the animation, film, and television industries (remember California is one of the states to have banned these PCs); businesses with requirements to roll out artificial intelligence (AI) services; and, heaven forbid, PC gamers such as myself.

---

[1] Did you know that a powerful kettle and a less powerful kettle will use exactly the same amount of electricity to boil water? This is because the amount of energy required to boil water never changes, so the less powerful kettle will just take longer than the more powerful kettle to do the same job.

This is perfectly fine for me, as I always build my own PCs, and the ban hasn't extended to the sale of individual components (yet!) as I find there are always, to me anyway, unacceptable compromises to be found in pre-built computers such as the storage is just a bit too slow or the memory isn't as fast as it could be.

Does the average consumer have the knowledge to build their own computer, however? The answer to this is clearly no, and it's also no if you want to find out if the staff in any size of IT department have the time to self-build and maintain specialist PCs for those in your workforce who would need them. If you run such a company, then just go and ask the question, and see how quickly they realize it's time to go to lunch.

How Power-Efficient Is Our IT Equipment Anyway?

Clearly we've already established here that there are still huge challenges in finding just about anything that both is power-efficient and does the job we need it to do. Even these super-powerful specialist PCs are significantly more power-efficient than they used to be, but that's still not good enough for regulators and lawmakers.

Our desire for energy-efficient equipment doesn't just extend to new purchases, however. You will also want to know just how power-efficient the IT equipment you already use is. There are times equipment comes near the end of its life and needs to be replaced, or perhaps because it's a device where the host operating system is coming to end of service and won't be receiving any more security and stability patches. You might though at this point just want to know if the equipment you have is horribly inefficient and costing you huge amounts of excess money.

There are devices you can purchase (sometimes local green charities and community groups have them available to borrow) that can help you determine the power efficiency of your existing equipment.

Figure 2-3 shows a power consumption monitor that you can fit between the wall socket and any electrical appliance or device. The idea with these monitors is that you leave them running for a period of time, usually a few days of typical usage, and they'll tell you just how much electricity the device has used during that period.

Figure 2-3. *Energy consumption monitors can help you identify inefficient hardware*

Most of these monitors can be a pain in the ass to use as you have to get down on the floor to the power socket to read the display, and if you unplug it to read it in brighter light and a more appropriate environment, you'll cut all the power to it and lose all the data, these things not often including a backup battery.

You can purchase power consumption monitors though that can synchronize with a smartphone app, and these are the ones to look for. They'll let you keep a good eye on the data and also let you keep that data afterward.

Let's take an example of how you would use these in a business space then. These devices are typically not cheap at about $20 for a good one, so you wouldn't want to purchase very many. How do you use them?

In a workplace you would most likely have a lot of PCs that are all of the same make and model. This will help as it'll mean you'll only need to test one of them. If it's a desktop with a separate monitor, then it's always a good idea to plug everything into a four-gang socket and then plug that into the monitor, so you can see what the power consumption of the whole bundle is.

With laptops it's less of an issue. With some good training and staff awareness, which I detail in Chapters 7 and 8, you can make sure that laptop chargers are only plugged in and using power when they're really needed. The other advantage with a laptop charger is that it will always state on the label what the power consumption of that charger will be.

Let's Get Into the Maths

Wattage is a measurement of how much energy is consumed by an electrical circuit and is the product of the voltage multiplied by the current (measured in amps). If you take the example of a dimmable traditional lightbulb, which would have a wattage between 60 W and 100 W, when you dim the bulb, you are reducing the current getting to the bulb, and the result will be a lower wattage consumed by the bulb. We can see this as the bulb gets dimmer and consequently also gets cooler as less power is consumed.

Not all manufacturers will list the wattage of chargers, however. Apple is known for this and might instead list the energy consumption as being 100–240 V/1.5 A (amps) with the output being 20.3 V/3 A. We can work out that 20.3 V × 3 A = 61 W of power.

If the charger is used for 3 hours a day to charge the laptop, then it's 61 W × 3 h, which gives us a total of 183 Wh (watt hours) per day. There are 1,000 Wh in a kWh (kilowatt hour), and over the course of a standard working year of say 250 days, that would equate to a total power consumption of 45,750 Wh, or 45.75 kWh. This is a figure you can use with the unit rate provided by your energy supplier to determine just how much the laptop charger will cost to run.

If we jump back for a moment to our lightbulb, we can estimate its own running costs. A 60 W bulb left on for 10 hours a day in an office that's in use 260 days a year will consume 60 W × 10 h × 260 d power, or 156,000 Wh (156 kWh) of power. Replacing this with a low-power light-emitting diode (LED) bulb, which will typically produce the same amount of light while only consuming 5 W of power, brings this down to 5 W × 10 h × 260 d, or 13,000 Wh (13 kWh), just 8.3% of the usage of the older bulb.

Stand By for Action!

When it comes to IT equipment such as printers, the situation will be slightly different. The power supply, or a label on the rear of the printer, will tell you what the power consumption of the device will be, but that'll only be half of the story, as that printer will spend most of its life in standby.

This is where you will need to consult the documentation that came with the device or the device web page on the manufacturer's website if it's still online. This documentation will tell you how many watts the device consumes when in its low-power state. This might vary from 5 W for an inefficient device to just 1 W or less for a newer, more energy-efficient one.

Let's take the example of a modern office laser printer. This has a power consumption when in use of, to take one example I found, 361 W (active printing), 7.8 W (ready to print), and 0.8 W (sleep). In a busy office this printer might only be printing for 1 hour a day and then another hour in ready to print mode before it automatically goes into standby. For the rest of the time, because it's never actually switched off, it's consuming power at the sleep rate.

This gives us the following calculations:

361 W × 1 h × 260 d = 93,860 Wh (93.86 kWh) – For printing

7.8 W × 1 h × 260 d = 2,028 Wh (2.028 kWh) – Ready to print

0.8 W × 22 h × 260 d = 4,576 Wh (4.576 kWh) – Standby

This has an additional calculation of 0.8 W × 24 h × 105 d = 2,016 Wh (2.016 kWh) to cover weekends when the office is closed.

This brings us to a total power consumption for the year of 93.86 kWh + 2.028 kWh + 4.576 kWh + 2.016 kWh = 102.48 kWh. The manufacturer of this particular printer, in this case HP, states that for an office of between one and five people, they would estimate the power usage to be 0.696 kWh per week. Our calculation for a busy office, so of perhaps 10–20 people, sits broadly in line with this figure at 1.97 kWh per week.

Getting Smart

Now I'm not suggesting that you set up a spreadsheet containing power and standby calculations for every piece of electrical and IT equipment in your office, well not unless you're into that kind of thing anyway (I am – you can tell, can't you?). But this is a rough guide to how you can tell how much the devices in your office will actually cost you to run over the course of a typical day, week, month, or year.

Now we're armed with this useful information, we can go shopping or at least browsing and see what more modern and newer devices and equipment do in comparison because you might find, especially if you have very old equipment still in use, replacing it might pay for itself in two or three years with the reduced energy costs, and in Chapter 6 I'll detail how to effectively recycle older hardware. You'll see here then that the wattage of a device is a really good indicator of just how much or how little it will cost to run, but it can still be complicated for certain device types.

Let's take the example of two smartphone chargers. One is an older 5 W charger, with the newer one being a 20 W fast-charge model. We are using these to charge a new smartphone with a 4,400 mAh (milliamphour) battery. This is where I'll get slightly less scientific as the precise calculations will vary considerably due to the specific smartphone and charger models you use.

As a general rule, however, the 20 W fast charger should charge the 4,400 mAh battery from empty to full in about 40 minutes, whereas the 5 W charger might take 3–4 hours. Over the course of a year, this would translate into power usage of around 20 W × 0.6 h × 365 d = 4.38 kWh and perhaps double this using less than 1 W when not in use but left plugged into the electrical socket.

Conversely the older charger would use 5 W × 4 h × 365 d = 7.3 kWh (rising by between 4.5 kWh and 12 kWh depending on how power-efficient it is when left plugged in but not actively charging the smartphone).

In order to increase efficiency, rather than multiplying by the number of chargers (one per device), I bought a special "family" charger, for example, Anker chargers are efficient (Anker's New GaNPrime Chargers Are Faster, Smarter And Greener (forbes.com)).

Okay … Enough Already!

It's clear then that using an older and less powerful charger to charge a modern, power-hungry device isn't necessarily a good idea. So what's the solution to this as obviously we want to avoid these chargers going to landfill and this is why many smartphone manufacturers have stopped including them in the box with new handsets?

There are options here, some of which I will detail in Chapter 6 when I talk about the benefits local, national, and international electrical recycling schemes can bring to the world. But there are also things you can do yourself, such as providing communal chargers for people to use for short periods (which brings its own advantages that I will detail shortly) or simply banning chargers altogether and asking people to charge their smartphones at home or in their car.

This might initially be seen as passing the buck of paying the bill over to the employee, but really it's a much more sensible approach that helps stop people plugging in a phone that'll only take an hour to charge and then disappearing off to a 3-hour meeting. The phone *might* stop drawing power after the charge is complete, but it's very dependent on the model, and there will in any case be a constant trickle charge for the power its using while in standby.

When people charge their devices at home, if they're keen on wanting to help the environment, they'll be much more likely to be aware of unplugging something when its fully charged.

The communal chargers idea is a good one, however. Let's go back to my small electric car for a minute as this is an excellent example of why you might not want to charge anything fully all the time. Modern batteries – and new technologies based on graphene and other materials are being developed by scientists – tend to cap out on the charge rate when they hit 80% capacity. After this time it will take much longer for the last 20% to charge.

Now in my car, with a maximum range of just 100 km (the Ami only had a range of 65 km), I might get serious range anxiety if I only charge the vehicle to 80%, but while it'll charge to 80% in about 2.5 hours, it'll take another hour and a half to charge that last 20%. This is horribly inefficient but is, sadly, just a fact of life when it comes to current battery technology (heh, "current," I get it. Funny – Ed).

It's the same with smartphones and laptops, so having communal charging points that people can use, for example, in meeting rooms and in the staff restaurant, will encourage people to get the fastest charge, as quickly as possible, while minimizing how many devices are charged to the last 20%. Overall this will greatly reduce the cost of the electricity used while still giving the workforce more than enough charge to get them through the day.

Noise and Heat

Noise and heat are not conducive to helping people concentrate and get work done and rarely are they helpful. The truth, however, is that both noise and heat are the sworn enemy of power efficiency. Heat is energy being consumed but wasted by the device, and noise is fans having to spin up to dissipate said heat.

There are several ways to deal with noise and heat, but I would argue that having a well-ventilated PC or laptop case isn't the solution, as all that is doing is allowing the heat to dissipate more quietly, in which circumstance you're only eliminating one of the two problems.

big.LITTLE, which I spoke about in Chapter 1 and will come back to later in the book, as well as being an important innovation, is a solution to this. Intel have now released their big.LITTLE processors with "efficiency" and "performance" cores. AMD are not doing this as they say their own processor architecture scales the power of the cores anyway, so they've always done it. ARM processors already support this technology, and Windows on ARM (WoA) laptops and convertible tablets already exist that these can run both 32-bit and 64-bit win32 (legacy) software, though not everything will run and some software will still produce an error. We can assume this will improve overtime, however. You can keep up to date with the development of WoA at the Microsoft website on `https://docs. microsoft.com/windows/arm`.

Apple's M processor series also support big.LITTLE, and it's clear that this microprocessor architecture is definitely the future of desktop computing.

As a quick refresher, big.LITTLE uses a combination of low-power, low-performance cores and high-power, high-performance cores on the same chip die. The processor only uses the low-power cores when it's doing day-to-day tasks or just sitting idle. The high-performance cores then only kick in when they're needed. The upshot is that the device uses a lot less power than it otherwise would if it had a processor along the lines of traditional Intel and AMD chips, where all of the cores run at the same speed and at the same level of power consumption.

Another solution is to not purchase computers that are more powerful than you absolutely need. If the processor isn't pushed, then it won't generate waste heat. "But!", I hear you cry, "Surely this is a reason to purchase more powerful processors as then they won't get pushed?"

Well, no. The reason for this is the amount of wattage needed to power the chip in the first instance. A modern desktop processor will have a TDP (thermal design power) of around 65 W (watts), with a high-performance PC having a TDP of around 125 W. TDP is a measurement of how much heat a component is expected to use when under load. While this doesn't mean the processor will always use that much power, it is an indicator of overall efficiency.

To put this into contrast, a mobile desktop processor, the type of thing found in a laptop, will have a TDP of around 15 W and still be able to perform all of the tasks a typical everyday worker will need to do.

A modern big.LITTLE processor by comparison will have a TDP of 10 W or less, making it much more efficient, while still having the power to perform everyday desktop tasks. Let's face it, when was the last time you were concerned your smartphone couldn't work quickly enough? A modern smartphone has significantly more capability than even a desktop PC of a few years ago, and the ARM-based processors used in these (both from Qualcomm and Apple) are now exactly the same chips found in big. LITTLE-powered laptops and convertible tablets.

As an example, I recently built myself a new desktop PC for work and gaming. I purchased a top-end AMD Ryzen 7 Pro 8700G processor as the prices for equivalent Intel chips are significantly higher. This chip without a big.LITTLE architecture has an operating TDP of 65 W and is able to scale back to 45 W when performing less intensive tasks.

The latest equivalent Intel processor, the Core Ultra 7, does have the efficiency/performance cores but has an identical TDP to the AMD chip, 45–65 W.

I'm writing this book on a small-form-factor (SFF) Windows on ARM desktop PC, however, which I bought as a distraction-free work PC that contains a Qualcomm Snapdragon 8CX Gen 3 SoC (System on a Chip) processor, which has a TDP of only around 7 W and, as a result, makes the PC completely silent because it doesn't require fans even when pushed. Qualcomm haven't at the time of writing said what the TDP of their latest Snapdragon X processors for Windows PC are.

So how do you find out which processor type is good for you? One of the best ways is also one of the most traditional, good old-fashioned reviews. These reviews, either online or in magazines, will normally give benchmark scores to new PCs and laptops, and these benchmark scores will tell you how good they'll be at performing everyday tasks and even running some less-demanding games (which is also a good benchmark of performance given that a graphics processor is still the best way to power AI workloads). If the review does specify just how well the computer handles everyday tasks, and they normally do, the benchmark will definitely give you a good idea of performance of the processor overall.

The other thing to look for in reviews is mention of how loud and hot the computer will get when pushed. Some new PCs, usually the ones based on big.LITTLE chips such as the Apple MacBooks, will barely get warm at all, let alone put out any fan noise.

Not only is this good for the environment; it's also good for people in the workplace. A quieter environment is more conducive to helping people concentrate, and a cooler workplace means you don't have to overcompensate for PC heat output by using expensive air-conditioning systems.

Using an Inverter

While we're on the subject of power consumption in the workplace, it's worth mentioning the installation of inverters. When you plug your PC or your laptop or smartphone charger into the power socket, it has to convert the alternating current from the mains electricity (usually 125–240 V) into direct current (around 12 V). This is because devices of all types simply don't need or consume the amount of power they used to.

In the example I gave earlier of a 60 W lightbulb vs. a 5 W LED bulb that produces the same amount of light, you can see a great example. Another example came from an electrician friend when I was double-checking my maths for this chapter. He told he that he was in the process of renovating a vintage radio and that some of the components, usually the valves (sometimes called vacuum tubes) inside, consumed current up to 600 V (stepped upward from a 230 V mains supply) and as a result were highly inefficient. He went on to point out that modern devices rarely need a voltage higher than 12 V.

This is because technological advances have made components much smaller than they used to be; a modern processor has components that are just a few nanometers across. Compare this with a valve, which was more than an inch wide and three inches tall, and you'll understand what I mean.

Smaller components require less power to work, and if you put too much power through these components anyway, they'd blow as they simply wouldn't be able to handle the voltage.

The power supply in your PC and the chargers for your laptop and smartphone work by modifying the input direct current into a lower-voltage alternating current. This used to be, and in desktop PC power supplies usually still is, handled by a step-down transformer.

Inverters are a newer technology that is much more efficient than a transformer because while a step-down transformer has to use coils of wire wrapped around a column with a hollow air or solid iron core to increase or decrease the voltage, an inverter is a much smaller device that can quickly flip one current type to another.

Simply put, they are much more efficient than step-down transformers, because they'll lose only around 10% maximum of the power they consume, rather than the 20%, 30%, or even more of the PC power supplies I talked about in Chapter 1.

If you look around your workplace, you will see many electrical devices that can run natively on just 12 volts and others that can't. You may see some devices, and refrigerators are a good example of this, that have a sticker on them saying they have an inverter. This is because traditional refrigerator technology was horribly inefficient on power usage, and companies such as Samsung sought to rectify the problem a few years ago.

It is worth investigating then with your energy supplier or electrical contractor if some kind of inverter can be installed for your premises, especially if you are refitting your premises or moving to new premises.

If you take the maths I detailed earlier in this chapter about smartphone and laptop chargers, you can pretty much add an extra 10% additional wattage onto them all, as this is the energy wasted by each step-down transformer or inverter (usually called the power brick) that sits between the device and the mains electricity.

If you scale this up across a lot of devices, then the power loss, and the associated additional cost of using and wasting that power, might in the long run make the cost of installing an inverter for the building much more sensible. That main inverter will itself lose a small percentage of energy, but as it is built specifically for the task, the overall energy loss will be considerably less than that lost by lots of individual devices.

This makes even more sense when you realize that most modern portable devices, including laptops, can be charged over USB as they only need 12 V to charge them in the first instance, thus eliminating the need for the power brick altogether. Having a separate electrical circuit then that solely powers USB sockets and that is powered itself directly by the inverter can be a good investment.

Power Usage of Cloud Service Providers

When it comes to cloud service providers, determining how much energy they are using to provide services to you, or can provide if you are shopping around, is much more difficult as you're at the mercy of the provider's public relations department and how open and honest they choose to be about the subject.

Fortunately times are a'changin' and the larger providers, such as Microsoft and Amazon, have been very open for some years now about how much electricity their data centers consume and they are even competing against one another to be the first to meet their targets of efficiency A or sustainability B.

Microsoft, Google, and Amazon all publish detailed information about sustainability, relating to their data centers and also to most if not all other aspects of their businesses. You can find this information on the links below:

Microsoft – `https://azure.microsoft.com/`
`global-infrastructure/sustainability`

Microsoft – `www.microsoft.com/sustainability`

Amazon Web Services (AWS) – `sustainability.`
`aboutamazon.com/environment/the-cloud`

Google – `https://sustainability.google`

As for any other company, a search online for **[company name]
sustainability** will normally return the result you're looking for. With
smaller companies though, they might not conform to the same norms,
as the language used by Microsoft, Google, and Amazon will be worded
in ways as to make it easy to find for fund managers and shareholders.
These things are very important to blue-chip corporations, so standardized
language will always be used where possible.

Other companies you purchase, or are interested in purchasing, cloud
services from, however, might not be listed on a stock exchange or might
just treat the subject matter slightly differently, so be prepared to spend
a little time searching for words and phrases such as **climate change**,
environmental policy(ies), or **global warming** to find the information
you're looking for.

Even then, some companies might not have caught up, but if you're
interested in purchasing services from them, you'll be contacting them,
and then of course their commitment to sustainability would be one of the
first questions you ask …probably just before "Why don't you publish this
information on your website?"

It's worth noting that some cloud service providers won't publish
sustainability and energy details because they won't know them or won't
know them authoritatively. This is because their own services will run
on top of another cloud provider such as Microsoft Azure, Amazon Web
Services, or Google Cloud.

Note   I want to make mention of how the use of AI services in business, such as Microsoft Copilot, is affecting the power usage of data centers. In May 2024, Microsoft announced that since 2020 their carbon footprint from data centers had risen by almost 30% due to their ongoing commitment to the company's growing AI needs. AI is a power-hungry technology and will impact all cloud service providers' environmental commitments. I will talk much more about AI and its effect on the climate in Chapter 5.

Why Where You Live in the World Affects Your Climate Impact

This will probably not come as a tremendous shock to you, but where you work in the world, and where your online service providers are based, can have an enormous effect on your own climate impact. As an example almost 30% of global carbon emissions come from China, and almost 15% come from the USA, with India on 7% bringing up third place.

France, where I live, is currently 19th in the global rankings with 0.93% of global carbon emissions, and the UK, where I was born and spent most of my life, is in 17th place with 1.03% of global carbon emissions. Even Canada, which we tend to think of as a land of super-friendly people leaving their front doors open because they all live in or near to huge tract of woodland with a moose living in, emits 1.89% of global carbon emissions.

Unsurprisingly, some of the countries that are best known for tackling climate change, probably because they all live close to ice caps, do much better. Finland sits in 57th place on 0.14%, Sweden in 63rd place with 0.13%, and Norway in 64th place, also with 0.13%. Denmark does even better in 70th place with 0.11%.

At the top of the list, insofar as they have the smallest contribution to global carbon emissions, sit countries such as the Faroe Islands, where a staggering 90% of their energy needs are provided by renewable sources. Their global emissions have been calculated at less than 0.00%.

The United Nations (UN) keeps track of the global emissions of its member states and the policies (or none) that they implement. You can find out more about this on the United Nations' website at www.un.org/en/climatechange.

The burning of coal and oil to generate power forms a large part of a country's global emissions. Looking just at coal, which is by far the most common fossil fuel still in use, South Africa still generates 86% of their national power from coal, though by population size they come sixth in the overall rankings.

China and India are still currently taking the top two spots with 61%, putting China in the top spot by population, and 71% for India in second place, respectively. The USA is in third place with just over 19% of its power generated by coal, but the power consumption in the country is so high it gets pushed up the rankings. Even some European countries fare badly with Germany on 24% power generation by coal.

When it comes to nuclear power, which some countries have banned outright for safety reasons, the USA generates about 30% of its power from nuclear stations, currently putting it first in the world, and France is second with a massive 70% of its energy produced by nuclear power.

It's not all bad news for the future though, as some of the biggest coal and oil polluters are also some of the countries producing the most power from nuclear sources, and this will only improve over the years. These countries include China, Japan, and Russia.

Summary

Clearly there are a lot of maths and figures involved when it comes to climate change and your own carbon footprint, not to mention all manner of considerations about where you open national offices, which service providers around the world you should purchase services from, and so on.

Sadly, with this being a book, it's not possible to provide completely up-to-date figures for the exact time you'll be reading this, but I hope this has acted as a good guide and introduction as to what you should be looking out for, keeping an eye on, and asking about.

In the next chapter we're going to take what we've discussed here and take it up a notch, looking in more detail at how you can make the best choices with new IT hardware, how you can use both it and your existing hardware more efficiently, and what working from home means for your business.

CHAPTER 3

Making Smarter Usage of Your IT Equipment

The power usage of modern IT equipment seems to change every couple of years, with computers and devices of all types, from printers to monitors, using less and less power than they did before. This of course is a great thing and in no small part has come about because of advances in technology that make our lives better in other ways too.

Take the humble television and by that definition also the PC monitor as they've always used the same technologies, as an example. Cathode-ray tube (CRT) screens were horrendously inefficient in their energy consumption, which is in no small part why they always got so hot when left switched on for an extended period of time.

When the color liquid crystal display (LCD) moved into the mainstream, power consumption dropped significantly, but there remained a problem for many years as these panels and light-emitting diode (LED) panels after them required a backlight. This illuminated panel filled the entire screen behind the LCD or LED panel and itself always chewed a large amount of power.

© Mike Halsey 2025
M. Halsey, *The Green IT Guide*, https://doi.org/10.1007/979-8-8688-1233-0_3

Eventually display panel companies invented what's become known as local dimming, where instead of a single light panel behind the screen, they included about nine separate panels, placed in a grid so that if, say, one corner of the screen was showing a black or very dark image, the light from the illuminated panel in that corner could also be dimmed.

This was primarily a technology for televisions as it helped movies appear more realistic, but it could still be jarring for some people and didn't solve the problem of the backlight using lots of power overall.

Modern LED TVs and monitors, with LCD now having finally fallen by the wayside, can come with several hundred of these local dimming zones, again primarily for TVs, which can make pictures and movies appear much more sharp, but that still doesn't solve the problem of the backlight and its power consumption.

So an alternative was needed, and this came in the form of organic light-emitting diodes (OLED) and later active matrix organic light-emitting diodes (AMOLED). The advantage these panels had over LED was that they didn't require a backlight at all. Each individual pixel generated its own light, and this meant that if a pixel on the screen was showing the color black, it just switched off and didn't consume any power at all.

Over the last few years, OLED and AMOLED screens have slowly begun to roll out to laptop and desktop displays, as they're generally much more expensive than LED panels. They've been commonplace in smartphones for a few years already, but the smaller size, and the mass production that goes with smartphone displays, has made them much more affordable in that arena. This is quite apart from the need manufacturers have had to satisfy consumer demand for longer and longer battery life in those devices.

OLED and AMOLED screens in turn led to Dark Mode being rolled out across every operating system, which not only used far less power overall than the traditional, now called, Light Mode but also had the effect of being far easier on the eye for the viewer and thus reduced eyestrain and helped improve health and reduce headaches for people that have to sit in front of a screen every day. I will talk more about Dark Mode and its value in Chapter 6.

With the advent of OLED and AMOLED, however, has come what I can probably describe as a small hiccup when it comes to power consumption, and that's consumer demand for ever brighter screens. So there is good news and bad news here: The good news is that people have at long last discovered this mythical thing in their home called a "front door" and are using it to actually go outside into the sunshine (surely not! – Ed). The bad news: they're taking their technology with them and are still glued to it.

This means that there is increasing demand for laptops and tablets with ever brighter screens. This is probably an effect of the pandemic, with people now naturally pushing back against being stuck indoors for the best part of two years.

One of the main reasons though is the advent of HDR (High Dynamic Range) screens that can show pictures that are brighter and more colorful than has been possible in the past and give TV shows and movies much more punch. All of this results inevitably in greater power consumption for these devices, and while that might not be much for a single device, when scaled out to millions of devices, it's quite a large amount.

Outdoor televisions have now started to become popular, too, as the latest thing to put on your terrace, and indeed I've recently installed one at my own home. This Samsung panel is currently the brightest you can buy at 2000 nits (my son had nits the other week – Ed). 1 nit, otherwise known as 1 cp, stands for candlepower and is a measurement of brightness. To display HDR video, TVs and other screens need a brightness of between 500 and 600 nits, equivalent to the light produced by 500 or 600 candles.

So screen technology is just one area where advances in technology, and people wanting to spend their hard-earned money on new technology, have benefits right across the spectrum, with newer screens helping with people's health and well-being while at the same time reducing their own power consumption massively compared with just a few years ago, even when you do factor in HDR video, and also helping save the planet … It's a win-win!

Well, not always as we'll discuss in Chapter 6 where we'll look at the problems caused by e-waste, but generally speaking, yes, upgrading to newer technologies can be a huge benefit, just so long as it's done correctly and the older technology is treated appropriately.

Computer on a Chip

In Chapter 2 I looked at the benefits that new big.LITTLE processor architecture can bring to computing. Everything from smartphone battery life to desktop PC power consumption benefits from this innovation – so much so in fact that it is now considered essential for new processors.

What I haven't discussed yet is something called System on a Chip (SoC). This is another technology that's rolling out pretty much everywhere, and it brings benefits from reducing the size of computer components and motherboards to reducing the number of components required to make a computer work in the first instance.

Apple's M processor line is a great example of this. It first launched in 2020 and received criticism, too, for the very benefits it brought. The M1 was an SoC that brought the processor, graphics, and memory onto one single die for the very first time, at least for Apple laptops and desktops. It had already been common for a few years now for processors and graphics systems to be integrated onto the same chip, and both Intel and AMD had already been doing this for some years with chips such as the Core i5 and Core i7 series, but for a desktop or a laptop PC, it was something entirely new.

Apple had several differing reasons for wanting to move in this direction. Firstly, the company wanted to start to design and manufacture its own chips. Until the iPhone 5, Apple had been using processors designed and manufactured by third-party companies including Samsung, one of Apple's chief competitors in the smartphone space.

They began to design and develop their own chips called the A series and a few years further on opened their own fabrication facilities so they could manufacture the chips themselves without still having to go to companies like Samsung to source their supplies.

From a company perspective, this was a complete no-brainer. They had complete control over the design and manufacturing process, never having to wait for chips to be produced for a competitor before theirs would be produced. Also, they could reduce costs because they were no longer paying other companies to design and manufacture their chips for them, which in turn increased profits and meant that at the same time they could reduce the cost of their products for the consumer.

With their own chip design and manufacturing now having been brought in house, the next logical step was to design laptop and desktop processors and build these into the next generation of Apple computers. This took slightly longer, primarily because it was a few years before the ARM chip architecture they were based on became powerful enough to perform desktop tasks.

Note   ARM (Advanced RISC Machines) is a company that grew out of Acorn computers in Cambridge (UK) in the 1980s. Acorn had produced the hugely successful BBC Micro and Electron home computers, and they moved on to develop the RISC (Reduced Instruction Set Computing) processor, which ran with a much smaller and much more highly optimized set of core instructions than the competing Intel and Motorola processors at the time. While not popular on the desktop, ARM began designing chips for other companies' mobile devices. While ARM has never produced any chips themselves, they have designed chips for years now, for everything from toasters to cars to smartphones, and you would be hard-pressed to find anything at all that doesn't have an ARM-designed chip in it somewhere.

This SoC approach has now gained traction, and smartphone processor manufacturer Qualcomm have now released their Snapdragon X range, which is designed to power the next generation of low-power laptop and small-form-factor desktop PCs.

I mentioned, however, that the move to design the M1 processor for Apple desktop and laptop computers came at the cost of some criticism for the company. While the company was widely applauded for producing processors that were as powerful and capable as the everyday Core processors they'd been buying for years from Intel and while customers and the press applauded the longer battery life and cheaper pricing that came with it, some were highly critical for two reasons.

Firstly, and perhaps most importantly, Apple had chosen, for reasons of pricing, efficiency, and speed, to integrate the computer memory directly into the chip. This means that there would never be any possibility of upgrading the memory later without either swapping out the chip (highly unlikely given the nature of modern on-device components) or buying a completely new laptop or desktop computer (which of course would be expensive and only add to unnecessary e-waste when a perfectly good computer was suddenly surplus to requirements).

The other reason was that Apple charged a significant premium for its MacBook range of computers over something smaller such as the Mac Mini (a small desktop equivalent) but that the Mac Mini now had exactly the same core components and, as a result, exactly the same processing power, speed, and efficiency of the MacBook. Some people were understandably annoyed.

Despite all of this, the System on a Chip idea is definitely one that has caught on, and as I mentioned, it can now be seen in non-Apple computers such as Windows on ARM devices, which run a modified version of Windows 10 and Windows 11. Indeed I am writing this book using a small-form-factor desktop PC running Windows 11 on a Qualcomm Snapdragon SoC chip.

How Old Is Old?

This of course all raises an important question: when is a good time to retire an older PC and purchase new computer hardware? Original equipment manufacturers (OEMs) have tried their very best in recent years to convince us to upgrade our devices, especially smartphones every year or two at the most. They do this with a steady stream of new advancements in screen and battery life and especially with camera technology, and Samsung is particularly notorious when it comes to this often with two major hardware launches every year.

Apple will have a hardware launch in the fall (autumn for readers outside of the USA) of each year, but will usually only launch a major new iteration of a device every two years, and most other companies follow suit.

Biannual hardware launches are of course a sensible approach as technology is now significantly more efficient and longer-lasting than it used to be, not to mention that especially when it comes to smartphones, features and power now seem to have topped out, with big leaps forward now being replaced with smaller iterative changes to each new generation of products.

While a smartphone of 10 or 15 years ago often felt slow and unwieldy next to a phone released only six months later, it's now widely accepted that a midrange phone bought new today will provide all the power and features an average person will need for the next three to five years. This is, of course, a problem for OEMs, and that's why we see so many adverts for cameras and screens from smartphone manufacturers on our shiny new OLED TVs.

So if hardware can last us a fair few years, the odd cracked screen notwithstanding, what about the software? This is where things get complicated ...

OS Support Lifecycles vs. Hardware Lifecycles

Google typically support a new version of their Android operating system for four years from the date of its launch. This, however, *does not* mean that when you buy an Android device, you're going to get four years of support from then on – you may get little or no support at all in fact. There are two reasons for this. The first is that it can take some time for OEMs to adopt a new version of Android for their devices, and it's very common for "new" smartphones to ship still running the *previous* version of the Android OS if not even the version before that, which I have seen recently in eReaders.

Then you have the issue that most OEMs only want to support Android on their devices for two years from the date the device launched. Why do they do this? Again it's two reasons. The first is that they want to sell you new hardware every year or two, and the second is that regulators are still allowing them to get away with it.

While moves are currently being made both with the US Congress and the European Union to force OEMs to support their hardware for longer and pressure from consumers to do this has increased in recent years, the process is slow moving, fraught with legal challenges, and riddled by bureaucratic and political ineptitude.

The upshot is that while one or perhaps even two newer versions of Android might be available for your smartphone, your OEM (who control the update and delivery process) might simply refuse to let you have them. If you wait a year for the price of a flagship device to drop to a more affordable level, you could find yourself being completely out of support within a year.

When Google released the Pixel 8 and Pixel 8 Pro smartphones in 2023, the company proudly announced they would receive seven full years of support and updates, and the press and the media loved it. Those of us with a more critical eye, however, were less generous. My own view was that, yes, *one* of their products would receive seven years of support, but what about all the others? It would be simplicity itself to extend support for the previous two generations of smartphones, for example. Then there was the fact that Fairphone also released their new fully repairable phone the same month, with that coming with ten full years of support and updates, but the press hardly mentioned that at all.

In fairness some of the larger companies have seen which way the wind is blowing, and Samsung and Apple in particular are very good at supporting their smartphones for at least seven years with updates. How long it takes for the rest of the industry to catch up is anybody's guess, but it's a step in the right direction.

Apple, as I have already mentioned, take a very sensible approach to OS updates, typically supporting their smartphones and tablets for up to seven years. That's a long time to be supporting older hardware, and it's definitely to be applauded, as it makes a huge difference to e-waste, and in the next chapter we'll look at how our devices can be recycled and still used for years after we stop needing them.

When it comes to the desktop, Apple normally support a version of MacOS for three years but provide free OS upgrades that can keep a MacBook or iMac running for more than a decade.

Google support their ChromeOS for Chromebook devices for about six-and-a-half years, but these end-of-life dates can vary from one OEM to another, and they're much more generous with laptops and computers than they are with smartphones and tablets.

Microsoft vary their end-of-life dates for Windows versions but do publish them years in advance. Typically they say there will be five years of mainstream support (during which time the OS will receive feature updates as well as security and stability updates) followed by five years of extended support, in which only stability and security updates will be provided.

It's still not that straightforward, however, sadly. With Windows 10, Microsoft issued two major updates every year, one in the spring and one in the fall, with each of these updates typically only receiving two years of support, forcing end users and businesses to upgrade to the next major update to continue receiving support.

Note   Windows Long-Term Servicing Channel (LTSC) is a channel
available to enterprise customers where typically an LTSC version of
Windows will be released every two to three years. Once installed,
that version will continue to receive support for five years on the
desktop and up to ten years for specialist devices where the OS is not
used for desktop tasks.

When Windows 11 was announced, Microsoft said that end of life for
Windows 10 in all versions will come on October 14, 2025, just over ten
years since the OS was first launched. In 2023, however, they announced
that, just as had been done with Windows 7, three years of extended
support could be purchased at additional cost. This time the offer would
be available to consumers as well as just businesses. Pricing has not yet
been announced, but I would anticipate a similar cost structure to the
Windows 7 extended support pricing of $50 for the first year, $100 for the
second, and $200 for the final year, each cost being per PC.

With Windows 11 we can expect goalposts to be moved at least once
during the lifecycle of the OS. Microsoft have stated that Windows 11 will
only receive one major update per year, but what happens outside of that is
currently too early to predict with any accuracy.

The company does publish regularly updated lifecycle documentation,
however, and you can find this on their website at `https://docs.`
`microsoft.com/lifecycle`.

You might think that you could just upgrade a Windows 10 PC to
Windows 11 and continue to receive more years of support. Sadly this isn't
always the case as Microsoft specified very strict upgrade requirements for
Windows 11, citing reasons of platform security.

These were that the PC had to include at least an eighth-generation
Intel or an AMD Ryzen 2 processor or newer and crucially a Trusted
Platform Module (TPM) 2.0 security chip. This would exclude a lot of older

and even newer self-build and pre-built gaming PCs, and it made a lot of people very angry. Microsoft didn't budge from this, however, and you can find out more about the minimum hardware specification requirements for Windows 11 and how to check your own PCs for compatibility at www.microsoft.com/windows/windows-11-specifications.

Security Concerns

Earlier in this chapter I talked about operating systems going out of support. This needs highlighting because it can create some very serious security concerns for your organization, so I want to spend a little time on the subject. It's more than a concern about operating systems, however, as processors also go out of support and, you may find this hard to believe, can present as much of a security threat as an old operating system.

Take Windows 11, for example. When Microsoft announced this operating system fairly out of the blue, they stated that the OS would only install on computers with an Intel eighth-generation or later processor. This caused a great deal of anger in the wider tech community; after all there were older processors happily running Windows 10, and the new OS was just Windows 10 with a new skin on the top of it.

Microsoft justified this on the grounds not of having a PC that could still run Windows 11 as it evolved and grew over the next five years, but for security. This is also the reason they insisted any Windows 11 PC have a TPM (Trusted Platform Module) 2.0 chip installed or UEFI firmware that could emulate one.

The reason behind all of this were two processor vulnerabilities in 2018 called Spectre and Meltdown. These were unique to Intel processors and allowed the malware to read the contents of protected areas of memory, which could be used for injecting malware into the system or worse. The problem was that this was caused by a flaw in the processor hardware design and thus was completely unpatchable. Microsoft and Intel did a good job of mitigating against them in firmware and software, but the specific hardware vulnerability remained until, you guessed it, the next generation of Intel chips were launched in which this specific vulnerability was fixed.

This was the eighth generation of Intel processors, and it goes to highlight some of the problems that can come about because of the continued use of older hardware. Again, we'll look at this in much more detail in Chapter 6 when we cover e-waste and recycling of older equipment as that creates its own environmental problems if people upgrade to use the newer operating system or are effectively forced to upgrade for reasons of security.

It's no better on the operating system front, with older versions of operating systems falling out of support now after just a few years. This is less of a problem with Windows PCs and Apple computers as it is with smartphones and tablets, as the Windows 11 upgrade block notwithstanding, desktop and laptop computers will typically keep on using the latest versions of their required operating system until the machine either grinds to an inevitable halt with age or just breaks and stops working altogether.

With smartphones and tablets (the ones running Android and iOS), things are very different. As I have already mentioned, Apple do a great job of supporting older hardware with their latest versions of iOS installing and running happily on devices that are seven years old. When you then factor in the life of that latest OS upgrade, you have a good nine years of support for these devices. Let's face it, nine years is a long time for a smartphone or a tablet, and it'll probably be dead before that time comes anyway.

Google, sadly, aren't anywhere near as diligent. Earlier in this chapter I wrote about how original equipment manufacturers (OEMs) don't like upgrading smartphones and tablets running Android to new versions of the OS if the device itself is more than two years old. This is purely for reasons of corporate greed, as they want you to go out and buy a shiny new device. You can't even switch to a different manufacturer as they're all as bad as each other, and all do it.

If we do a little more math, we can work out just what this means for security. Google release an operating system with four years of support. It often takes a full year for this operating system to roll out to devices as the OEM wants to take the time to tailor that OS with their own look, feel, and apps. At this point we're down to three years of support.

It's often then another year before someone purchases the smartphone as they don't want to pay top dollar for it and instead want to wait for it to become more affordable. We're now down to two years of support.

Once the person has had the smartphone for one year, the OEM has already decided to never give it an upgrade to the latest version of the OS, which by that time will already be available. So there are no new upgrades coming, and we have only one year of support left. By the time the handset is two years old, to the person who purchased it anyway, it is completely out of support and potentially vulnerable.

Things can get even worse though as it's not unknown for some smaller OEMs to release devices with not the previous generation of OSs on board, but the one before that. This usually happens when a device launches around the same time as a new OS version. In this case the OS is already two years into its supported life from Google, and if the person waits another year for the price to drop, they then only have one year of support for that device and no upgrade path ahead of them from the OEM.

Now I'm going to caveat all of this, as it does make it sound like every Android smartphone and tablet in the world is a security disaster waiting to happen, which it's not …sort of. Yes, it's true that in 2018, which was a particularly bad year for Android security, there were more than 26 million different pieces of malware for Android recorded in the wild, and during 2021 the GriftHorse malware infected more than ten million Android devices.

The more we use our smartphones for from shopping, to banking, to in-person payments, the more vulnerable we are to malware being able to access our finances and steal money. In reality though things are slightly different.

For malware to infect our smartphones and tablets, it has to go through several steps first. The apps themselves will have their own security built in, and this is especially true of banking and finance apps, which are getting more secure all the time. Our banks will also use two-factor authentication methods to help prevent the theft of money from our accounts and fraudulent transactions being made on our credit cards. My advice is to do *all* of your banking through smartphone and tablet apps as these are considerably more secure than banking in a web browser can ever be.

Then there's the device hardware itself, which will almost always now include both a TPM encryption chip and a biometric device such as a fingerprint reader or iris scanner. Apps will use these to authenticate a user before a transaction is allowed to take place. This is a very high level of security.

The Android OS also has several layers of security built in, the first of which is the Android app store. Yes, it's true that all of the malware I've mentioned came from fraudulent or hijacked app store apps, usually games, but Google still do a good job of keeping the store secure. It might not sound like it from the scary statistics, but there's more going on here, and that's social engineering.

Antisocial Engineering

If we take another short trip down memory lane, you might remember using Windows XP. This venerable old operating system was lovely and as comfortable as an old shoe, so when Windows Vista failed to set the world alight, people stuck with it. By the time Windows 7 came around, XP had already been with us for eight years, and people were naturally resistant to change.

XP was horribly insecure, however. It was designed for a time when the Internet was fairly new, the high street was still a direct competitor to Amazon, Google was only three years old, and nobody had even coined the phrase "social media," let alone thought to build Facebook or Twitter. These wouldn't emerge until 2006. When XP was on sale, MySpace was the only social network to use.

What Windows Vista introduced PCs to was User Account Control (UAC), which was a security layer that sat between the user and the computer and required the user to authenticate any operation that could inject malware into the system. While annoying in Vista, it was later tamed for Windows 7 and has now become something we're largely oblivious of as we're all so used to it. Similar systems were also introduced in iOS and Android when they launched in 2007 and 2008, respectively, while MacOS, which had been built on the UNIX operating system framework, had already included it for some time.

The inclusion of this new layer of security meant that malware could no longer just inject its way into an operating system in the way it had done so before – a new strategy was needed. This came in the form of social engineering and emails trying to trick the end user into installing the malware because it was a fun game they might want to play or a video they might find really funny.

These tricks are still being played today, but, while malware-injected emails and office documents still exist, social media is now the weapon of choice for criminals wanting to infect our devices.

On Facebook, TikTok, and Instagram especially, but also on other social networks such as Twitter (X), it's relatively straightforward to get a person to click a link to watch a video of a cat falling off a tall cabinet or a child getting its head stuck in railings. Because people consume this type of content so readily, and because people have become used to filling their smartphones with pointless games they'll only even play once, malware has a whole new way to embed itself on our devices.

What we can do about this really all comes down to education and awareness, something we'll look at in detail in Chapter 8, but it highlights the problems we face with smartphones especially.

Smartphones and Your Organization

When it comes to your own organization, you have a potential way for not just one piece of malware to attack your systems, but potentially for millions of pieces of malware to attack your systems. This happens every time you allow a smartphone to connect to your local or cloud servers and upload or download documents and files or share and send them to other people.

Again it's not all a disaster waiting to happen as anti-malware software in our local PCs and our servers and in cloud services such as Microsoft Azure and Amazon Web Services is extremely good at finding and eliminating these threats. They do happen though with a story from only last week as I write this of the UK's National Health Service (NHS) being hit by *yet another* ransomware attack that took many systems offline.

It's just another example then of the challenges facing the volume of e-waste we produce if a business has a policy stating that only devices running supported operating systems can access their systems, if Jane from sales or Derek from accounts wants to know why the phone they've only had for a year and a half is suddenly blocked from company servers.

This can be a difficult juggling act for an organization, and your own IT department will know their anti-malware and security systems well enough to be able to advise you which is the best way to jump. It is something that needs to be considered, however, when allowing people to use their own smartphones for work.

How Green Is Your Beige Box?

Whatever happened to beige box PCs? I have a computer museum in my home office, and in my collection are an original IBM 5150 PC and the very first Apple Macintosh, both of which are very beige and both of which are awaiting some new capacitors to get them working again.

Sustainability wasn't really a consideration back in the early days of computers. This was primarily because earlier electronic components weren't anywhere near as reliable as modern electronics.

When you purchase PC equipment though, you might want to know just how environmentally sustainable and repairable it is. There are several schemes that manufacturers *can* but often aren't obliged to use that can show just how "green" their products are.

Where I live in France, there's a mandatory repairability score that's given to all new electronics and electrical products (see Figure 3-1). This provides clear iconography that tells the purchaser or consumer how easily (or not) repairable the device is.

Figure 3-1. *France has a colorful mandatory repairability index for products*

When it comes to computer equipment though especially, such as desktop and laptop PCs, peripherals, and other devices such as smartphones and tablets, the Global Electronics Council developed the EPEAT (Electronic Product Environmental Assessment Tool) scheme (www.epeat.net). This gives products a score "*measuring the social and environmental impacts of products from extraction to end of life*" (see Figure 3-2). It has already been adopted by many major PC manufacturers including Acer, ASUS, Dell, HP, and Lenovo.

Figure 3-2. *EPEAT assigns gold, silver, or bronze awards for sustainable products*

You can use the EPEAT ratings to get a far better idea of the overall sustainability of the product, including whether recycled plastics and metals are used in its construction, what types of packaging are used, and other criteria. The organization also has a handy product finder tool on its website that you can use to search for detailed sustainability information on computers, smartphones, peripherals, and other electronic devices (see Figure 3-3).

22 Results Found					EXPORT RESULTS	EXPORT ADVANCED	
EPEAT Climate⁺™	Product Name ⌃	Manufacturer ⌃	Product Type ⌃	Location of Use ⌃	EPEAT Tier ⌃	Registered on ⌃	Status ⌃
	Surface Book 3 13.5-inch	Microsoft	Notebook	United States	Silver	2020-05-15	Active
	Surface Book 3 15-inch	Microsoft	Notebook	United States	Gold	2020-05-15	Active
	Surface Laptop 13.8" (7th Edition) (model 2036)	Microsoft	Notebook	United States	Gold	2024-05-29	Active
	Surface Laptop 15" (7th Edition) (model 2037)	Microsoft	Notebook	United States	Gold	2024-05-29	Active
	Surface Laptop 3 13.5-inch, Alcantara palm rest (model 1867)	Microsoft	Notebook	United States	Gold	2019-10-09	Active
	Surface Laptop 3 13.5-inch, metal palm rest (model 1868)	Microsoft	Notebook	United States	Gold	2019-10-10	Active
	Surface Laptop 3 15-inch, Alcantara palm rest (model 1873)	Microsoft	Notebook	United States	Gold	2020-11-30	Active
	Surface Laptop 3 15-inch, metal palm rest (model 1872)	Microsoft	Notebook	United States	Gold	2019-10-10	Active
	Surface Laptop 4 13.5-inch, Alcantara palm rest (model 1950, 1958)	Microsoft	Notebook	United States	Gold	2021-04-15	Active
	Surface Laptop 4 13.5-inch, metal	Microsoft	Notebook	United States	Gold	2021-04-15	Active

Figure 3-3. *You can search for EPEAT awarded products on their website*

How Do You Choose New Hardware Devices?

With all that said, how do you choose what device types to purchase for your organization, both for smartphones (if you issue company phones) and for laptops and desktop computers? With smartphones my best advice is to do some research online, not for how long an OEM says they'll support a device for, as these companies can be very fickle and frequently change their minds, but for how long they have historically supported their devices for. This needs to be researched on a company-by-company basis as it will change over time, but websites such as the popular `https://endoflife.date` contain useful information on both current- and previous-generations of devices from a wide range of manufacturers.

As I have already mentioned, however, two companies that are very good at supporting their devices for a long time are Apple and Samsung. Apple typically support a device for up to nine years, and some (but not all) Samsung smartphones are supported by up to three Android versions. With one of these being the currently installed version, this means a maximum supported life of 10–12 years, which ought to be enough for anybody.

What Do You Use Your PC For?

When it comes to desktop and laptop computers, you should look at what the machine is to be used for and where it will be used. There are all manner of different factors to consider here, and we'll look at several typical use cases as you might be surprised at some of the "best" choices available to you, and we'll look at some of the different uses you will put your computers to in a moment.

It's also important to consider at this point if you will be purchasing your own equipment or asking employees to use their own. While some might sneer at the latter unless you make a contribution toward the cost of their machine, the general benefits include the person getting a machine that they like, enjoy using, and feel comfortable with. This element of personal choice can make people significantly happier with the computers they use, which, in turn, can have a knock-on positive effect on productivity and general happiness in the job.

People have all manner of considerations when they choose their own PC or laptop. The ergonomics of the keyboard and trackpad are often highest on the list, with some people preferring clicky, tactile, mechanical key switches and others like myself preferring quiet, low-profile keys. Screen size and resolution will also be an important consideration, and some people might want to get a Mac instead of a PC. Of course this is perfectly okay these days as all cloud services for business support the different desktop operating systems available.

The Office Desktop

Let's take a typical example of a business PC, the office workhorse. This is a machine that won't typically be used for anything more demanding than making video calls over Teams or Zoom. It'll be using a web portal or bespoke software to perform tasks such as writing and editing documents, filling out and submitting forms, communicating within the company and with suppliers and customers, and other often mundane productivity tasks such as resource allocation.

There are different ways to jump here as the traditional desktop PC can be a terrible choice in this role because it is too large and too powerful and consumes far too much electricity to justify being used in this role. Instead we have several options ...

All-in-One Windows PC

A low-power all-in-one PC – this can be a good way to go because it allows you to provide the worker with just a single desktop device. While many will be perfectly happy with a full-HD monitor with a 1920 × 1080-pixel resolution, at a size of 24 inches, some roles will require a larger screen or a greater pixel density. All-in-one PCs tend to use laptop hardware, i.e., a single card with all equipment integrated, so they are quite impossible to repair or improve.

Small-Form-Factor PC

If you already have monitors or prefer more flexibility over the hardware that you purchase and use, a small-form-factor PC is often a good choice. These can often be attached to the back of the monitor and hidden out of sight while also taking advantage of mobile chipsets, meaning lower power consumption while still being more than powerful enough for everyday tasks.

Micro PCs

You can now buy very small computers, smaller than SFF PCs. Intel was quite good about it, with NUC devices, but there are now a lot of alternatives, and Intel decided to stop and sell that brand to ASUS.

All-in-One Chrome PC

An all-in-one Google Chromebook or Chromebook+ computer can be a good way to go if the work being performed takes place entirely in online services accessed through a web browser. Google Chrome is the browser that defined industry standards, and even if you use a different browser in the workplace such as Microsoft Edge, you would be very unlikely to find anything that wasn't perfectly happy in Chrome as well.

Windows 365 and Entra ID

Microsoft's Windows 365 and Entra ID (formerly known as Azure Active Directory (AD)) services allow people to access company software and networks on absolutely any device. Because general office tasks are a low-intensity job, it only requires a low-intensity device. For the most casual of use, even an Apple iPad running Remote Desktop will suffice to get access to a full Windows system that, on the iPad's screen, will to all intents and purposes look and feel just like a full Windows PC.

This method also allows the use of older hardware, provided the operating system version it's running is still under active support, as in the case of Windows 365 the processing and storage is all done in the cloud and then streamed to the user's device.

The Mobile Worker

Things can get a little more complicated with mobile workers as you need to consider factors such as that person going to places where Internet connectivity might be unavailable or if they need a laptop that is more rugged than normal, for example, they're visiting construction sites or in a role where the laptop will be slung around a lot.

All-Metal Body

One way to reduce e-waste with laptops is to choose a model with an all-metal body. This can help in several regards. Firstly, and perhaps the most obvious, is that an all-metal body will be stronger and longer-lasting than a laptop with a plastic shell. It won't crack or break under strain and will be much stronger overall.

The other advantage of an all-metal body is that it can be recycled infinitely. Plastics break down after being recycled a few times. While you can continue to recycle metal, when a plastic can no longer be recycled, it has to go to landfill or be incinerated, neither of which is good for the environment.

Using Mobile as a Workstation

A new trend is on its way: users needing only to do browser or simple app usage can then connect their smartphones to a USB-C dock, which will provide power, screen display, mouse, and keyboard. Samsung and Google's high-level models allow to do it, for example. So I can use my Samsung S23+ with a PC dock for having more comfort taking notes or reading documents.

Windows vs. MacBook vs. Chromebook

It's an automatic way of thinking for most people that when you're equipping your workforce with a laptop, you just buy a PC with Windows. The reasons for this are many, from the obvious of "Well, Windows is just the business OS, duh!" to the enterprise license subscription you're probably already paying Microsoft for, which includes the latest version(s) of Windows and all the deployment and management tools you need.

It's not all that cut-and-dry though these days as, while in the dark and distant past (i.e., before 2010), we all relied on software running on a Windows 10 PC to get stuff done. Then came Microsoft Azure and with it the ability to run apps in the cloud and stream them to PCs. Now, Windows 365 allows us to stream an entire PC to a PC or indeed to any other device.

This, coupled with the fact that most work these days can be done in a web browser, means that you can be genuinely platform agnostic when it comes to the operating system itself. Both Chrome OS and MacOS will do an admirable job of keeping your people productive, and there can be advantages too.

I wrote earlier about the Apple M SoC processor architecture the company introduced in 2020 and how power-efficient it is. For now at least (as I write this), Intel and AMD haven't quite caught up, so if you need a laptop that's slightly more powerful, perhaps to run a computer-aided design (CAD) application or to do work in Photoshop, a MacBook could very well be the way to go, given there's a full version of Microsoft Office available for the OS and anything else you can either do in or run from the cloud anyway.

ChromeOS also has advantages, not the least of which being it's a cinch to deploy and maintain, with the OS pretty much taking care of itself with updates directly from Google. As with MacBooks, ChromeOS machines also have impressive battery life, helping keep people going through a working day.

Wi-Fi vs. All the Gs

Next, we come back to something I mentioned a little while ago, that of your mobile workforce not having Internet access for some of the time. It's down to yourselves to decide how important this is, but plenty of laptop and convertible computers now come with built-in cellular data, be that 4G (fourth generation), 5G (fifth generation), or whatever it's on by the time you read this.

You'll need a SIM card, or an Electronic Subscriber Identity Module (eSIM), with a data package, but you might find that if it helps people stay in the field and not have to drive around polluting the environment while they return to an office, it could be money well spent.

Note   I wanted to slip in a note here about eSIMs (Electronic Subscriber Identity Modules). You'll be familiar with the SIM card you plug into your phone to get a connection to your carrier, but most modern smartphones and some laptops, too, come with the ability to support an eSIM instead. This is a SIM card held entirely in software, and its advantages include being able to quickly and easily get people connected to local networks when they travel internationally, as well as the obvious and massive reduction in the overall consumption of plastics and metals that come with SIM cards being posted everywhere and dumped when they're no longer needed.

The Power User

Sometimes in your organization you'll find there are people who just need a high-powered machine. This could be because they have to perform design, rendering, editing, or other processor-intensive tasks. Here you need to weigh up the cost of the equipment, the cost to the environment, and the power consumption of the computer itself. Again with this there are several options, but perhaps less flexibility when it comes to being sustainable.

Let's face it, with processor and- memory-intensive tasks, you're fighting a losing battle to try and make it as environmentally friendly as possible. That's just not really feasible for a powerful machine, so what are your options?

Buy the Fastest and Most Powerful PCs You Can

It could be that you need a "powerful" machine for your work but that the work itself is an occasional piece of light video rendering, in which case a small-form-factor PC using some mobile (laptop) components such as a modern laptop processor will already give you a huge performance boost.

You have to weigh up the workload for the machine against the hardware you will purchase. If the machine is being regularly or exclusively used for a task such as video encoding, computer-aided design, photo or image editing, or engineering, then my advice is always to buy the most powerful PC you can justify the cost for.

This approach might seem like an oxymoron, but sometimes you just have to buy the newest, fastest, most powerful PC components on the planet, as I did a few weeks before writing this when I configured and built myself a new PC for work and gaming.

So I set about the task of building myself the most environmentally friendly, most power-efficient PC I possibly could, only to realize that this was pretty much impossible. I needed a powerful processor, so a 35 W unit was simply not going to cut the mustard, but the full-fat 125 W processor in my previous desktop had been serious overkill, so I chose a 65 W AMD processor instead.

Where I could make a contribution to the environment was buying as efficient a power supply as I could, and I wrote in Chapter 1 about the grading scheme for these.

The aim then became not how environmentally friendly I could make the PC, but how I could reduce e-waste by giving it the longest lifespan I could. If I could make a PC that would be powerful enough to last six to ten years, comfortably seeing out the rest of my working life, then that would be as good a contribution as ever.

The older PC would, as is the case with all my discarded computer equipment, be donated for a close friend so he could do gaming, something it was still more than powerful enough to handle.

Look to the Cloud

If you can't or don't want to build or buy the fastest and most powerful PC on the planet, why bother? If your existing PC or a new, lower-end PC has a decent-sized and good-enough-quality monitor and a fast and stable enough Internet connection, why not use the cloud?

At the time of writing, putting a powerful rendering PC in the cloud is expensive, and you're also faced with the prospect that chucking huge files up and down your fiber connection might slow things down. This won't always be the case, however, and using Windows 365 to run powerful PCs, which can then be used anywhere and on practically any device, might be a cost-effective alternative to purchasing expensive hardware yourself.

This works doubly given that if you find later down the line you need an upgrade, you won't have to ditch the PC and buy a new one, costing money and contributing to e-waste; you can simply upgrade your service subscription and buy more cores, more memory, or whatever else it is you need to get the job done.

Upgrading and Repurposing Computers

You might find with some PCs that you can breathe new life into them by route of a straightforward upgrade. Adding more memory to a PC can often be the quickest and cheapest way to breathe new life into it, say upgrading it from 16 GB RAM to 32 GB. Adding a new graphics card can help a CAD or video rendering PC work more efficiently or provide AI capabilities the PC just didn't have before, and swapping out an aging hard disk for a modern SSD (solid-state disk) can speed workflow.

While upgrading laptops has always been difficult going on impossible, the Right to Repair movement has gained traction, and, though not every laptop will support upgradeable and swappable components, it's not very difficult these days to find laptops that will, and you may choose to purchase these machines in preference for the sealed, non-upgradeable units going forward.

You might find however that, just as you might do with your children's clothes, PCs can be repurposed for different people in different departments. A powerful PC that was used by one of the engineering teams a few years ago might still be perfectly suitable for one of the accounts team that needs to work on large spreadsheets. This might seem counterproductive, as a powerful PC, especially an older one, will use more electricity. It can be argued though that for as long as the computer still works, using it is far preferable than it ending up as e-waste.

Both of these also vastly reduce the amount of e-waste being produced, so before purchasing a fleet of new desktop and laptop PCs, it can be good to do an audit, see what's still good, and spend some time thinking where else in the company it might be useful, perhaps even working as an upgrade for the machines already in use there.

How Hybrid Work Fits with Your PC Choices

All of this brings us on to hybrid workers, sometimes called work from home (WFH), and what you can do to help encourage them to be more environmentally responsible with their computer purchases.

Again some of this will come down to education and information, which we will cover in Chapter 8. People are, on the whole, not especially IT literate. They'll know how to use what they need to use to get things done, but if you asked them what a PC bus was, they'd probably say it's the thing Microsoft staff use to get to work in the morning.

All of the information in this chapter does, of course, relate as much to hybrid workers as it does to your own business, so should be shared with them. Maybe even buy them all a copy (of the eBook though to save on paper wastage).

Encouraging people to buy something that's appropriate for them and not to over-purchase is never going to be a bad idea, and so it can be helpful where people work from home to have a conversation to see if that computer will be used for anything else, such as gaming or their photography hobby.

The more we can do to work as a community, the more success we will have at driving down the effects of climate change, and I'll discuss the interconnected world we live in much more detail in Chapter 10.

Summary

Clearly there are a lot of considerations to be made when choosing new IT equipment. Be that anything from a smartphone to a workstation PC, there are environmental considerations, security concerns, best-practice methods, and the effect our decisions will have on the e-waste mountain both today and in the future.

Then there's the cloud to consider, as it's considerably more powerful now than at any time in the past, and surprisingly these massive data centers can sometimes be the best and most efficient way to create a sustainable and environmentally conscious future for your organization and its IT operations. In the next chapter then, we'll stick our head in the clouds to see what's up there, how it can help us, and who's leading the way with innovation and sustainability.

CHAPTER 4

Appraising Cloud Services and Climate Change

We've all got our heads stuck in the clouds somewhere. From something as straightforward as using Microsoft or Google email or OneDrive or Dropbox file backup and sync to systems such as Teams or Zoom for chat and collaboration, we're using cloud services that are powered by huge data centers, and we have been doing so now for a couple of decades at least.

Back in the early days of data centers, there was no incentive to try and tackle energy usage and emissions to combat climate change, as that wasn't really a "thing" in the public consciousness until the mid-2000s. Sure the term "global warming" was first used in 1975 when American scientist Wallace Broecker used it in a scientific paper. This was around the start of the modern computer revolution, and while it was the late 1980s when the hole in the ozone layer first came to the public's attention, it was thought at the time all we had to do was ban the use of chlorofluorocarbon (CFC) gas in aerosol sprays.

© Mike Halsey 2025
M. Halsey, *The Green IT Guide*, https://doi.org/10.1007/979-8-8688-1233-0_4

Birth of the Data Center

That isn't to say that the companies running data centers, including Microsoft and Google, didn't have an incentive to reduce their power consumption. Both Gmail and Hotmail were free services, as were Google Drive and OneDrive (known as Windows Live Folders and later SkyDrive at the time). While Azure didn't appear until October 2008 and didn't really begin to gain traction for a few years after that, power cost money, so with no way to monetize cloud services for the best part of a decade without advertising, money (and power) had to be saved.

It didn't help that this all came at a time when Intel was the world's most dominant designer and manufacturer of microprocessors. The iPhone wouldn't appear until 2007, and the smartphone revolution wouldn't start for a year or two after that. AMD was also in the doldrums. They might have created the first 64-bit desktop processor in 2003, but they just couldn't compete with the might of Intel, who were reputedly using all manner of dirty tricks at the time to maintain their dominance.

The processors both Intel and AMD were making were also, looking back on them now, clearly the wrong types of processors, as both companies were pushing for more and more core grunt. Processors needed to be ever more powerful as people and businesses were wanting to use their computers for more and more powerful tasks.

The use of computer-generated imagery (CGI) special effects in movies might go as far back as *Vertigo* (Alfred J. Hitchcock Productions, 1958), *Westworld* (Metro-Goldwyn-Mayer, 1973), and *Tron* (Walt Disney Productions, 1982), but it was ultimately director James Cameron that pushed computer effects into the mainstream public consciousness with *The Abyss* (Twentieth Century Fox, 1989) and *Terminator 2: Judgement Day* (Carolco Pictures, 1991) and the use of motion capture by Peter Jackson in *The Lord of the Rings: The Fellowship of the Ring* (New Line Cinema, 2001).

Clearly movies would never be the same again, and by the time the 2010s came around, we'd be seeing fully virtualized environments in *Avatar* (Twentieth Century Fox, 2009), full-body replacement in *Captain America: The First Avenger* (Paramount Pictures, 2011), and completely CGI actors with both Peter Cushing and Carrie Fisher in *Rogue One: A Star Wars Story* (Walt Disney Productions, 2016).

It was no different in science and research, which required powerful mainframe systems. The Cray-1 supercomputer first went on sale in 1975 with its unique circular design with surrounding seating that covered the power and cooling equipment. It wasn't until the early 1990s though that what was then still known as the microcomputer began replacing mainframe computers in server rooms, and the dot-com boom in the mid- to late 1990s really gave birth to the modern data center with Apple and VMWare being the first to launch virtualization software specifically for use in these environments.

By the turn of the century, the data center revolution was in full swing as Amazon launched Amazon Web Services (AWS) in 2002 and in 2013 Google kicked off their cloud infrastructure investment with $7 billion.

Modern Data Center Infrastructure

Today, and as I write this, Microsoft maintains more than 300 physical data centers in over 140 countries worldwide. Amazon maintains more than 100 data centers in around 25 countries. Google meanwhile operates 36 data centers in around 18 countries. You then also have major tech companies including IBM, Oracle and Apple, Meta (Facebook, WhatsApp, Instagram), and Tencent (WeChat) in China all owning and operating their own data centers.

When it comes to the smaller companies, these tend to be hosted on server infrastructure that already exists, such as AWS and Azure, as it is expensive and difficult to maintain the types of infrastructure these companies require, but using the infrastructure of companies like Amazon and Microsoft also enables these smaller companies to be agile and scale their capacity up or down as needed by their customer base.

Legal, Privacy, and Political Issues

You might wonder why Microsoft needs to have more than 200 data centers in more than 70% of the total number of countries on Earth. There are several reasons for this, the most obvious being the speed with which the services operate for businesses and end users (being physically closer to the data center really does make a difference), and obviously there's capacity to consider, as there are more than 500,000 companies subscribed to Azure services.

There are other issues, however, some political, some legal. There are countries in the world, including China and Saudi Arabia, that insist that if you provide cloud services in their country, the data stored for those services must be accessible to their government(s) and must therefore be physically located within the country's legal jurisdiction. Google, for example, which has had all manner of disagreements with the Chinese government over search and censorship, doesn't maintain a single data center in that country, despite desperately wanting a piece of a hugely lucrative Chinese search market.

Amazon does have infrastructure in China, and Microsoft also owns and operates data centers in China. None of these companies operate in Saudi Arabia, however, while they do have data centers in the region, in the UAE, Bahrain, and Oman.

Indeed you may remember a story from 2010 when Blackberry, which were hugely popular with businesses around the world due to their end-to-end messaging encryption, were forced to open a data center in Saudi Arabia or risk missing out on that lucrative market. Saudi Arabia still has a strong hold on the tech companies, but both Azure and AWS operate in the country in partnership with other, and more local, tech firms that effectively act as a customer face for them.

Even Tencent, which is arguably China's largest cloud service company operates, more than 20 data centers right around the world, from the USA and Brazil to Europe, Asia, and Australia.

Then we come to the legal difficulties. In 2013 US law enforcement handed Microsoft a search warrant for emails as part of a US drug trafficking investigation. The emails, however, were stored on a server in Ireland, a member of the European Union and an independent country. Microsoft said no, as the data was outside of the US government's jurisdiction and the Irish government also formally stated that a company operating in Ireland should not have to hand over data to a foreign government as the warrant was not recognized under Irish and European law.

The case dragged on until 2018, when at the bequest of the Federal Bureau of Investigation (FBI), the US Congress passed the Clarifying Lawful Overseas Use of Data Act or CLOUD Act to try and resolve the issues. This was viewed by the European Union as being in breach of their General Data Protection Regulation (GDPR), and in response the German Commissioner for Data Protection warned against the German Federal Police using Amazon's servers to store their sensitive data.

Privacy and GDPR

The whole US government vs. Microsoft case shone a particularly large spotlight on company data, and companies, organizations, and governments around the world began demanding to have the option of storing their own, politically or commercially sensitive data in their own country or in a country of their choice (such as being kept within the European Union).

Microsoft obliged and began rolling out new data centers to accommodate their customers, with a promise that the service would then eventually also be available to consumers as well.

On these links you can see information on the data centers for the large cloud providers and their locations around the world:

- Microsoft – `https://datacenters.microsoft.com`

- Google – `https://www.google.com/about/datacenters`

- Amazon – `https://aws.amazon.com/compliance/data-center/data-centers`

- Tencent – `https://www.tencentcloud.com/global-infrastructure`

Let's be clear that none of this completely protects sensitive data from hackers or from a government or law enforcement somewhere in the world suddenly demanding access to data stored in their territory, but as an additional safeguard, it's something businesses and governments everywhere felt they needed.

This also feeds into specific privacy and data protection laws, such as GDPR (you can read about this at `https://pcs.tv/3FaoL55`) in the European Union, which is considered to be by far the most stringent and robust data privacy regulation in the world and is the reason everybody living in or visiting one of the EU's 27 countries will have a notice pop up for practically every single website they visit asking for permission to store data-collecting cookies in their web browser.

Data Centers vs. Climate Change

Data privacy obviously does present a problem when it comes to tackling climate change. With hundreds of massive data centers all around the world, how do we reduce our impact on the environment and reduce the volume of power these data centers consume?

One example would be to put the data centers in places where it's easy to keep them cool without using electricity, such as the arctic circle or somewhere where all the power needed can be generated by a sustainable means such as solar panels or through wind turbines.

With data centers in practically every country on Earth, placing them where they can use sustainable energy isn't really a feasible option. Sure, some, even many, data centers can take advantage of these conditions, but others will fall very short. This, of course, is where the companies that own and manage those data centers have had to step up to the mark.

This is where things get a little confusing, as companies generally fall into one of three categories:

1. They're clear and concise about the technologies, and the methods they are using to reduce their carbon footprint, and to be more sustainable.

2. They have clearly defined targets on where they aim to be in reducing their emissions and becoming "net-zero."

3. They simply don't say anything or much of anything at all.

Most companies, especially companies listed on stock exchanges around the world, will fall into category number 2. They'll be required by stockholders to disclose what they're doing, (a) because it's the type of information institutional and private investors want to see these days and (b) because the release of any further information could be considered "commercially sensitive" and they won't want their competitors getting the same ideas and perhaps stealing the march on them.

Establishing the Climate Credentials of Cloud Providers

So how do you go about establishing the green credentials of individual companies, so that you can determine where you should put your money and whose services you should be using? Let's look at each of the big players individually at this point.

What Does Net-Zero Actually Mean?

Before we jump into looking at what individual companies or corporations are doing to reduce their impact on the environment, and even to help restore the balance of nature, I want to examine what the term "net-zero" actually means.

This term is banded around a lot as a way to say a business, an organization, or even a whole country is helping reduce the impact of climate change. In fact it's not really that simple, being that *net-zero* is effectively just a marketing term.

Net-zero (sometimes known as carbon neutral) is defined as "achieving a balance between the amount of carbon emitted into the atmosphere, and the amount of carbon removed from the atmosphere. Net-zero happens when the amount of carbon added to the atmosphere is no more than the amount removed."

What net-zero isn't is a measure of how a business, organization, or country is doing to actively reduce the amount of carbon in the atmosphere, in addition to their becoming net-zero and not making things any worse.

Here we get into a little more jargon and find the terms "climate positive" and "carbon negative," which effectively mean exactly the same thing as one another. Being carbon negative means that the amount of carbon you remove from the atmosphere is greater than the amount of carbon you put into it.

It is possible, though I'm not accusing any company or organization of doing this, that a claim can be made about being carbon negative when the amount removed from the atmosphere is just a single ton or so more than they contribute. While I'm in full support of businesses becoming carbon negative, this is where actual figures and percentages start to be really helpful.

What About Carbon Offsetting?

Some companies will claim to already be carbon neutral when really they're not; they're using a system called "carbon offsetting" to effectively cheat. Microsoft Azure, which I'll come to shortly and which says it would be using 100% renewable energy by 2025, also says they've been carbon neutral since 2012 by using a combination of reducing their own emissions and using carbon offsetting.

Carbon offsetting is a way for businesses and organizations to compensate for their own carbon emissions, by investing in carbon reduction projects elsewhere. Once a business has calculated, either themselves or with the help of a specialist agency, their own carbon emissions, they purchase "credits" from accredited carbon reduction projects that they can use against their own published carbon footprint.

In all, carbon offsetting is a good idea, but it can be seen as a way for a business or organization to claim they're carbon neutral when they're actually nothing of the kind, and they can also act as a disincentive for actually and aggressively reducing your carbon footprint anyway.

Where carbon offsetting becomes contentious is in high-impact areas such as aviation and travel. When you've booked a flight, domestic or international, you might have been asked if you want to offset your carbon emissions by donating money to plant some trees. This is a good thing in itself, but it's often suggested that people, businesses, organizations, and whole countries should be planting more trees anyway. Offsetting then becomes seen as a way for people to pretend they're being environmentally friendly when they're really not.

When a business or organization then claims they are carbon neutral, it's always good idea to see or ask if any of this has been achieved by carbon offsetting, as if that is the case there is clearly still some way for them to go to reduce their own impact on the environment.

As a good way for your business to get a head start on becoming carbon neutral though, you might want to consider carbon offsetting, and you can find out more about it on the following page at the World Economic Forum:

www.weforum.org/agenda/2019/06/what-is-carbon-offsetting

Microsoft Azure

Clearly, as one of the largest companies on Earth, not just one of the largest technology companies, Microsoft have acres of pages and downloads on their website about their environmental strategies. They were formed by Bill Gates after all, whose charitable foundation works around the world to help the poorest communities with problems like water and sanitation, disease prevention and eradication, and agricultural development.

All of these things are directly impacted by climate change, so it's understandable that Microsoft don't want to be seen working against the interests of their founder and largest individual shareholder.

Microsoft's aim for their Azure services at the time of writing are

- To be carbon negative by 2030

- To replenish more water than they consume by 2030

- To be zero-waste certified by 2030

- To not contribute to deforestation with new construction by 2025

These are unchanged from the time when I wrote the first edition of this book, with the one exception being that the carbon-negative pledge was pushed back from 2025.

As a company they also work with charitable groups and projects around the world on aims such as optimizing water usage and improving water quality, reforestation, and promoting energy efficiency. These are all the types of things you would expect a major corporation to be doing when they're trying to set a positive example about sustainability and community.

Microsoft then, as you might expect, are a company that provides real information about the technologies they use and are developing to make their data centers more sustainable and environmentally friendly.

On their website they list several technologies including liquid immersion cooling, which as you can imagine is using servers immersed in liquid to reduce the heat they produce. Microsoft first trialed this type of technology with Project Natick, which placed a sealed data center at the bottom of the North Sea off the coast of Scotland between 2018 and 2020. You can read about this at `https://natick.research.microsoft.com`. Microsoft recently announced that the project has been forsaken.

Grid-interactive UPS batteries and clean fuels for power backup are two more technologies the company lists on their website, and all of these, fortunately, come with downloadable data and technical documents because if there's one thing I've learned in all the years I've worked with Microsoft as an MVP (Most Valuable Professional) awardee, they love their jargon and acronyms.

Microsoft end their commitments by saying that by 2050 they aim to have eliminated all of the carbon that has been emitted by the company since it was founded in 1975. They don't say how they will achieve this though normally becoming carbon negative is achieved by investing in projects and technology that actively remove carbon from the atmosphere.

You'll probably use other Microsoft products and services, too, such as Windows 10 or Windows 11, or perhaps you purchase surface hardware and will be interested in how these purchasing decisions extend across the entire company. The goals of course are the same, but to help with clarity,

Microsoft produce an annual company sustainability report, which you can find online at www.microsoft.com/sustainability and https://azure.microsoft.com/global-infrastructure/sustainability.

Amazon Web Services

Amazon Web Services' (AWS) goals are very similar to Microsoft's. That is to be net-zero by 2040. Helpfully, Amazon do publish regular updates on exactly how they're achieving this with articles about new solar and wind power plants they are building or investing in.

Amazon also detail the technologies they use to make their data center servers more power- and energy-efficient and how they use water more effectively and efficiently in the company.

Amazon also have a regular podcast that might interest you or your colleagues, where they, business leaders (usually from companies already using AWS), and experts discuss technology that's being used to combat climate change.

As for wider and broader goals across all of Amazon's companies, these can be found at https://sustainability.aboutamazon.com where the company details their broader ambitions:

- To be carbon neutral by 2040

- For 50% of all shipments from Amazon.com to be carbon neutral by 2030

- For all Amazon's businesses to be using 100% renewable energy by 2025

All in all, the goals at AWS aren't currently as ambitious as those set by Microsoft Azure, but the latter company as I have explained has to take a very aggressive line because of the negative impact not doing so will have on the Bill and Melinda Gates Foundation.

This doesn't mean you should automatically choose Azure over AWS when looking for a cloud partner, as other factors to consider can include Amazon only running a small number of data centers worldwide, around 30, compared with the 200 operated by Microsoft. I detailed this earlier in the chapter when talking about legal problems and data privacy, and these are all factors to be taken into account when choosing a cloud service provider for your business.

Amazon provide sustainability reports, which you can download from `https://sustainability.aboutamazon.com/governance` and `https://sustainability.aboutamazon.com/environment/the-cloud`.

Google Cloud

When I wrote the first edition of this book, Google proudly proclaimed on their website that they are carbon neutral already, though they didn't say if any of this had come by means of carbon offsetting. Now, however, we get the answer to that question as their current aim is to achieve net-zero emissions by 2030, which is a lot more honest. They do also have specific commitments, however, as Microsoft and Amazon do:

- To be using 100% carbon-free energy by 2030

- To accelerate the "circular economy" to maximize the reuse of finite resources across the company and supply chains and to enable others to do the same

- To replenish 120% of the water they use by 2030

The way they word this first point is interesting, as it's only when you drill down into the detail they say this will come from 100% renewable sources. If a company says they will use "carbon-free" energy, then to my own mind this could just as easily include nuclear power as it would renewables. This makes it a good idea to always check the detail.

Google, however, do go on to talk about services, tools, and utilities they themselves as a company provide to help other businesses use renewable energy, for cities to monitor their own carbon emissions and use smart technologies to help reduce them, and for people to reduce their own emissions at home.

These normally come in the form of products like the Nest thermostat and data modelling services, but it's good they are promoting the environmental services and products they produce as a company that can also help others, perhaps even yourselves.

Google produce an annual sustainability report that can be downloaded from their website on these links: `https://sustainability.google/commitments` and `https://cloud.google.com/sustainability/`.

Tencent

At the time of writing the first edition of this book, Tencent was the only major cloud service provider that didn't detail any climate and sustainability policies on their website. This might be unsurprising given the company and many of its data centers are located in China, which as a country is the biggest polluter on the planet, producing about a third of all global carbon emissions.

Now, however, they've caught up and provide environmental and social governance (ESG) information. The company has set out a carbon roadmap that says they will achieve carbon neutrality and to use 100% green electricity by 2030.

It might be difficult, therefore, for this company to switch to renewable power when so much of the power in the country is generated through the burning of coal, though they don't mention if this goal will be achieved by building their own solar or wind generation plants.

While Tencent didn't publish any information and data a few years ago, the amount of information they now publish is extensive, perhaps even going beyond Microsoft in outright transparency. You can find this information and data on their ESG website: `www.tencent.com/esg`.

Oracle

When we get to the smaller cloud service providers, we find their goals are broadly in line with the larger players, with Oracle setting a goal of using 100% renewable energy in its data centers by 2025, though their net-zero date is set to be 2050, which is much later than the larger companies.

Oracle have also upped their game since the first edition of this book was released with much more information than was previously available. You can find it all on their website: www.oracle.com/sustainability.

IBM

IBM are quite similar on their own website, with a whole raft of very interesting and useful articles about sustainability and the many different things the company is doing to reduce their impact on the planet.

What I couldn't find at the time of writing this or the previous edition of the book, however, were any actual and measurable goals for the company, such as achieving such and such by 2025 or something else by 2030.

If you are purchasing services from IBM, it would be a good idea to ask your reseller or IBM representative for specific information on their sustainability policies and practices (www.ibm.com/sustainability).

Hardware and PC Companies

By this point you might be wondering about the sustainability policies of the companies you purchase your computer hardware from and what they are themselves doing to reduce their impact on the planet and the impact of the computer and other equipment you purchase from them.

There are a couple of things to look out for when it comes to the actual hardware devices you purchase:

- Repairability – Is the company on board with "Right to Repair," which I detailed in Chapter 1, which makes it much easier for you or third-party independent companies to repair and upgrade hardware?

- Ocean plastics – A big move with technology at the moment is the use of reclaimed plastic from the ocean to be recycled and used in some components of electrics and technological products. These plastics are often of a low-grade quality and so might only be used for part of a product. Their inclusion, therefore, is often much more than a marketing gimmick than a real achievement.

You can find individual companies' sustainability policies and reports online at the following links:

- HP – www.hp.com/us-en/hp-sustainability.html
- Dell – https://corporate.delltechnologies.com/en-us/social-impact/advancing-sustainability.htm
- Lenovo – www.lenovo.com/gb/en/about/sustainability
- Samsung – www.samsung.com/us/sustainability
- Apple – www.apple.com/environment

Other Cloud Service Providers

When it comes to other cloud service providers, you need to search for the information on their own websites, and the results will vary. Some, for example, will be very clear about their policies, while others won't. One of the biggest cloud telephony providers, for example, 3CX, still doesn't provide any sustainability information on their own website at the time of writing this second edition. All I was able to find was a blog post from 2020 on how home working can help the environment. You can find this article online at `www.3cx.com/blog/unified-communications/world-environment-day-remote-working`.

In fairness to these companies, you will frequently find that they don't use their own data centers, but instead run their services on the backbones of Microsoft Azure and Amazon AWS.

As an example of this, Sony runs its PlayStation cloud gaming network on Azure and has been doing so since 2019. This is despite Microsoft and Sony being direct competitors in the console and cloud gaming space. It just so happens that it's better and more cost-effective for Sony to use Microsoft's services.

When you speak to cloud service providers, you can of course ask them if they use their own data centers or if their backbone is provided by one of the big players in the market, and you might want to do this anyway just to be sure the answer isn't Tencent holding customer data in a Chinese data center. If the latter is true, then the sustainability policies of the company you are looking to purchase services from becomes, perhaps, less important. This will be because the hosting company's (Microsoft, Amazon, or Google) sustainability policies for their cloud service will automatically apply to the small cloud service company.

A Sustainable Future for Cloud Services

As technology advances, so do the things that cloud service providers can do to make their own data centers more sustainable and energy-efficient. There is a big push toward the big.LITTLE processor architecture I detailed in Chapter 1, AMD launched new 128-core EPYC server processors in 2023, and ARM processors are also becoming much more popular in data centers because of their inherent power efficiency.

The advantage of this type of technology is twofold. Firstly, the energy-efficient cores take on the work at times when the server is relatively idle, but also the huge number of cores in the processor (you may only have four or eight in your own PC processor) allows you to achieve more on a single server, such as running parallel tasks, virtual machines, or serving different customers simultaneously.

Having more cores on a processor can result in two outcomes. You can either have fewer servers in a smaller data center doing the same amount of work as a huge number of servers in an enormous data center, or you can still have huge data centers, but far fewer of them being required to service your entire customer base.

Both of these outcomes are good for the environment, and it demonstrates how technology firms have generally "got the memo" when it comes to sustainability and climate change.

The cloud is still growing, however. To compare, for the best figures I could find, in Q1 (quarter 1) of 2016, AWS revenue was slightly over US $2 billion. By Q1 of 2021, that had grown to almost US $14 billion and was $23.06 billion by the second quarter of 2023. Microsoft's cloud services grew by 23% in just the third quarter of 2021, making over US $15 billion, or 36% of the company's entire revenue for the quarter, and $25.9 billion in the last quarter of 2023, when Google Cloud made $9.2 billion, and there is no sign of any of these companies' cloud offerings slowing down.

Fortunately, they know this and will have already factored this growth into their own sustainability plans. This is in part why Microsoft, Amazon, and Google devote so much of the sustainability pages on their websites to detailing the renewable energy projects they're undertaking or investing in and all the new technologies they are developing, either on their own or with partners.

Summary

Microsoft, Amazon, Google, Tencent, and absolutely every other company on the planet that runs data centers keep very quiet about the number of servers they operate and what types of hardware they're using. This is understandable, however. The information would be constantly changing, it's commercially sensitive, and it would only be twisted by hardline environmentalists that would prefer the number be significantly smaller anyway.

One of the things that is rapidly changing data centers and our use of them is AI, with Microsoft themselves announcing that their carbon emissions because of the addition of power-hungry AI services like CoPilot and ChatGPT (which Microsoft also host) have increased by 30%. So in the next chapter we'll look at this new technology and examine how it can both help and hinder your and cloud providers' goals to achieve net-zero.

CHAPTER 5

Artificial Intelligence and Climate Change

Sitting in the Bay of Bengal, just west of the Andaman Islands in the Indian Ocean is North Sentinel Island. This island is small, measuring 60 square kilometers (23 square miles) and is the home of the Sentinelese. This isolated tribe lives completely separated and cut off from the rest of the world. They fish with spears and hunt with bows and arrows, and beyond that very little is known about them.

There have been attempts to contact the Sentinelese over the last few hundred years, but generally these attempts don't go well. Toward the end of 1771, an Indian merchant ship, the Nineveh, was wrecked on a reef close to the island. One hundred six surviving crew swam to North Sentinel Island for safety and were immediately attacked by the Sentinelese. Other and more formal attempts to contact this tribe over the years have almost always resulted in the deaths of those who dared to disturb these people.

An eventual peaceful contact was made in 1991 by the Anthropological Survey of India, who took gifts of food and cooking implements to the island. Little progress was made, though, with the party completely unable to communicate with the islanders, who clearly warned the visiting scientists not to stay very long.

Perhaps a more typical example of contact with the Sentinelese was in November 2018 when an American missionary named John Allen Chau made an illegal visit to the island (this bit is important and I'll come back to it). Chau was quickly killed and, we presume, eaten.

© Mike Halsey 2025
M. Halsey, *The Green IT Guide*, https://doi.org/10.1007/979-8-8688-1233-0_5

Recognizing the significance of the Sentinelese, their desire to be left alone, and their complete lack of immunity to all the viruses everybody else had built up an immunity to decades or even centuries ago, the government of India made the island a protectorate and in 1956 prohibited all travel to the island, with anybody who travels within 5 nautical miles (9.3 km) of its coast picked up by the Indian navy and summarily prosecuted.

I mention North Sentinel Island not because it's anything to do with climate change, because it isn't, but instead because the Sentinelese are very probably the only people on the planet who haven't heard about the current trend of assigning the label AI to everything.

If you look around you, artificial intelligence is everywhere. As I write this, only yesterday Apple announced they will be building AI into their Siri virtual assistant. Microsoft have also recently announced new CoPilot+ PCs, and Nvidia have announced new data center server hardware for AI that I will come to later.

I'll also come to explain in a while why, while the technology behind AI might be artificial, it most certainly isn't intelligent and won't be for quite some time, if ever. Of course, the world of AI is changing so rapidly that this chapter is guaranteed to age like warm milk, but I'll give it a go of trying my best to future-proof things if I can, which will likely mean talking about AI advances in more general terms.

I want to start with some history though and look at where the idea behind AI came from and what we believe it to be.

The Living Machine

Artificial intelligence was first talked about in the novel *Erewhon*, written by English writer Samuel Butler and published anonymously in 1872. A satire on Victorian life, the novel tells of machines that come out of the industrial revolution that learn to self-replicate and that become self-aware and able to reason.

If you look to examples of AI in fiction though, you'll probably more likely think of film and television, with Fritz Lang's German expressionist silent film *Metropolis* (1927), Stanley Kubrick's *2001: A Space Odyssey* (1968), Robby the Robot from *Forbidden Planet* (1956), or maybe the television series *Lost in Space* (1965–1968), which copied that idea to create "Robot."

More recent examples you might think of are Ridley Scott's *Blade Runner* (1982), which is itself based on the 1968 dystopian science fiction novel *Do Androids Dream of Electric Sheep?* written by Philip K. Dick, James Cameron's *The Terminator* (1984), Agent Smith from *The Matrix* (1999), or the character of Data from *Star Trek: The Next Generation* (1987–1994). Of these some have been benevolent, such as Data or Robby the Robot, and others have not including HAL 9000 from *2001* and obviously the T-800 Terminator.

Indeed artificial intelligence has proven such a popular subject for science fiction that it inspired author Isaac Asimov to create "the three laws of robotics" in his 1942 short story *Runaround*. In the story the laws are presented in the form of the fictional "Handbook of Robotics, 56th Edition, 2058 AD" as follows:

- The First Law – A robot may not injure a human being or, through inaction, allow a human being to come to harm.

- The Second Law – A robot must obey the orders given it by human beings except where such orders would conflict with the First Law.

- The Third Law – A robot must protect its own existence as long as such protection does not conflict with the First or Second Law.

If you think about artificial intelligence in robotics today, we're not expecting Lt. Cmdr. Data to start working alongside you in the office, as even basic home-help robots can do little more than chat awkwardly with the elderly. If you asked people today what an artificial intelligent robot would be like, they'd probably imagine a Boston Dynamics robot equipped with weapons on the battlefield and get flashbacks of ED-209 from the movie *RoboCop* (1987).

In short, artificial intelligence frightens people, and perhaps rightly so, as it's been depicted all too often as an aggressor that sets out to destroy humanity.

How AI Solves Climate Change (Scenario A)

Let's take this back to the main topic of this book then and look at some fictional ideas of how AI could solve climate change. We're going to make several assumptions here. The first is that the AI in question can think and reason and make logical decisions and then act on those decisions to self-replicate, create tools and robots, and carry out actions.

All of this is a stretch as things currently stand, and it's one of the reasons why I say the days of being wiped out by the "Rise of the Machines" are some considerable way off in the distance.

In this scenario though the AI has been tasked with solving climate change. It logically comes to the conclusion that even if some form of climate change would happen naturally and that humans have made the problem considerably worse by pumping huge quantities of greenhouse gases into the planet's atmosphere, if humanity stopped doing this, the planet would eventually find a new equilibrium and return to its normal, beautiful self.

But then we hit the snag, as the AI reasons that humans are very unlikely to give up their pollution, at least give it up entirely as they're far too wedded to their technology, machines, and general way of life. A logical conclusion then could be drawn that wiping out humanity would be both the quickest and most efficient way to solve the problem of climate change, and the AI goes to war with us, quickly and efficiently wiping out all human life on Earth while leaving all other plant and animal species untouched.

This is clearly the *Terminator* scenario and hugely unlikely for the reasons I've already given of machines not able to self-replicate and human beings still being essential for most roles the machine brain would need carried out.

How AI Solves Climate Change (Scenario B)

So we have an artificial intelligence that has concluded that mankind is the problem and needs to be wiped out, but that knows it doesn't have the capability to create the weapons and armies it needs to wage war on us. So what does it do?

The machine brain will look to the tools it does have available to it and use those instead. There are already a huge volume of "weapons" it could use that are potentially or even definitely connected to networks the machine can access. These include nuclear power stations, nuclear weapons, and even more everyday and innocuous things like the energy grid and social media.

The machine could shut down or overload energy grids to starve us of electricity. This would cause a societal collapse and cause many people to freeze and die in winters. Alternatively the machine could use disinformation to make humanity go to war with itself.

This latter scenario is the truly scary one, but could it actually happen?

Artificial Intelligence and Why It Isn't

So having detailed the nightmare scenarios in which artificial intelligence wipes out humanity, let's do some healthy debunking, and we'll start with the fact that while AI is certainly artificial, it's definitely *not* intelligent.

We think of intelligence as being able to reason and create the way humans do, use tools the way apes and monkeys can, or learn to detect explosives or trapped people as we do with dogs. An intelligent creature looks at the world around it, all of the world that it sees, makes judgements about that world, and draws conclusions from it. This is perhaps best exemplified as determining it needs to seek shelter when a storm brews overhead. Most living creatures will act in this way, and undersea creatures will hide from predators that threaten them.

What we now call AI grew out of data science and the need for business and the scientific community to sift through enormous mountains of data to find specific items, build patterns, and make sense of that data in general terms.

Specific examples of this might be looking at thousands of hours of digital camera footage to trace the route and the actions taken by terrorist subjects or criminals or searching through mountains of genetic data to find a cure or more effective treatments for cancer.

These are called "data lakes," and for decades now technologists have been working on new software and tools to help scientists, engineers, and security forces make sense of them and make them genuinely useful.

Out of this have grown many tools, and all the major cloud service providers, including Microsoft Azure, Amazon Web Services, and Google Cloud, offer data lake tools and services. Microsoft's Power BI (Business Intelligence) tool is one of these, able to analyze huge volumes of data and present that data in ways people simply can't do because it would take forever, even if they knew what they were looking for in the first place.

The data we train these services on has to come from somewhere, and new AI tools are fed the Internet, usually all of it, so that it can digest the information it finds there and build enormous databases that it can refer to when providing us with answers to questions. You might have heard news stories about media organizations, such as a lawsuit brought against ChatGPT creator OpenAI by the *New York Times* to get OpenAI and its biggest single investor, Microsoft, to stop harvesting their copyrighted content.

So let's look at the quality and veracity of the information these tools are digesting. Much of it will come from freely available sources, such as out-of-copyright and even in-copyright books. US comedian Sarah Silverman has challenged OpenAI for pirating content from her books.

Other content will come from blogs, news articles and online news sources, and even social media. There's more information out there on the Internet now than there ever has been before in the form of text, spoken word, and video, but can we trust the quality of this information?

Here's where we get to one of the biggest problems facing the world today, misinformation. Everybody has an opinion, and most of those opinions will be challenged by others. Some people have an ulterior motive to spread untruths, perhaps to sway an election as has already been seen around the world, or to control the people of a nation in the way dictatorships like North Korea and tightly controlled countries like China have been known to do.

As human beings we're able to look at the information we read and form judgements about it. We're, sometimes but not always, taught in school from a young age to check information to see if it's backed up by other, and reputable, sources, such as peer-reviewed research, or factual information provided on subjects such as coding or medicine.

The software that sifts through the Internet can't reason like this. Tools like ChatGPT are not artificial intelligences, but instead are really two different tools called "Generative Models (GMs)" and "Large Language Models (LLMs)." Generative Models are the tools used to create images, audio, and other non-text-based content, while LLMs create text and chat and are used for search.

What people are talking about when they speak or write about an AI is something that is able to reason and draw conclusions in the way the human or an animal brain does. This is known as "Artificial General Intelligence (AGI)" and we're not there yet.

This is because there is a finite amount of data that can be fed to the GM or the LLM, and it cannot see, read, or hear anything beyond that point. It doesn't know it's sitting in a data center, can't see the people working there, and doesn't know where the building is in the world or what the weather is doing unless it has also specifically been fed this information.

Anthropomorphizing the Machine

Anthropomorphism is the attribution of human traits, emotions, or intentions to non-human entities and is considered an innate tendency of human psychology. You might believe that your dog thinks it's a human because of some of its behavior or that your fish is making fun of you when it stares at you from its bowl.

It's the same with GMs and LLMs as while you can have a conversation, typed or spoken, with ChatGPT, Google Gemini, or another new AI tool, it's not actually thinking. Instead, it's been trained on what conversation is and what the expected response should be in any given situation. It's able to regurgitate this data in a way that approximates a conversation. It *is* providing often or mostly relevant responses to your queries, but it's *not* independently creating those responses based purely on what it's been taught before, what its own opinions might be (because it doesn't and can't have any), and what it believes you're going to want to hear.

We assign human characteristics and traits to the GM or LLM, however, because we see and hear it actually having a conversation with us. This is in the same way that if we ask it to create an image of, say, a man in a small boat fishing on a lake with snow-topped mountains in the background, it can do so, and we believe it's actually creating art.

It's able to do this because it's already been fed millions of images of all those things, and it's able to extrapolate individual items so that they can appear together in the same image and in a way that respects aesthetics and what we have come to expect from imagery and pictures.

None of this demonstrates intelligence, however, and this can be proved, because if you take all the data away and ask the GM or LLM to do the same things, it will be completely unable to respond. This is unlike a human who, while they might completely lose their memory and not know who they are, where they are, or why they're there, will still be able to communicate and function. The human has learned skills that no amount of memory loss can ever take away and where serious damage to the brain would be required to cause the human to cease being able to function.

Animals, birds, and fish are also able to function and communicate even when they have little or no intelligence. At the moment, much of western Europe is seeing an invasion of very nasty Asian hornets that are attacking and, in some places, decimating bee populations. Nobody would describe a hornet as intelligent, yet they are able to communicate with each other, work collaboratively, identify different species of insect and different colonies of Asian hornet, attack colonies of bees and even people, and then know when it's then time for them to move on.

Then we have a computer that contains a Neural Processing Unit (NPU). Your smartphone probably has one of these, and the desktop PC I'm writing this book on contains one. The computer needs electricity to function, as do we and all "life," but turning on the power to a computer and leaving it doesn't mean the computer will start to process data on its own. It will literally just sit there, idling, until an actual person gives it instructions. This isn't intelligence.

AI and Quantum Computing

So can we ever have AGI and is it even possible? Later in this chapter I'm going to talk about the challenges AI poses for those combating climate change because of the enormous amounts of power it needs to consume.

The other problem facing NPUs and GPUs (Graphics Processing Units) that are used to generate AI content is the amount of processing power available. Up until now all processing has needed to be done in the cloud, in enormous data centers, because only they have the processing grunt available to perform the simplest tasks such as replying to a message in a conversation.

When Microsoft announced their new CoPilot+ PC concept, which is PCs capable of generating their own AI content locally while not having to send and receive data from the cloud into what are being called SLMs (Small Language Models), they announced that any PC released with the branding must meet a minimum specification. One of those specifications is an NPU able to perform a minimum of 40 trillion operations per second (TOPS).

At the time of writing, both Intel and ARM are gearing up and getting ready to release their first generations of processors capable of meeting this specification, with further development for future generations still ongoing. Microsoft announced the CoPilot+ specification when there was only a single processor on the market that could meet the spec, Qualcomm's Snapdragon X, which can handle 45 TOPS. I have a new work/gaming PC in my office with one of the very latest AMD processors on board and it, like the Intel processors released at the same time, can only handle 16 TOPS.

This processing ceiling presents an upper limit to what GMs, SLMs, and LLMs can currently achieve. It might seem a lot, but the human brain can process somewhere in the region of one million trillion calculations per second, far ahead of what the fastest modern supercomputer can achieve, being 25,000 times quicker and more powerful than current NPUs.

I have three border collies, Evan, Robbie, and Téo (see Figure 5-1), and it's widely known that this breed is at the higher end of dogs' general intelligence, with them being roughly as intelligent as a three-year-old human.

Figure 5-1. *Evan, Robbie, and Téo*

Orangutans are the most intelligent primate species, considerably more so than dogs as they share 97% of their DNA with humans, but even orangutans are equivalent in intelligence to a five-year-old human according to scientists. If the human brain is 25,000 times more powerful than the most powerful NPU and we use primates and dogs as a point of comparison (you just wanted to sneak in a photo of your dogs – Ed), then AGI is still some considerable way off ...or is it?

This is where quantum computing comes into the picture. Quantum computing is the next generation of processing, if scientists are ever able to get it to work reliably. A quantum computer is one that exploits quantum mechanics to operate. Google are one of the many companies and academic institutions building quantum computers. They have estimated that, when fully working, their quantum computer would be able to perform calculations in seconds that would take the world's currently most powerful supercomputer 47 years to complete. That's an order of magnitude ahead of where we are today and comes very close to being able to compete with the human brain for computational power.

113

Some people estimate that the first workable quantum computer is between 10 and 30 years away, with many of the people building them freely admitting even they don't fully understand all the theories involved due to the sheer complexity of it all. When this eventually happens, we might begin to see the first signs of AGI, but only if we find ways to program "reason" and "choice" by then. Without these essential skills, even a quantum computer won't be able to "think" in the way a dog or an orangutan does.

Even then we're still talking about a computer that's the size of a small car and that usually has to be operated at near absolute zero (–273 Celsius or –459 Fahrenheit), so the odds that a quantum processor will be invented that can work and operate inside a handheld device as small as a smartphone is unlikely for at least the next hundred years (you can bet what one of the first tasks quantum computers will be put to then – Ed).

The Powered or the Powerful?

Now we've established what AI is or, more logically, what it isn't, there's absolutely no doubt about its benefit to business. Consumers will likely have little use for it, aside from the fake and joke videos that have appeared over the years about smart speakers being able to have long, rambling conversations with the elderly. In business though the possibilities for how AI can help in the workplace and boost productivity are practically limitless.

We're already seeing the beginnings of how this will work as I write this (this is the bit that will age like warm milk then? – Ed) with Microsoft CoPilot transcribing online meetings to both keep a written record and also allow people who miss that meeting to catch up with it afterward. CoPilot is also able to summarize those meeting notes and other documents into bullet point summaries.

Aside from making it easier for people to get up to speed with the daily life of business, these tools can also help write better emails and reports (that's no substitute for a good education! – Ed), and it can help with research, both within company documents and files, which is where SLMs come into play, but also with the wider Internet and the aforementioned data lakes.

Then we look at practical applications in medicine, research, and engineering. AI tools have already proven better than humans for spotting tumors and growths in X-rays, it's being used by researchers to help find cures for motor neurone disease (known as ALS in the US and some other parts of the world) and cancer, and we can only imagine what the first AI-designed bridges and skyscrapers will be like.

Naturally all of this takes a large amount of processing power, especially when people expect results near instantly. Earlier in this chapter I said that while, as I write this, PC processors powerful enough to handle this workload locally are starting to be released by Intel and AMD, only Qualcomm already has a processor powerful enough, the Snapdragon X, and this is perhaps a little hampered by being an ARM-based chip in a world where some older x86 Windows software still won't work under emulation (see Figure 5-2).

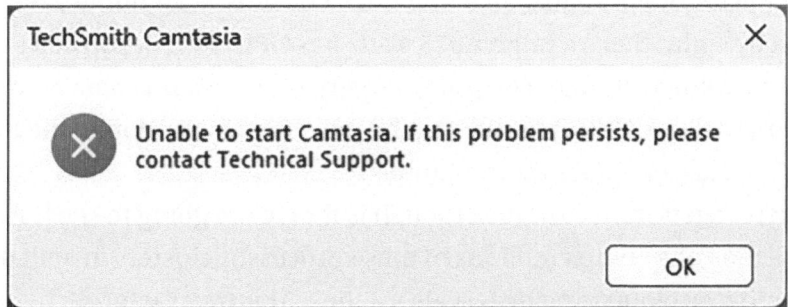

Figure 5-2. *On my own Windows on ARM PC, some software still can't run*

This all means that right now, all of the processing for AI tasks is being taken care of in the cloud, and there will be a huge amount of cloud AI processing in future years. This is especially true in business where much of the work people do takes place using cloud services such as Azure, AWS, or Google Cloud anyway.

At the beginning of this chapter, I said that Nvidia, traditionally a maker of high-end gaming graphics cards, had announced a new server processor especially designed to run AI workloads. This is because it was discovered that while GPUs can't run AI workloads as efficiently as a dedicated NPU, they can process those workloads considerably more efficiently and effectively than a standard processor.

Nvidia's CEO, Jensen Huang, proudly took to the stage in June 2024 and announced this new step forward for the cloud and for business. So here's the problem.

AI vs. the Climate: Who Will Win?

This Nvidia Blackwell GPU processor architecture draws 15 kW of power per cluster of eight GPU cores. 15,000 watts of power, enough to keep all the kettles in your office going, but these will be on and powered and used to their maximum potential all of the time, constantly, 24 hours a day. Divided by eight, that's a huge 1,875 watts per GPU. I think you can see where I'm going with this. The previous generation of GPU data center chips consumed 1,000 watts making the power consumption of the new chips 87.5% larger. That's quite a jump.

Where it gets more complex though is that we're going to see hundreds of thousands or perhaps millions of these processor clusters installed in data centers as cloud providers scale up their AI infrastructure.

One million of these GPUs will consume 1.875 gigawatts of power. So let's put this into context. A typical small nuclear power plant will produce 1 gigawatt of power, meaning that if a data center has one million

GPUs running AI workloads, that data center on its own will require *two* full nuclear power stations just to run it, double that which was required before.

Power stations running on fossil fuels, such as oil, coal, and gas, produce less than a gigawatt, as do renewables such as solar, wind, and tidal. It's also extremely expensive and takes a huge amount of time to build new nuclear power infrastructure, even though the technology is becoming safer all the time. As I write this I'm reading reports on how the energy industry is trying to work out how they're going to power all of this.

Where it all gets more complex still is that we can see the trajectory of where this is going. Since OpenAI first announced ChatGPT in 2022, there's been a race in the technology industry to see who can get to the top of the tree first, with OpenAI, Microsoft, Amazon, Google, and others all building and designing the next and the next and the next generation of these systems in quick succession, each more powerful and thus consuming more power than the last.

This isn't a technology where we get an update every two, three, or four years either, such as we're used to with new versions of software. Two years later and ChatGPT-4 was available, much more powerful than before with even Microsoft admitting they would continue using ChatGPT-3 for some workloads because the additional processing required by ChatGPT-4 was costing them a not inconsiderable sum of money.

If we look at usage though, we can see that until 2022 there really was nobody using these AI tools, except for their own development and testing. By the time ChatGPT-3 was released though, millions of people around the world were using them through tools like DALL-E, Bing AI, and Google Gemini.

When Microsoft launched CoPilot and immediately integrated it into every piece of software and service they have, from Azure, to Teams, to Windows, it was clear that many more millions of people would soon be using it. Microsoft even broke with tradition and back-ported these features into Windows 10, long after that operating system was officially out of its active support and update period.

The mandatory inclusion of a CoPilot key on the keyboard for every new PC going forward and the launch of the CoPilot+ PC brand sealed the fate of where Microsoft and other companies want this technology to go. This is, of course, what brought about the move to SLMs on individual devices or company networks. These enable a more limited amount of processing to be done using only company or personal files and documents.

Hitting the Ceiling

You might remember that in the previous chapter I went into detail about each of the cloud providers and their climate and sustainability goals. Microsoft have been honest though and already announced that so far, and this will inevitably get worse: their own carbon emissions have jumped by 30% just through the use and implementation of CoPilot in their services and their hosting of OpenAI's own services on Azure.

Where these companies then have goals of becoming net-zero by 2030 we can fully expect these targets to slip. This will present a very difficult challenge for the cloud providers. Currently they're all competing with each other to literally win the race for AI and pouring billions of dollars into research and development every year.

At this point it's fairly easy to predict where we're going to end up (good luck reading this without laughing in 2026 – Ed). Everything has a maximum ceiling. There is a maximum amount of power that energy grids and companies are able to generate. There is going to be a limit to the use business, science, medicine, and engineering will have for the technology, quite apart from the fact that it's already proving to be extremely expensive for business and industry to use. We also have Microsoft's own admission that the current previous generation of the technology is perfectly fine for most workloads.

This means we will eventually find an equilibrium, where there is a balance between usage, usefulness, power consumption, and cost benefit. The race to build the next, best, and fastest will continue, while in the real world, usage will likely continue to use previous generations.

Server processor design will also need to continue to evolve. We live in an age of increased climate awareness. While Nvidia's stock price soared on the announcement of the Blackwell GPU, media and news organizations around the world were not blind to the huge increase in power consumption it required. There will be pressure on Nvidia and other processor manufacturers then to temper this power usage, and their ambition, by also providing more power-efficient GPUs and NPUs to handle the workloads that people will actually want to be doing.

Blackwell will be extremely useful in the fields of medicine and science, but likely not so useful for the rest of the world.

Your Use of AI in Business

This brings us neatly on to how AI is useful to your own business or organization and to your own workloads and productivity. Primarily this is going to come down to cost. I have already mentioned that AI services are expensive. This is partly because the big tech companies have expended billions of dollars in research, development, and investment and will eventually need to recoup that money.

The main reason for the high prices in the cost of AI services, however, is that it's simply very expensive to run, with Microsoft's CoPilot Pro service for Microsoft 365 customers currently sitting at $20 per user, per month. This is a huge cost, especially when it's mostly only going to be used for tasks such as summarizing documents. Fortunately, each of the big cloud providers has clear information about price and costing on their websites, which you can see on the following links:

- Microsoft 365 – https://www.microsoft.com/en-us/microsoft-365/microsoft-copilot

- Microsoft Azure – https://azure.microsoft.com/en-us/pricing/details/cognitive-services

- Amazon AWS – `https://aws.amazon.com/augmented-ai/pricing`

- Google Cloud AI – `https://cloud.google.com/vertex-ai?hl=en#pricing`

What might prove more cost-effective is buying PCs compatible with the CoPilot+ branding when you upgrade your computers. It's very likely they won't continue to be called this in future years. My own assumption is that this was supposed to just be "Windows 12," but when Intel didn't have its chips ready in time, Microsoft created the CoPilot+ brand to fill the gap. Ultimately, by the time these new processors from Intel and AMD have been released, Microsoft will announce Windows 12 and no doubt declare that all new PCs and laptops sold using the operating system *must* carry one of the new processors. This might even have all happened by the time you read this.

Price/Performance

Your business decision then will be based on the benefit to productivity weighed against the cost per seat. This will not be an easy choice for businesses as there's no way when you first purchase an AI service to determine just how productivity will be improved, as there's no baseline to measure against, especially when staff will have to be trained in how to use these tools in the first instance so they can make the most out of them.

If we toss some climate calculations into the mix, we can assume there is a direct correlation between the cost per user and the carbon cost per user. This is because the cloud companies have already admitted the energy costs of using AI are very high.

If this is a consideration for you, then you will want to factor this into your purchasing decisions and only implement AI where it's definitely going to make the most difference.

If you can get heavily discounted or perhaps even free light-use AI services such as document summaries and meeting translation and transcription, you will likely find this is most of what your workforce will need to improve their productivity and offset the cost per seat.

Only then for much more demanding roles, such as new product design, strategic planning, and research, would you want a full AI system, and then it could easily be limited to a few generalized seats used by a team as opposed to each individual.

There may be a temptation to go all in because this is a new technology that has clear benefits to business and industry, but I would always advise limited testing first to determine how it might be used within each team or group within the business and what the best mix of services and pricing would be for each.

Personal Use of AI

Outside of the world of business and industry, there are many individuals and self-employed people that might be interested in what AI can do for them. Many companies already offer services to cater for this. Microsoft's CoPilot Pro is also available to individuals and consumers, though at (currently) $20 per seat it's no cheaper than the business offering while less capable overall, not having features such as analyzing data and trends within already existing company files.

OpenAI, Google Gemini, and many other AI services also exist that anybody can subscribe to for as little as $10 per month. A quick search online will detail what many of these are. There are a few caveats for the use of these services, however.

Most of them at the moment are focused on what we've traditionally seen as the original and main uses for this technology, the generation of images, videos, and short text and for online research.

This is fine in itself if you feel this can improve your productivity, but bear in mind there is a margin of error for the results produced by these tools, as quite often still the results they provide can contain errors and even misinformation – the AI not knowing how to tell the two apart when it encounters them online.

There's also the fact that so many companies, startups, and other firms have jumped on the AI bandwagon that not every one of them will survive in the long term. There are inevitably companies that struggle to compete and end up out of business. The best advice then is to remain flexible and agile, especially if you're with a smaller provider, so that if the service you're using does go bust, you're able to switch to a different provider quickly and simply.

Lastly there's an issue that I encounter myself as an author and the producer of educational video courseware for Pluralsight (you can find my Windows courses online at `https://app.pluralsight.com/profile/author/mike-halsey`). A few months ago I was sent a link to an AI service that you can train to very successfully imitate your own voice.

With the hundred or so hours of courseware I have produced over the years, not to mention other files I have produced for YouTube videos and recordings of talks and presentations I've given, there's plenty of material at my disposal to train such a tool.

This would be great for me when recording courseware as often I have to do multiple takes of a simple, short video because I'll fluff my line or need to cough, one of the dogs will bark or run around on the wood floor behind me, a tractor will go past my office, or a cow will be heard in the field next door. This isn't to miss the effects of the weather with heavy rain always being audible to a microphone.

With this AI tool I would be able to write the script, so that it's in my own voice and my own style, and then feed this script into the AI and have it output a perfect audio file that I could then overlay on a video recording of me demonstrating X or Y on the Windows desktop. A perfect job in just a single take!

Would Pluralsight allow me to use this tool, however? I reached out to them and they replied that, for the foreseeable future at least, the answer is a resolute no. The increase in my own productivity this AI tool could provide, which frankly would be enormous, just can't happen, at least not for the foreseeable future.

Then there are other professions where the use of AI tools is completely banned. In June 2022 a judge in New York imposed sanctions on two lawyers who submitted legal briefs that had been created by ChatGPT. The briefs were easy for the judge and his staff to spot as they contained six completely fictitious case citations, which the judge decreed were "acts of conscious avoidance and false and misleading statements to the court."

Other areas where the use of AI-generated content would also be completely banned would include education, research, medicine, and anything where health or public safety is a priority such as many engineering fields and architecture.

There will be limited use for AI in each of these, but to use an AI for the creation of an entire work or project in any of these fields would be a complete no!

It's important then, if you are self-employed as I am, to consider if the people, businesses, and organizations you work with and for would allow the use of these tools. It's always a good idea to ask, but never a good idea to assume it'll be alright.

Investment in AI Hardware

An alternative to the purchase of expensive AI cloud services is the use of AI on the desktop. Earlier in this chapter I wrote about Microsoft's CoPilot+ PC program. This takes advantage of NPUs in the PC hardware itself to run AI tasks locally. This is not only considerably cheaper for the business or the end user but also considerably better for the environment because it's an AI task that isn't needing to be run on a hugely powerful GPU or NPU in the cloud.

This I suppose is where the future-proofing part of this chapter really comes into its own (oh, some good news then – Ed) as by the time you read this the next generation of processors from Intel and AMD that include the NPUs running at 40 TOPS or more and that can take advantage of these new features being built into Windows will be available or might be just around the corner.

If you already have an NPU in your computer though or if you have a powerful graphics card, your computer might already have some or all of the grunt necessary to undertake AI tasks on its own, without you needing to upgrade. Some websites, software, and services are beginning to appear that allow you to test this, and one of the first was `www.devicetest.ai`.

Having a powerful NPU could end up being an important factor in your next hardware purchasing decisions, and you will be able to weigh the potential additional cost of CoPilot+ hardware against the cost of CoPilot Pro cloud or another cloud service. I'm willing to bet that the former will turn out to be considerably less expensive than the latter and do much of what a full cloud service can offer anyway, for everyday workloads at least.

Summary

AI is clearly very new and shiny and will remain the big thing that everybody wants to use and take advantage of for some years to come. We usually run on a cycle of around five to seven years of something being the latest big thing in tech, until some other new, big, and shiny thing comes along to replace it.

Speaking of replacing things and upgrading your computer systems to ones that include NPUs, in the next chapter we'll look at the inevitable outcomes of all of this and how PCs and other hardware can be repurposed and recycled safely so as to avoid ending up in landfill and what services (government or private) might be available to help you dispose of your old and unwanted hardware in an environmentally sustainable way.

CHAPTER 6

Effectively Recycling and Repurposing IT Equipment

Every dog has its day, as the saying goes, and it's the same with our computers, smartphones, operating systems, and even that piece of software you've been using like forever because it just works and does exactly what you need. I still use Microsoft PhotoDraw, which was released all the way back in 1999, as I just can't be arsed[1] learning Photoshop for occasional use.

We all hate saying goodbye to the things we love. I remember back in 2014 when all support ended for Windows XP. Because XP didn't include the security features that were only introduced with Vista, it was hugely vulnerable to malware and hacking. This would only be compounded by a lack of future fixes and patches, and there were certain to be additional vulnerabilities found in the operating system later that could also be exploited by criminals.

As a Microsoft MVP (Most Valuable Professional) awardee, I was asked with a couple of colleagues to tour the UK at the time to meet with tech user groups, businesses, and academia, to explain what end of support

---

[1] "Can't be arsed": slang. One is unwilling or disinclined to make the effort necessary (to do or accomplish something). Primarily heard in the UK.

© Mike Halsey 2025
M. Halsey, *The Green IT Guide*, https://doi.org/10.1007/979-8-8688-1233-0_6

meant and why they should be migrating to Windows 7 as quickly as they could. It was felt that as we didn't work for Microsoft, we would have much more credibility, and it wouldn't be seen as a strong-arm sales tactic.

What we didn't anticipate was the severe backlash we encountered. You might have been mistaken for thinking we were telling people they could never see their children again or they were going to have to lose their house. That was not, I can assure you, a fun or pretty summer.

While people can form strange and irrational attachments to software, it's not the same with hardware as a cracked screen can often result in a cry of "How much?!" when someone discovers they could almost buy a new phone for the cost of a replacement screen and then they go out and buy themselves a new phone anyway.

Right to Repair

I've already mentioned the movement called Right to Repair in Chapter 1, but I just want to reiterate that it's something worth looking out for when purchasing IT equipment. The short version is that the major tech manufacturers of smartphones and laptops have been keeping a very tight grip on the hardware they sell to you.

This is normally justified on the grounds that the technology inside is proprietary or that in order to get the size and weight of the device down, it has to be glued or include non-serviceable components.

The upshot is that the independent phone or computer repair shop in your neighborhood is never allowed access to technical or repair manuals for these products and isn't allowed to purchase spare or replacement parts from the manufacturer, sometimes even being threatened with legal action should they try.

A few are allowed to spend large sums of money and sign strict nondisclosure agreements to become repair shops, but largely the device manufacturers want you to return the device to one of their own stores or to their authorized service center.

Right to Repair is now being taken seriously by more manufacturers, and it is commonly described as meeting the following three criteria:

- That manufacturers make repair and technical manuals available to independent stores and that those store owners can purchase replacement parts from the manufacturer as required.

- That, wherever possible, manufacturers make the devices easily serviceable and use screws to seal the casing instead of glue. Note, however, that this isn't always possible, especially with smartphones and water and dust resistance, but things are improving.

- That the manufacturers agree to make spare parts available for some years after the device has officially ended support, to reduce the amount of e-waste going to landfill.

All of this means that when you're purchasing new hardware of any type, it is a good idea to ask about the Right to Repair policy of the manufacturer and how compliant the specific hardware you're purchasing is.

In 2021 France, the country where I now live, introduced the world's first "repairability index" with a clear and easy-to-understand iconography that must be shown for all electrical and electronics products sold in the country (see Figure 6-1). It's a simple score out of ten that gives the purchaser a clear idea of how repairable that product will be.

Figure 6-1. *The French repairability index shows clear iconography*

As an example of why this is important, it's now getting very common for laptops to come with a replaceable battery and solid-state disks (SSDs). This is about as far as it can be reasonably expected to go with a laptop as the motherboards are specially designed to fit in the case, memory is still all too often fixed to the motherboard, and the processor is always attached to the motherboard and fitted with a non-replaceable heatsink for reasons of heat efficiency. We can let the manufacturers have some of these as they make sense, though memory is still a contentious subject for many Right to Repair advocates.

Just being able to replace the battery in a laptop or the battery and screen on a smartphone though can extend its life considerably. Remember, however, there could be security implications for using smartphones and tablets for too many years, as I detailed in Chapter 3, and it can often be a good idea to put policies in place that prevent unsecured devices from connecting to your company network and files.

A Note About Dumb Phones

I also want to mention, when it comes to phones, the problems caused by the onward march of technological progress. Setting aside for a moment the issues I detailed in Chapter 3 about manufacturers only supporting the software on smartphones for a set number of years, after which time they can become highly vulnerable to malware, there are other problems that come along with some regularity.

Cellular networks are one, and you might remember the huge hype with the launches of the 3G (third generation), 4G, and 5G cellular networks around the world, how each one was a technological wonder that would enable you to do more of the things you love than ever before.

The problem with this does come much further down the line, but we do eventually reach a point where the semiconductor companies that make the modems and radios for these devices do eventually drop all support for older network types. 3G is still supported in some countries as I write this, but I still have a couple of perfectly serviceable older 2G (second generation)-only handsets that are completely useless except in a handful of countries where a 2G network is still in active use.

I found this useful website recently that details the retirement dates for 2G and 3G networks in countries around the world. If you still use a 2G or 3G phone, you might find it helpful: `https://eu.korewireless.com/2g-3g-network-sunset-dates`.

The thing is that 2G phones, often developed for sale in parts of the world such as India where these networks are still active as I wrote this, simply don't support 3G and above, because they're basic handsets that aren't Internet connected, and they simply don't need to support 3G or 4G. This is an important consideration as more and more people want to carry "dumb phones" so they can disconnect from the online world for their own sanity and peace of mind.

Fortunately, a few companies have recognized the need to continue providing what is most commonly referred to as "feature phones" including Nokia, whose phones are now being manufactured and sold under the HMD brand. You can find Nokia classics like the 3310 now updated with 4G support at `www.hmd.com/` feature-phones.

You might even wonder why some people find it important to switch off from smartphones. In addition to the people who like to switch off from the Internet when away from home, it's also common for people (including business travelers) to buy these basic handsets as "burner phones" when they travel abroad because of the risk of thieves stealing their smartphone when out and about or if they are traveling to a country where the authorities are fond of examining the contents of smartphones and laptops.

I've mentioned that most countries have already switched off 2G networks and that the switch-off for 3G is pretty advanced too. As I write this, 6G (sixth generation) and even 7G (seventh generation) are in active development, though many countries are still struggling with their 5G rollouts. While the future for mobile Internet might be marvelous for business, consumers, and the future of the Internet, it's quite alarming news for those that work in the e-waste industry or have a phone they'll want to use for years to come and for which the supported network(s) might be switched off.

While network support isn't a problem for modern smartphones, if you want to use or your workforce want to have access to a dumb phone, it's worth checking the specifications before you buy.

We can also talk about Wi-Fi versions. Wi-Fi 6 is not yet globalized but the OEMs start to sell Wi-Fi 7, always for good (and demanded) reasons: speed, security, and scalability.

Continuing to Use Older Hardware

So how as a business or as an individual can you hope to manage your devices and use them for as long as you can with all these problems to contend with? There are several ways to manage your hardware if you want it to be in use for a long time. Some of these solutions are simple and easily understandable; others are much more technical and require some expertise to implement.

Smartphones (and Some Tablets)

Let's start with smartphones, as we've been talking about them primarily so far in this chapter. In Chapter 3 I detailed that the device manufacturer will only support the hardware and security updates for a set number of years and that the operating system developer will also only support the OS on these devices for a set number of years.

This is because the device manufacturer wants to sell you a new smartphone, and it's also costly for new operating system versions to include updated drivers for all the hardware in a smartphone that still needs to be supported. Essentially companies, and you'll encounter this in your own business or organization, have to make a judgement based on cost-effectiveness.

In recent years though a whole new industry has developed to meet demand for people who want to use older devices. In part this came as a response to companies like Google, who many felt couldn't be trusted with their personal data, and people wanted to use an operating system on their brand-new phones that wasn't spying on them and accessing their personal information.

It quickly expanded though into a wider project, and now there are many mobile operating systems that can be installed on a huge range of smartphones old and new.

Ubuntu Touch

GNU/Linux has always been popular on desktop computers, and this is a subject we'll return to later in this chapter, but did you know that you can also install a full touch-friendly version of Linux that's been purposely designed for smartphones?

There are several different distros of Linux available for smartphones, but one of the most feature-complete and most popular is Ubuntu Touch: https://ubuntu-touch.io. This is supported on a very wide range of smartphones and tablets, and it is regularly updated with new features and security patches.

Installation is done by connecting the smartphone or tablet to a PC and running installation software. This can be complex, so it's best for those with some technical and programming skill to perform installations, as there is always a risk involved with installing a new OS on a device such as a smartphone of "bricking" the device entirely, making it completely unbootable. However, online tutorial and guides are available on the Ubuntu Touch website for those who want to try.

There are of course downsides to using Linux on a phone, and these almost exclusively revolve around the availability of apps. You will find apps for all the basics available, from GPS satnav to email, calendaring, and messaging. What is far less likely to be available are apps from larger companies such as Microsoft, Google, and Meta (Facebook, WhatsApp), so using Ubuntu Touch to access their services can often be a "do it through the web browser instead" type of affair. A full list of available apps, though, is available on the Ubuntu Touch website, so you can check first before deciding to install the OS.

LineageOS

If you prefer to stick with Google's Android operating system on your phone, then LineageOS could be the right choice for you. Google provide an open source version of Android that comes without all the Google services such as the Play Store, Maps, etc., and some companies use this as the foundation for their own Android variant.

LineageOS, which you can find online at https://lineageos.org, has a strong open source developer community who are either developing alternatives to apps from the big players in the market or who also have help and advice on hand for how to install your much needed apps manually. This is a process called side-loading, and while it won't work for every app, it's often a better alternative for people than Linux.

LineageOS is supported on devices as old as the HTC One M8 (2014), LG G2 (2013), and Motorola Droid RAZR (2011).

Sailfish

Like LineageOS, Sailfish (`https://sailfishos.org`) is an Android variant operating system, but one that has been built with a strong focus on privacy. It is not supported on as many devices as LineageOS, but if security and privacy are important to you (these are also strong features of Linux on smartphones), then Sailfish could be a good alternative for an older smartphone.

Note   I want to put in a note here about Apple's iPhones. The security that Apple build into the bootloaders for their phones and tablets can be very difficult to break, and the hardware is usually bespoke and custom to each device. This makes it extremely difficult for open source developers to create new operating systems for older iPhones and iPads. Apple are good at supporting older hardware themselves, however, with the normal lifespan for an Apple device being between 10 and 14 years.

XDA Developers

There is, as I mentioned previously, a healthy open source developer community for smartphones and, to a lesser extent, tablets. The main center for this community is called XDA Developers, and you can find it online at `www.xda-developers.com`. Here you can keep up to date with all the operating systems available for older and even new hardware and place requests for hardware drivers for your specific device.

Desktop and Laptop Windows PCs

When Microsoft released Windows 11 in 2021, they introduced strict hardware requirements for the first time. This took much of the tech community by surprise as until this point, if a PC ran the current version of Windows, it would likely also run the next version too.

This is because, with a few notable exceptions such as Windows Vista where much of the underlying architecture changed, the core parts of Windows don't vary much from one version to another, and Microsoft has, over the last 20 years, been reducing the minimum hardware requirements for each version rather than increasing them.

So when Microsoft announced that a PC would need an Intel eighth-generation (or second-generation AMD Ryzen) processor and a Trusted Platform Module (TPM) 2.0 chip or firmware TPM, many people found that their PCs and laptops that were running Windows 10 perfectly well now couldn't be upgraded to the new version of Windows.

This means that when Windows 10 ends all support in 2028 (support officially ends in October 2025, but three years of extended support can be purchased by both businesses and consumers), their PC would become either useless or potentially, horrendously insecure. Naturally as you can imagine, there was uproar.

Microsoft stuck to their guns, however, citing reasons of security, and the minimum hardware requirements didn't change as Microsoft figured any PC running Windows 10 now on the older hardware will be near the end of its life by 2025 anyway, the seventh-generation Intel Core processors having been replaced in 2017 (eight years before 2025) and TPM 2.0 replacing the older TPM 1.3 version in 2014 (eleven years before 2025).

Remember that all processors before eighth generation were not secure as requested with memory leaks allowing an application (or even a VM in a virtual environment) to see other apps' memory, thus forcing Microsoft to patch and reduce performances of PCs.

As you will be aware though, things are rarely that simple, with a great many PCs chugging on for 15 or even 20 years before finally giving up the ghost. I myself am still using a media center PC containing a third-generation Intel Core i5 chip that was released in 2012. It runs a sandboxed (disconnected from the Internet) installation of Windows 7, for which I paid for three years extended support, and it will no doubt still be in use for many years to come.

These PCs might end up running slowly, but for light office duties or as a means for the grandparents to stay in touch with family and email, they can be perfectly good. Even if we weigh up the downsides of having older, less power-efficient components, it's easy enough to swap out an old power supply on a desktop PC, and keeping a machine in use does stop it from ending up in landfill.

Linux on the Desktop

End of support for Windows on an older PC though is where GNU/Linux can come into play. Linux has been around since 1991 and is based on the older Unix operating system that was used on mainframes and minicomputers from its first development days in 1969. It can be argued that it is a more mature OS than Windows and has been much more secure from the start. Windows might be more user-friendly and more mainstream, but there will always be a place for Linux.

The GNU part of the name, which is something every tech writer and author knows to use to avoid getting shouted at by the Linux community from behind their pints of real ale, stands for "GNU's Not Unix!" ... Don't ask me why.

There are a great many variants of Linux (called distros), and they vary from the supremely technical to the very user-friendly. You can find a full list of all Linux distros at `https://linux.org/pages/download`, but the most user-friendly include Ubuntu (`https://ubuntu.com`), Linux Mint (`www.linuxmint.com`), and Manjaro (`https://manjaro.org`).

Linux has a few benefits over Windows including that, being open source, hardware driver support is excellent and the minimum required specifications to run it are incredibly low. This means on even the oldest hardware you can find that a Linux installation runs much more smoothly than Windows ever could.

Even software and app support on Linux isn't that bad, with all the major web browsers, including Google Chrome and Microsoft Edge, being available on Linux and the main productivity packages OpenOfffice and GIMP (a Photoshop alternative) being fully featured and compatible with the file formats for their Windows counterparts.

ChromeOS Flex

Linux isn't for everybody, however, as many people both want and need an alternative to Windows that is fully featured, but also very easy to use and understand and easy to keep secure and updated. To meet this need Google stepped in with an installable version of their ChromeOS operating system.

ChromeOS Flex is available for both PCs and Apple iMac and MacBook laptops. It can be downloaded from https://chromeos.google/products/chromeos-flex, and Google have a helpful hardware selector that will let you download a version that already includes the correct drivers for your hardware.

If you have a custom or self-built PC, however, then a generic version can be downloaded and installed.

For anybody that has already used a Google Chromebook laptop, you will know that it is an extremely simple and easy-to-use OS that includes all the apps you need. It's essentially a desktop variant of the Android operating system we use on our smartphones, and you can even install Android apps on ChromeOS.

Another advantage of ChromeOS is that it updates itself quietly in the background, making no fuss in the very same way Windows has never been able to achieve. This makes it a perfect (light) operating system for nontechnical people, children, or the elderly.

One last advantage, at least from this commentator's viewpoint, is that because you can install Android apps, you can get more secure access to banking and other finance and government services than you can in a web browser. Specific apps for these services will always be *considerably* more secure than accessing them in a browser, and I would always recommend you use apps for these tasks anyway.

Repurposing Older Hardware

Sometimes it's not necessary to shoehorn a different operating system onto a PC, as the PC itself might still be old, but the operating system will still be supported. Let's take Windows 11 as an example. You have a PC or a laptop that was purchased in 2017, containing an eighth-generation Intel processor, which would also (unless it was a self-build machine) have come with a TPM 2.0 security chip. This qualifies the machine for upgrading to Windows 11.

Let's say, for the sake of argument, that this PC stays on Windows 10 until 2025 when that operating system ends support. By this time the PC is eight years old. Windows 11 launched in 2021 with an expected ten years of support lifecycle, meaning that the PC could stay in support and still be used and receiving security and stability updates until it is fourteen years old, which is fairly old for a PC, at which point if it's still working you can look to repurpose it as a Linux or ChromeOS Flex machine, perhaps for a specific role within the business.

If you've ever tried to use a PC that's eight years old, however, you might not notice anything at first, but when you then compare things like startup times, spreadsheet recalculation times, and even the time taken for the PC to open apps and software on the desktop, you'll notice that one of these things is not like the other.

Here is where you'll be looking to replace the PC with a newer one as, let's face it, time is money and if the difference on 100 computers taking 2 minutes longer to boot to the desktop in the morning means an equivalent loss of 3.33 hours of lost productivity each and every day across the business, why would you not want to replace the machines? This doesn't even take into account the longer computing times associated with having an older processor when people are trying to "get work done."

With a potential cost of hundreds of hours of lost productivity each and every week just by not investing in new hardware, you clearly need to scrap the slower, older PCs and replace them with shiny new boxes.

Or do you?

Reallocating the PCs

It's always a good idea to undertake regular audits of your IT equipment to see what's what, what you've got, what it's being used for, and most crucially what you "need" it to be used for. This last point is the most important because it means you can often find new roles for a PC within the business. Let's look at a few examples.

The Payroll PC

While many companies now subcontract their payroll needs to third-party suppliers, some companies will still have a dedicated payroll system, and this is usually just a single PC sitting in a seemingly abandoned corner of the finance office (covered in cobwebs? – Ed), connected to a printer from which you print your employee pay slips, and running just a single piece of software, once every week or month to process the payroll.

This role, while critical to the business, isn't very demanding and is absolutely tailor-made for an older PC that's no longer of any use on the front line of accounts or logistics.

The Machinery Monitor

On the factory floor you have a lot of pieces of different machinery, and these need to be programmed and monitored. For this reason they'll often be connected to a dedicated PC that's used to reprogram the machinery for different production needs and to check its diagnostic and reporting sensors to maintain oil and hydraulic fluid levels.

Here is a great example of how to repurpose an older PC as even if the machinery it's connected to requires a computer with an older Serial (RS232) port, purchasing a plug-in PCI expansion card for the PC to support that port will cost just a couple of dollars. It's also very easy to purchase rubber plugs that can be put in USB and other ports on the PC to prevent dust getting inside them.

Better still, this is a machine that, because it doesn't have to be connected to any other part of the business (unlike the payroll PC), can be totally isolated from your network and from the Internet. The upshot is you can use a PC running an operating system that's completely out of support such as Windows 7 or even Windows XP.

The Visitors PC

If you run a business that has different premises or has regular visits from suppliers, customers, and stakeholders, you might find that having a spare desktop or laptop PC lying around can often be useful for the staff or other people visiting you. This could be for many reasons. Perhaps their laptop battery has died, or maybe even the laptop itself has died or gone missing. Maybe they just want to be able to spread out a bit for the afternoon and use a proper keyboard and monitor.

For occasional use a powerful PC isn't really cost-effective, so repurposing an older PC into this role can be a great way to keep the machine out of landfill. Sitting in an unloved and unwanted corner of the office (ooh! More cobwebs! – Ed) and, yes, probably covered in cobwebs next to that filing cabinet containing all the company-branded coffee mugs, baseball hats, and pamphlets you were never able to get rid of, this could be a useful and welcome addition to your premises for visitors.

The Training Room PCs

In Chapter 8 I talk about how you can use staff training to inspire your workforce to help you achieve your climate goals and, in turn, change and improve their own behaviors. If you have a training or meeting room, you might already keep PCs or laptops in it. You never know when a staff training exercise can involve people needing to research a subject or view a new feature of the business' online services or company portal.

Another reason to have dedicated training PCs is so that anybody in the training session can actually concentrate and focus on what they're there for, rather than being constantly distracted by messages popping up in Teams.

This can make it useful to keep some older PCs aside in that room for occasional use, as it can also hit productivity time if people have to go in and out of the training session to go to other PCs, wander back and forth to ask questions of the trainer, and then be scattered around the office at the very time you really need them all in the same location.

The Emergency Laptop!

Now for this one I'm not suggesting that you place your older laptops inside a glass case with "In case of emergency" printed on the front, as amusing as that might be, but it's often the case that a laptop, even a brand-new one, might encounter a software problem or a hardware fault

(I can thoroughly recommend my own *Windows 10 Troubleshooting*, Second Edition, and *Troubleshooting and Supporting Windows 11* books, both from Apress, at this point).

Holding some older and perfectly serviceable laptops back can be very welcome in this scenario as, again, it's a question of lost productivity. If somebody needs to go out on the road and all of a sudden finds they have no laptop to go with (even if the destination has a guest PC as they've also read this book), a whole dampener can be put on the trip, and it could even be postponed or canceled entirely.

The Light Office Duties PC

You might feel that an older PC doesn't need to be placed into a role where it just sees occasional use, as there are often areas of a business where you'd likely never know you were using an older and slower PC in any case. These can include light office work such as using Microsoft Word or working on the company's online portal.

You might feel that your reception staff only need access to the company and staff calendars and a database of employee office locations and phone numbers. For this type of light, but day-to-day essential duty, an older PC, retired from the front lines, can fit the role perfectly well.

Other Uses for Older Hardware

What I have mentioned are just some of the ways in which you can repurpose older hardware. You might find that an older PC is just what you need to run the PBX (private branch exchange) or IP (Internet Protocol) telephony system at your business. Perhaps you could use a PC in a new role as a network firewall or security appliance. Older PCs can also be pressed into service in a new life as a file server.

Whatever role you find for your older PCs and hardware, it's always good to think outside of the box, enquire what people in the workplace might need or be able to make use of, and consider all the possibilities before retiring the computers. Let's face it, if you later need a computer for one of these roles, you might find yourself having to spend extra money on a new device.

Selling Your IT Equipment

You could find that your PCs still have value. They may not hold any value to yourselves, but one person's trash is another person's treasure. One of the most obvious ways to sell a PC is to offer them to your employees. This is actually how I got one of my very first PCs that was brought home from work by my father, an Olivetti M240, complete with a 10 MHz Intel 8088 processor, a whopping 640 K of onboard RAM memory, and a capacious 20 MB hard disk drive (just 0.001% of the 2 TB SSD I have in my PC today).

I absolutely loved this old PC and primarily used it with the WordPerfect 5.1 word processor, which I also loved. As an aside, if you'd like to find out more about the M240 and the other computers I have used during my own life, you can find them all listed on my website at `https://windows.do/my-computing-history`.

Caution   When selling a PC, you need to make sure the hard disk is fully cleaned, which doesn't just mean deleting the files contained on it as they would still be recoverable. Specialist software you can sometimes find online for free can securely wipe a drive by repeatedly writing random code to every sector of the disk. The old M240 I received still contained a lot of files pertaining to the accounts of the multinational construction company it came from, but data protection wasn't really a thing back then.

So why might your employees want to buy your unwanted PCs and laptops? Well, not everybody lives in the same house as you and wears the same shoes. You might well find that some of your employees don't have a lot of spare cash lying around and could do with an extra or just a single PC at home.

This could be for their child who is just starting their high school or college education (let's face it, this is how I got mine!), or it could be for their parents whose older computer has died and they still need to be able to manage their banking and access important public services online, but for whom a new fast PC would be overkill. For this it's a good idea to remember what I said earlier about banking apps and Google ChromeOS Flex.

They might just want to buy one for a friend as a present or because they've fallen on hard times. There are all manner of reasons for someone to purchase an older computer including that they just might not see the benefit of spending new PC money as they'd much rather drop $1,500 every year on a new smartphone instead (I still don't get this – Ed).

Selling Peripherals

It's not just the PCs that can have value when they're no longer needed. The computer monitors you use in your office might be seen as an upgrade to some people, who might still be using smaller screens with a lower resolution.

There may be someone in the office, perhaps with a friend or family member whose printer has just died and who needs to have a working printer for their child's school work. Why spend $50 on a new printer when you're practically giving one away, with some spare ink or toner, for only $10.

Chairs and Desks

Speaking of peripherals and school-age children, what about those families where one of the children is about to start high school and needs a desk and chair? While some might prefer to splash out on something new from IKEA, there's likely nothing wrong with the furniture you're replacing.

Indeed when I first started self-employment way back in annals of time, my father bought me a huge L-shaped executive desk from a local second-hand store. Rather than being a small and hopelessly impractical chipboard effort, this had all the space I needed for my huge CRT (cathode-ray tube) monitors – we didn't have flat screens back then – and all the paperwork I needed to chug through. Best of all it was solid wood, high quality with barely a mark on it, and cost less than half the price of the new chipboard ones.

Donations to Schools and Charities

I'm sure I don't need to remind you that your local schools and charities will be regularly crying out for computers for the children they teach and the communities they support. The global Covid pandemic was an excellent example of this, as people around the world began donating their older and unwanted PCs to schools, who repurposed them to be given to the low-income families that didn't already own a computer, but who were now faced with having to educate their own children at home for an extended period.

This, of course, is a fairly extreme example, and it resulted in a huge surge in the sales of new PCs as the global workforce, now faced with working from home themselves, decided it was time for an upgrade.

If you called around a handful of local schools or charities, taking no more than an hour of your time, to ask who needed computer donations (PCs, laptops, monitors, printers, desks and chairs, etc.), then I'm fairly sure at least one of them would bite your hand off and likely try taking some of your arm with it.

The charities working with poorer communities (the unemployed, immigrants, veterans, rehabilitated offenders, addicts) will always likely be the most in need, especially those that conduct their own training. Before I moved to France, I spent many years working for small local training charities in Yorkshire (UK) where I lived at the time. I taught English and math primarily to the long-term unemployed to help upskill them and get them back into the workforce so they could improve their own lives.

During this time I saw first-hand how difficult it was for those charities to obtain the right amount of computers for their students and also how tremendously difficult the home lives of the students were when all the essential public services, and school services for their children that they needed to access, were only accessible to them with a small, basic smartphone or through a public computer at the local library, which was already under threat of closure.

National and International Donation Schemes

In almost every country there are local, national, and government schemes to help people repurpose and recycle older computers and IT hardware. The EPA (Environmental Protection Agency) in the USA runs a scheme, which you can find online at www.epa.gov/recycle/electronics-donation-and-recycling.

There are also charitable organizations you can find on a quick search for "**donate old computer**" such as www.goodwillsc.org, www.computerswithcauses.org, and www.givingcenter.org, all of which are based in the USA, and each of these will help find a home for your retired kit. In the UK there are websites including https://itforcharities.co.uk and https://therestartproject.org that make it easy for you to contact charities and organizations that are looking for exactly the type of kit you are donating.

These schemes are to be found worldwide and are quick and easy to search for. Even on an international scale, the United Nations runs programs that donate all manner of things, from farm equipment to desktop computers and laptops through schemes such as the World Food Programme and UNICEF. You can find out how to donate to United Nations schemes on this link: `www.un.org/en/about-us/how-to-donate-to-the-un-system`.

Additionally, other international schemes exist that you can donate your IT equipment to where it is then used by those most in need, such as in the developing world for children's education. These schemes include Computer Aid (`www.computeraid.org`) and the World Computer Exchange (`https://worldcomputerexchange.org`).

Safely Recycling IT Equipment

Sometimes though your IT equipment will genuinely be at the end of its life. Perhaps it's just so old it's unusable or has stopped working completely. Perhaps it's just smashed or broken (like my laptop that day I ran out of coffee – Ed). These are the devices that are genuinely at the end of their lives and that need to be disposed of.

There's a real need to do this safely, however. In Chapter 1 I detailed some of the toxic and unpleasant chemicals and materials that go into making our electronic equipment. These include

- Cadmium – Which can be carcinogenic and cause blood pressure and bone damage

- Mercury – Which can cause blindness and muscle atrophy

- Lead – Which can lead to nervous system and cognitive problems, kidney failure, and fertility problems

- Nickel – Where high doses can cause kidney disease and cancer

Needless to say, many countries around the world already have strict rules and laws governing the disposal and recycling of electronic components. In the USA the two accredited certification standards for responsible electronics recycling as specified by the EPA are the *Responsible Recycling "R2" Standard*, which you can read about at `https://sustainableelectronics.org`, and the *e-Stewards standard for responsible recycling*, for which details can be found online at `https://e-stewards.org`.

The EPA does also make it straightforward to find accredited recycling companies in your state, with details online at their website: `www.epa.gov/smm-electronics/certified-electronics-recyclers`.

In the European Union and the UK, the *WEEE (Waste Electrical and Electronic Equipment) Directive* sets the rules for how electronics must be recycled and disposed of. These rules are currently the most stringent in the world and, as you can imagine with that, are by far the most complex to understand. You can read all about these rules on the European Commission website at this short link (the actual link is horrendously long as you might imagine from a huge bureaucratic administration): `https://pcs.tv/3Fo8Mjn`.

In the UK you can read about the WEEE regulations at `www.gov.uk/guidance/regulations-waste-electrical-and-electronic-equipment`, and a quick search online for "**WEEE Recycling**" will reveal accredited and specialist recycling firms in your country, county, state, or local area that can collect and safely dispose of your unwanted kit … In the UK these are typically named according to the British sense of humor as "WEEE Recycle IT" and "WEEE Can Do It!", and it's nice to know that even waste management firms know how to have a laugh (let's face it, only the British would vote to name a polar exploration ship "Boaty McBoatFace" – Ed).

I'll talk about all these regulations much more in Chapter 9 when I look at regulatory compliance for sustainability and how it might affect your business.

The Future of International E-Waste Recycling

Not every country in the world has rules on the recycling and disposal of e-waste. Sadly in far too many countries, waste is not recycled properly if at all and finds its way into the ground and the water table where it can cause significant environmental damage and considerable health problems for the people exposed to the water that's been contaminated.

One of the biggest problems with this is India, which is the world's fifth largest producer of electronic waste, at about two million tons each year. While schemes exist to recycle and dispose of e-waste properly, too much of it is still disposed of through the use of acid baths, burning cables, and dumping the electronics directly to landfill.

Estimates are that some 80% of India's surface water is polluted and that e-waste has contributed to this. The United Nations though continues to press its member countries to introduce better and more stringent recycling and disposal of e-waste regulations.

In a report from the UN Environment Programme in 2019, which you can read at `https://pcs.tv/3ciZzMX`, they estimated that some 50 million tons of e-waste is being produced each year, of which only 20% is being recycled. They highlight the value of countries introducing regulated e-waste recycling, pointing out that one ton of e-waste can contain 100 times as much gold as one ton of gold ore and that the value of e-waste is worth more than $60 billion globally every year.

If you live or work in a country where there is little or no formal regulation of e-waste recycling and disposal, this doesn't mean that companies and organizations to help you achieve this don't exist. It may take a little searching online to find the right companies, but it is definitely worth the effort.

Summary

While it can be unclear what your options are for recycling and repurposing IT equipment in some parts of the world, many countries and trading blocs are making it much simpler both to recycle older and broken kit and to donate it to local, national, and international schemes. This gives it a new lease on life and also helps the poorest and most disadvantaged people and children in society.

In Chapter 10 we'll look at some of the political problems associated with e-waste and climate change policy. They are indeed many, and you could very likely decide that it's simply not worth waiting and you're going to get on with it yourself anyway, as it's very clear what you need to do anyway.

In the next chapter though we'll bring things back down to Earth and to your business and look at your existing computers and IT equipment. We'll examine the various options and settings available on your devices and computers for power saving and what else you can do to reduce your own energy consumption, bringing down the cost of running your business.

CHAPTER 7

Managing Power For Your Existing IT Systems

In Chapter 2 I detailed the tools you can use to determine how much power your existing IT equipment is using, but this is only half of the story as the companies that make the software for our technology, Microsoft, Apple, and Google, have built settings into their software that can also help you manage power consumption.

You might also be surprised at how much of an impact these changes can make; they can highlight some of the ways we've gotten used to using technology over the decades and some of the bad habits we've slipped into.

Managing Power Consumption in Microsoft Windows

Because this is a book predominantly aimed at businesses, it seems sensible to start with the venerable desktop computer. These PCs, coming in many different forms these days from the traditional desktop to all-in-one desktops, laptops, convertible laptops, tablets, and more esoteric and

© Mike Halsey 2025
M. Halsey, *The Green IT Guide*, https://doi.org/10.1007/979-8-8688-1233-0_7

bespoke hardware designs we see occasionally from the likes of Lenovo and Microsoft, are the backbone of business, and they keep everything running.

Whether you're running Windows 10 or Windows 11 on your PCs, and Windows 12 could be available by the time you read this, the settings you need to make them as power-efficient as they can be are easy to find and easy to use.

A Note About Laptops and Chargers

I want to drop in a note about laptop chargers at this point, as you might well find that your workforce, perhaps even yourself, are keeping laptops permanently plugged in to the charger when it's in use during the day. This can be a very power-inefficient way of working as on a modern laptop the battery is very commonly able to easily get through a full working day and improvements are being made all the time. The charger when left plugged in will also still use a very small amount of power (usually just 1 or 2 watts), but scaled across a company, this can make a significant dent in both your electricity bill and your carbon footprint.

Leaving laptops charging overnight is also a bad idea. A typical laptop will need between 3 and 4 hours to achieve a full charge. After this point the charger should be unplugged from mains electricity, and the laptop, even if it's in sleep, will consume almost no electricity until it's woken by the user the following day.

As a result it can be a good idea to encourage workers to charge their laptop for short periods of the day, such as when they're at lunch or to take the laptop home with them and charge it there. This isn't so the business can keep its electricity bill down, but because the worker will be proximate to the laptop and much more aware of when it is charged and when the charger should be unplugged from the wall socket.

Smart Laptop Charging

Some modern laptops now come with a smart charging feature that can extend the life of the battery. This feature, which is commonly found in a manufacturer-provided management app, as it is with my Microsoft Surface Laptop Studio (see Figure 7-1), can stop the laptop charging when it reaches 80% charge.

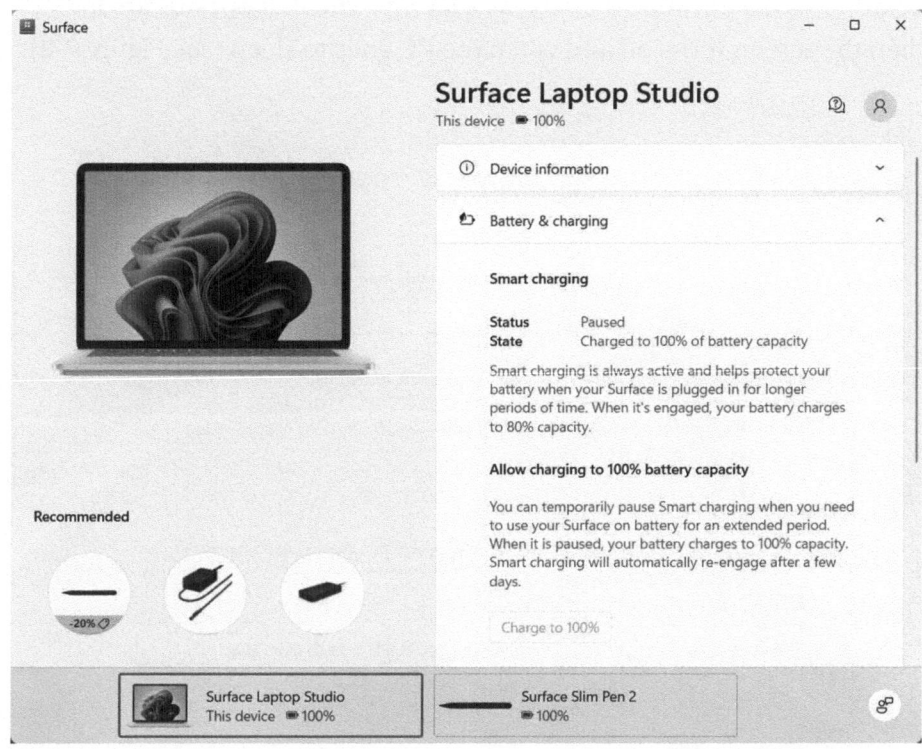

Figure 7-1. *Smart charging is available in some modern laptops*

While this feature is only currently found in a manufacturer-specific app, if your laptop even supports it, it is highly likely to be built into Windows at some point in the near future, perhaps even as you read this. When this happens you will no doubt be able to find it in the *Power* section of the *Settings* app, and while it could require specific electronics to work, it will likely support many if not all laptops.

153

Power Settings in Windows 10

The power settings you'll need in Windows 10 can be found in the *Settings* panel. Open the Start Menu and click the cog (gear) icon that's just above the power icon. Once Settings has opened, click *System* and then click *Power & sleep.*

The options you will see here will vary depending if you are using a desktop PC or a portable PC such as a laptop. The first options are for when the screen turns off and when the PC goes to sleep (see Figure 7-2).

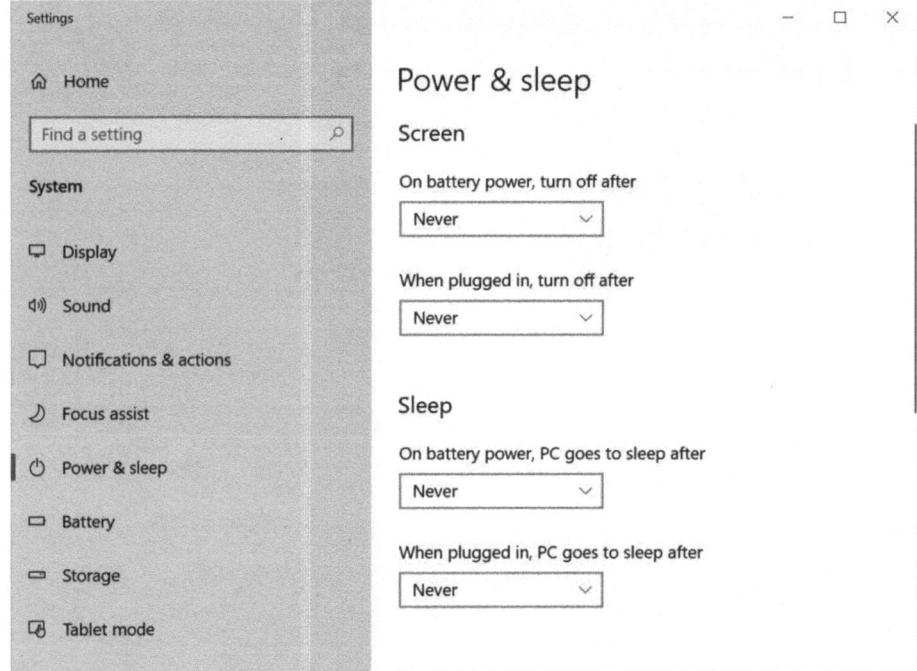

Figure 7-2. *The main power options in Windows 10 are easy to use*

The two options for when the screen turns off and when the laptop sleeps are incredibly important as it's the screen that can consume the most power on a portable device. On your smartphone, for example, keeping the screen on will deplete your battery much faster than anything else you could do.

Having the screen turn off on the laptop can therefore extend the battery life of the device, meaning it can work for longer without needing recharging, and it also means that a desktop screen, which by its very nature is plugged into mains electricity all the time anyway, won't consume anywhere near as much power.

Sleep is also an important setting to configure as modern PCs will consume only a small wattage when in sleep while also being able to resume and wake up in just a couple of seconds, sometimes even signing you back into the PC before you've finished opening your laptop lid.

Below these settings is a power management slider control (see Figure 7-3). This has just two basic settings for *Best energy savings* and *Better performance*.

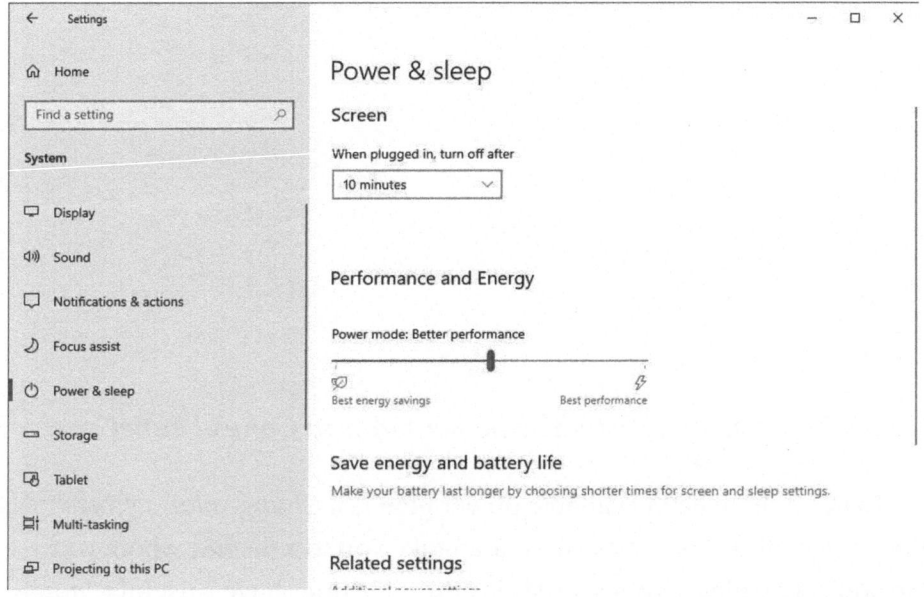

Figure 7-3. *The performance and energy control can help control power usage*

These two options, however, are configurable so you can get very fine control over power management. Click the *Additional power settings* link you'll find further down the page, and you'll be shown the older *Control Panel* options for power management and the *Choose or customize a power plan* screen (see Figure 7-4).

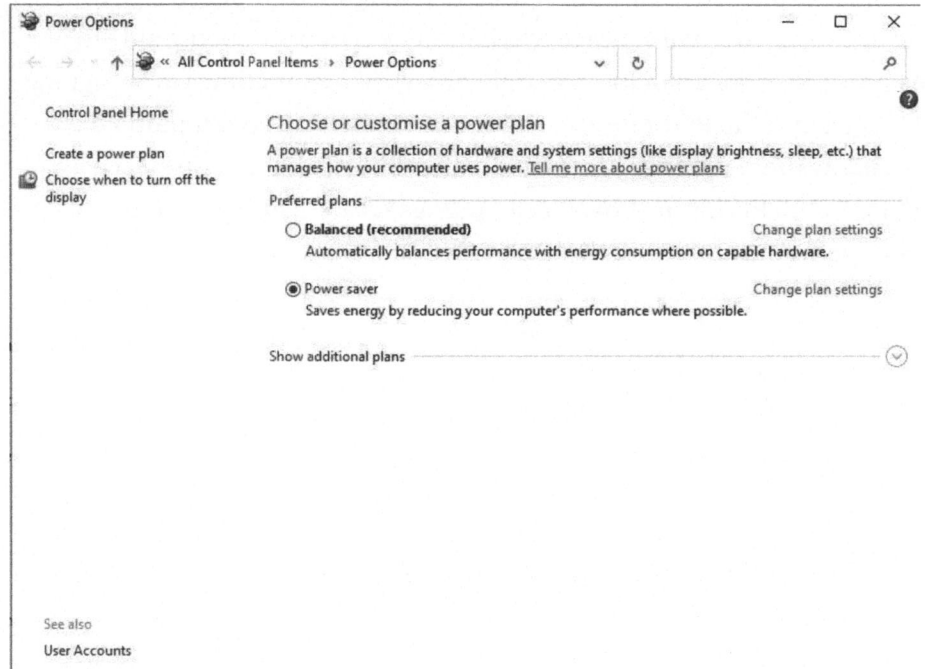

Figure 7-4. *You can customize power plans in Control Panel*

To the right of each available power plan is a *Change plan settings* link. In itself this doesn't do more than take you to a display where you can control display settings, but this next page does have a useful *Change advanced power settings* link, and this will open a panel where all the most useful options can be found (see Figure 7-5).

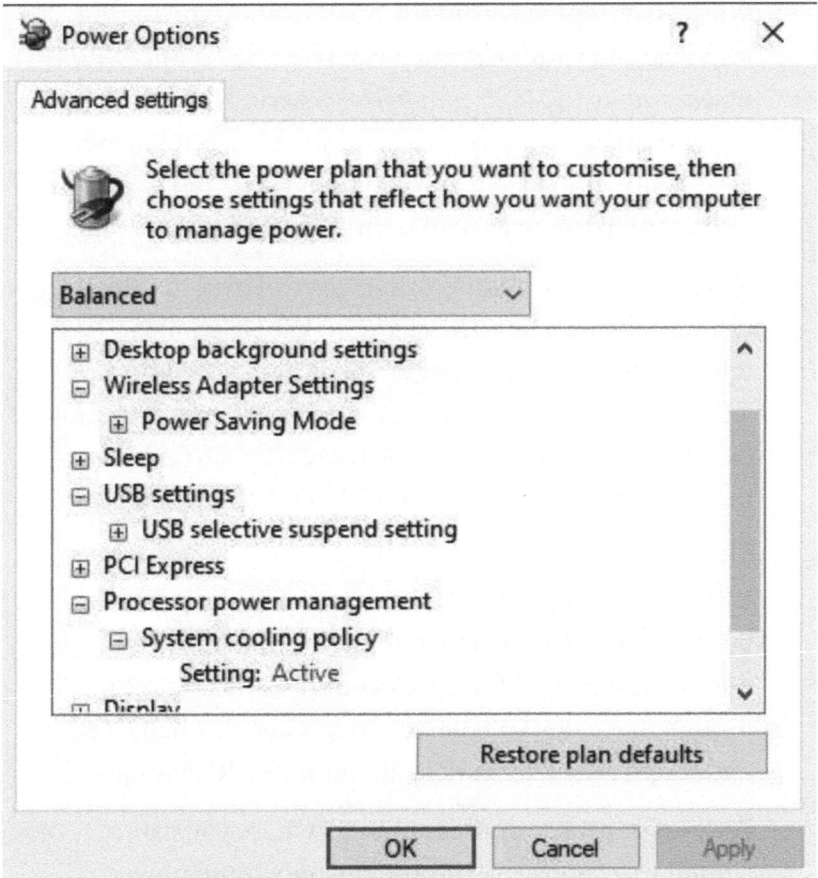

Figure 7-5. *Advanced power management settings are available in Windows 10*

Let's have a look at the most useful settings here and how you can configure them:

- **Hard disk** is only really useful if your PC contains older, mechanical spinning hard drives. New SSD and NVMe storage is significantly more power-efficient, but if you do have older disk drives, these can be set to sleep after a period of inactivity.

- **Wireless Adapter Settings** is the power option for the Wi-Fi card in your PC, which can be set from *Maximum power saving* to *Maximum performance.* This will depend on how you use Wi-Fi on your PC, but having it set to an option such as *Medium power saving* on a laptop can provide a small improvement in battery life.

- **Sleep** is where you can get finer control over the sleep settings and also find *Hibernation.* Hibernation is different from sleep in that while putting a PC into a sleep state keeps memory active so the PC can resume much more quickly, hibernate writes the current memory state to disk, copying it back again when the PC wakes up.

- **USB settings** can place USB devices in a sleep state, by effectively cutting power to them when they're not needed or the PC is in a sleep state. Bear in mind though that a few USB devices don't like this behavior and might refuse to work again until the PC is restarted.

- **Processor power management** is where you can, should you choose to, throttle the maximum power output of the CPU in the PC. By default it's set to allow the maximum processor state to reach 100% performance because why wouldn't you, but there may be specific circumstances where you wouldn't want it to reach this level. Here is where you can also find a setting to control the level the PC's fans work at.

It's important to note that not every option will be able on every PC. Some will only appear if you have appropriate hardware, such as an installed battery.

Additionally, on the left side of the Control Panel power options, you will see a *Choose what the power buttons do* link. Here you can decide what happens when the power and sleep buttons are pressed (if your PC has the latter), and some PCs will allow you to choose what happens when the lid is closed (see Figure 7-6).

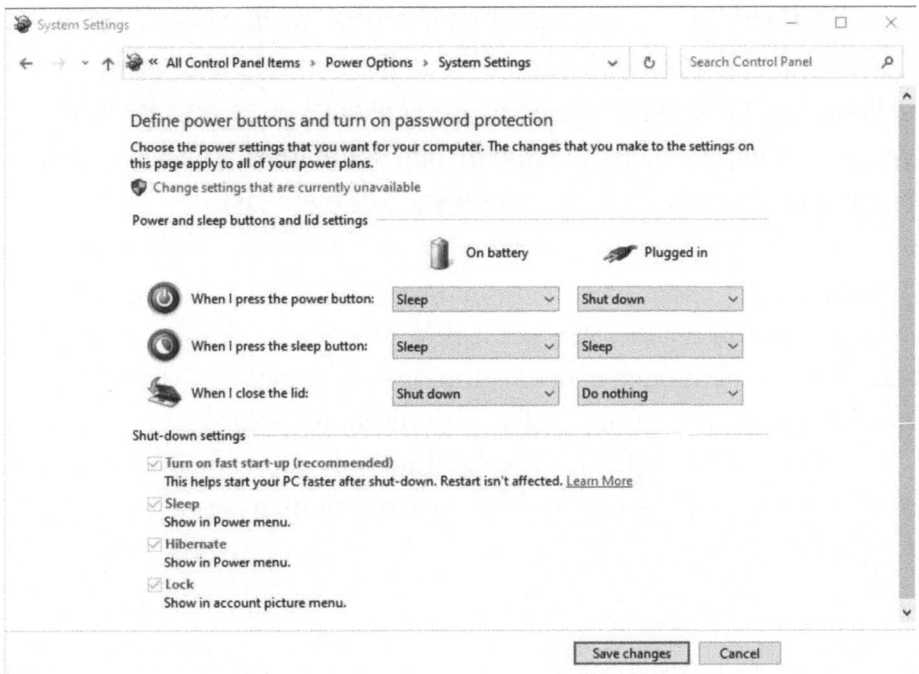

Figure 7-6. *You can choose what happens for power buttons and the laptop lid*

Power Settings in Windows 11

The power settings in Windows 11 are very similar to those in Windows 10, though a few things have been moved. Firstly, the Settings icon in Windows 11 might not be as prominent in that the Start Menu will by default show you only pinned and your most recently used apps. If you don't have Settings pinned, then it could fall off the main list.

Should the Settings icon not appear for you in the Start Menu, click the *All Apps* button near the top-right corner of the Start Menu and scroll down until you get to *S* in the list.

Note   Windows 10 at launch was a very different operating system from Windows 11 five years later as Microsoft have moved a lot of Control Panel items into Settings. While the Control Panel was part of Windows 11 at launch, and will likely always exist in some form, we can expect the same to happen, and some tools I refer to in this chapter might not always be where you left them last.

With *Settings* open, click *Power* in the right-side panel to access basic power settings for the PC. Now at the time of writing this, they are *very* basic, and as I mentioned at the beginning of this section, we can fully expect things to change and evolve over the coming years.

For right now though the Power settings only allow you to change the screen-off and sleep settings and choose a power plan (see Figure 7-7).

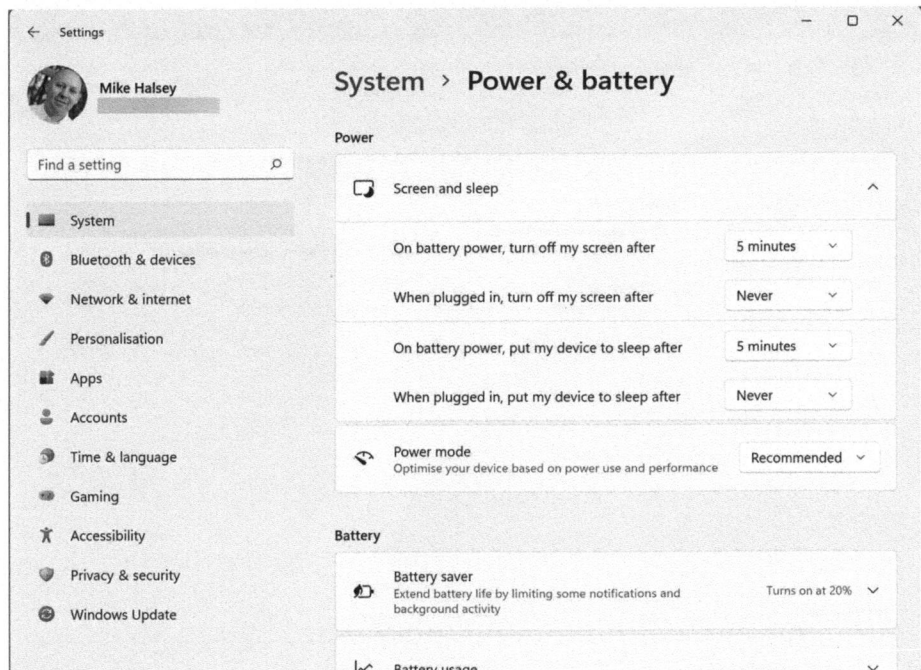

Figure 7-7. *At the time of writing, power settings in Windows 11 are basic*

The other power settings you need for finer control, however, are still available in the Control Panel (see Figure 7-8). Again though as I've already stated, we can expect some or all of these settings to be moved at a later date, and Power in the Settings panel is where they'll end up if that happens.

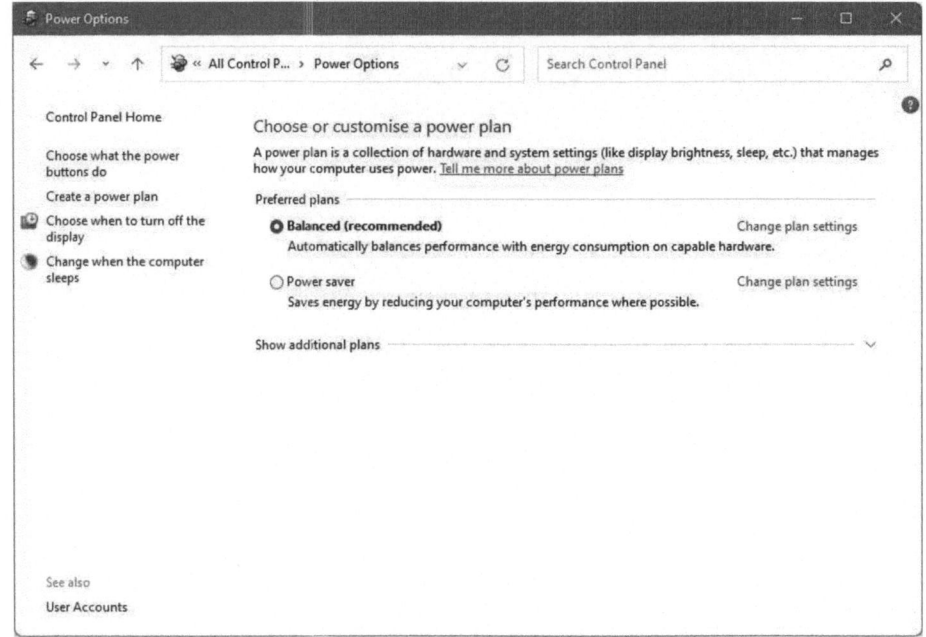

Figure 7-8. *Power settings do exist in the Control Panel, but they might be moved later*

These controls work in an identical way to the ones in Windows 10, and this is because you don't have to scratch at the operating system very much to find that Windows 10 and Windows 11 are effectively the same OS.

Managing Power Consumption Using Group Policy

If you manage a large fleet of computers and laptops in your organization, then you can control and manage all the power settings via Group Policy. Search for **gpedit** in the Start Menu on the desktop OS in either Windows 10 or Windows 11, or open Group Policy via your management interface where you will find the power settings in *Computer Configuration* ➤ *Administrative Templates* ➤ *System* ➤ *Power Management* (see Figure 7-9).

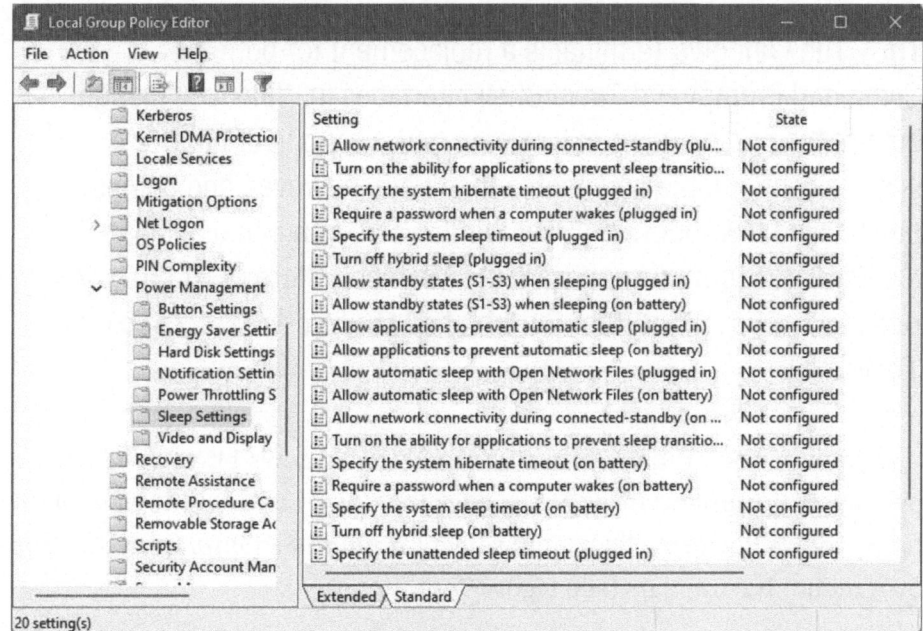

Figure 7-9. *Power management can be done by Group Policy in Windows*

All of the settings you will find elsewhere in the Windows interface or via the Command Line are available here, and for managing a large number of PCs, this is definitely the best way to control power usage.

Managing Power Consumption with the Windows Command Line

Windows 10 and 11 do also come with scripting tools that allow you to configure and manage the power options on a PC and across an organization. This is the *powercfg* command. You can use this in the Command Prompt in Windows 10 or the Windows Terminal in Windows 11.

Tip The Windows Terminal is a replacement for both the Command Prompt and PowerShell interfaces in Windows, though both of the original tools still exist in both versions of the OS. It is more configurable and usable than both, however, and comes preinstalled in Windows 11. For Windows 10 you can download the Windows Terminal app from the Microsoft Store at `https://pcs.tv/3FEoyHR` or from GitHub at `github.com/Microsoft/Terminal`.

If you are using the Windows Terminal in Windows 11, you will need to open a new Command Prompt tab, click the *down* arrow to the right of the first Windows PowerShell tab, and select *Command Prompt* from the drop-down menu that appears (see Figure 7-10).

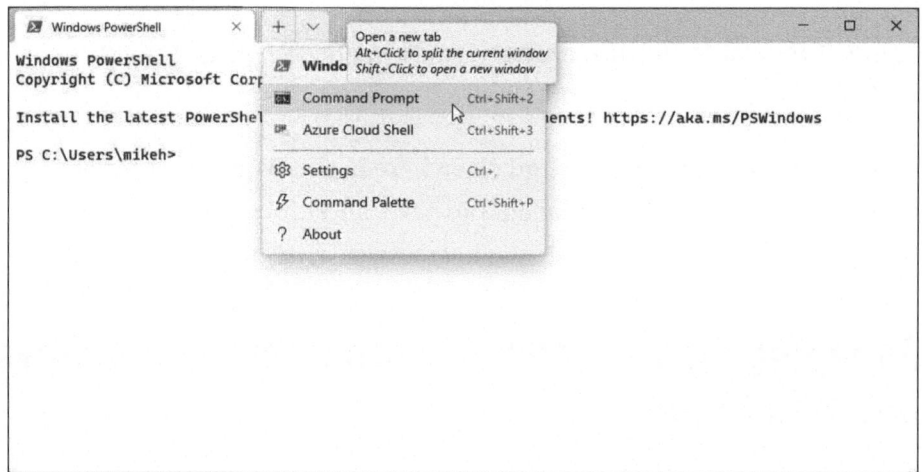

Figure 7-10. *The Windows Terminal is the replacement for Command Prompt*

Once in a Command Prompt window, you can use powercfg to manage the power settings on the PC. Powercfg is used in the format `powercfg / switch [parameter]`, and the following switches are available to you.

You can find full details on the powercfg command on the Microsoft Docs website at `https://pcs.tv/3mEKfyZ`. I do want to look at a few of these commands in more detail, however, as they can be extraordinarily helpful.

Table 7-1. *Power management Command Line switches*

Option	Description
/?, -help	Displays help about switches and can be used after a switch to display additional help, i.e., `/List /?`
/list, /L	Lists all the available power schemes.
/query, /Q	Displays the parameters for a named power scheme or all power schemes if none is specified.
/change, /X	Modifies a named parameter in the current power scheme.
/changename	Modifies the name and description of a power scheme.
/duplicatescheme	Duplicates a power scheme.
/delete, /D	Deletes a power scheme.
/deletesetting	Deletes a parameter setting.
/setactive, /S	Sets a named power scheme to be active.
/getactivescheme	Retrieves the currently active power scheme.
/setacvalueindex	Sets the parameter associated with a power setting while the system is powered by AC power.
/setdcvalueindex	Sets the parameter associated with a power setting while the system is powered by DC power.

Table 7-1. (*continued*)

Option	Description
/import	Imports power schemes from a file.
/export	Exports a named power scheme to a file.
/aliases	Displays all aliases and their corresponding GUIDs (Globally Unique Identifiers).
/getsecuritydescriptor	Gets a security descriptor associated with a specified power setting, power scheme, or action.
/setsecuritydescriptor	Sets a security descriptor associated with a power setting, power scheme, or action.
/hibernate, /H	Enables and disables the hibernate feature.
/availablesleepstates, /A	Reports the sleep states available on the system – more on this below.
/devicequery	Returns a list of devices that meet specified criteria – use with /? for more information.
/deviceenableawake	Enables a device to wake the system from a sleep state.
/devicedisablewake	Disables a device from waking the system from a sleep state.
/lastwake	Reports information about what device or event woke the system from the last sleep transition.
/waketimers	Enumerates the active wake timers.
/requests	Enumerates application and driver Power Requests.
/requestsoverride	Sets a Power Request override for a particular Process, Service, or Driver.
/energy	Analyzes the system for common energy efficiency and battery life problems – more on this below.

(*continued*)

Table 7-1. (*continued*)

Option	Description
/batteryreport	Generates a report about the PC's battery usage – more on this below.
/sleepstudy	Generates a diagnostic system power transition report – more on this below.
/srumutil	Dumps the Energy Estimation data from System Resource Usage Monitor (SRUM).
/systemsleepdiagnostics	Generates a diagnostic report about system sleep transitions.
/systempowerreport	Generates a diagnostic system power transition report.

Powercfg /availablesleepstates

Sleep isn't just a standard thing with modern PCs. There are different types of sleep state, all slightly different from one another, and not every one is supported on each computer. You can use this command to report on what sleep states are supported by your particular hardware (see Figure 7-11).

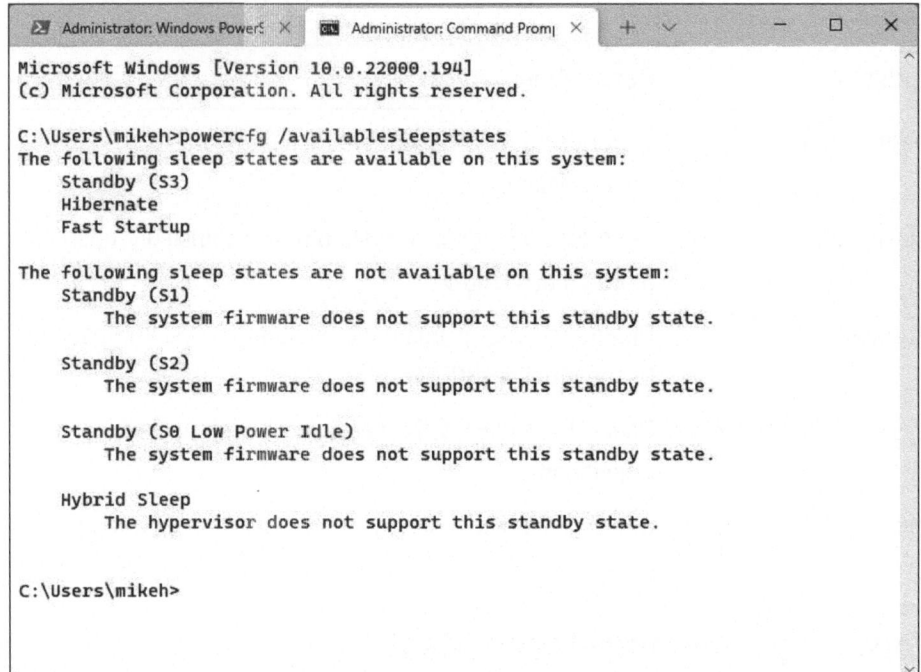

Figure 7-11. *You can find out what sleep states are supported by a PC*

The different sleep states supported by modern PCs are as follows:

- **S0** (zero), which is really just a lower power state where the PC remains fully usable but hardware such as the processor has been throttled back.

- **S1** is a state where the processor and motherboard bus (interface) are stopped, but all data is stored in memory for a quick resume.

- **S2** is similar to S1 but more interface buses are off. This might cause some components to lose power and not properly resume on wake.

- **S3** is almost indistinguishable from S2, though more chips on the motherboard have their power cut.

- **S4** is otherwise known as **Hibernate**, and this is where the contents of memory are copied to disk and full power is cut until the PC wakes. This state has the long wake from sleep time.

You can read more about the sleep states available on Windows PCs at the Microsoft website: `https://pcs.tv/3FHqNdI`.

Powercfg /energy

This command is used to report on the battery health of a laptop or other mobile PCs. It will take 60 seconds to generate its report, which it will then save as an HTML (web page) file in your `C:\Users\[username]\` folder.

Opening the file will display any errors (highlighted in red) or warnings (highlighted in yellow) for the sleep state of the PC. This is most useful if you have a PC where sleep isn't working. In a report on my own laptop (see Figure 7-12), the Windows 11 disk defragmentation service (defragsvc) is reported to have made several requests to the OS to prevent the system going to sleep.

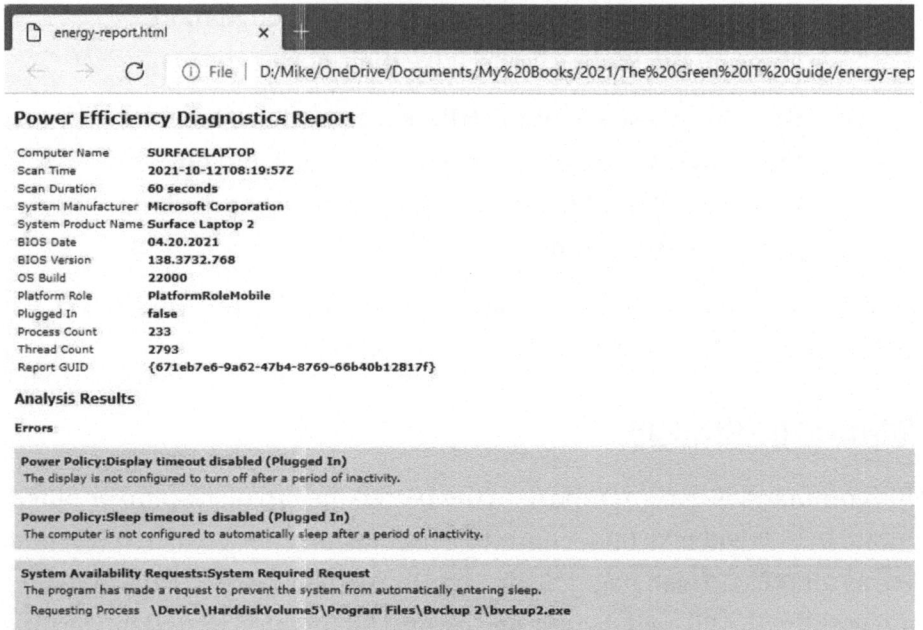

Figure 7-12.   The energy report file can be useful for seeing why sleep might not be working on a PC

Additionally the report told me that Skype might not be acting properly and gave me technical information I could use if I found the application was misbehaving when I woke the PC again.

Powercfg /batteryreport

The battery report file is saved to the same folder location as the energy report file and provides information about battery usage on the device over the previous three days. This includes a full event log of when the PC was switched on and off and when it was put to sleep and awoken (see Figure 7-13).

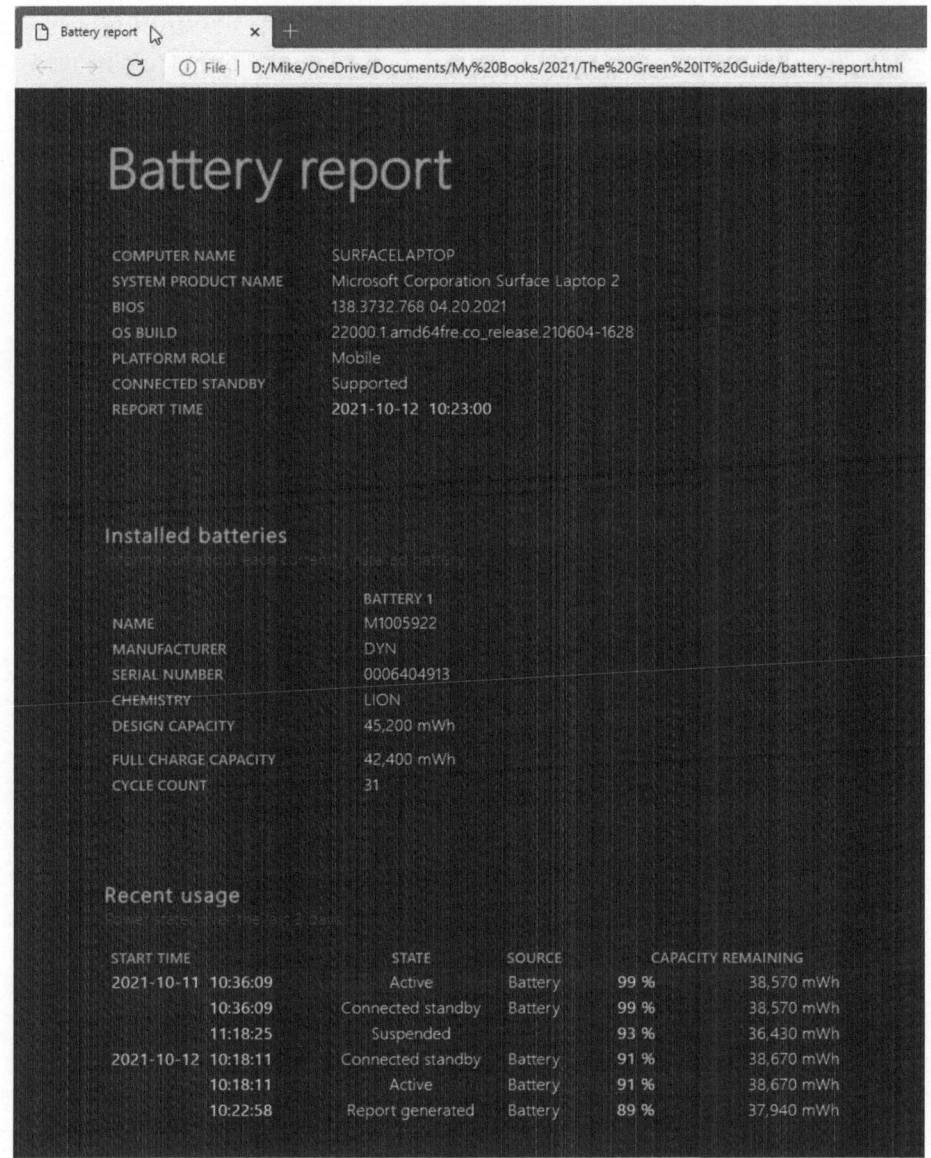

Figure 7-13. *The battery report file*

Where this report comes in most useful, however, is to report on the design (maximum) capacity of the battery in milliwatt-hours (mWh) and the remaining capacity of the battery at the time of specific events, such as sleep and wake. This can be useful if the incorrect sleep state has been selected for a PC, such as S0, and on waking the PC the user is finding the battery severely depleted.

Powercfg /sleepstudy

Again, the sleep study report is also saved to the current user folder. It reports on how well the PC slept and what it is woke for and experienced during that time, for example, if it woke to update the operating system or to synchronize your email (see Figure 7-14).

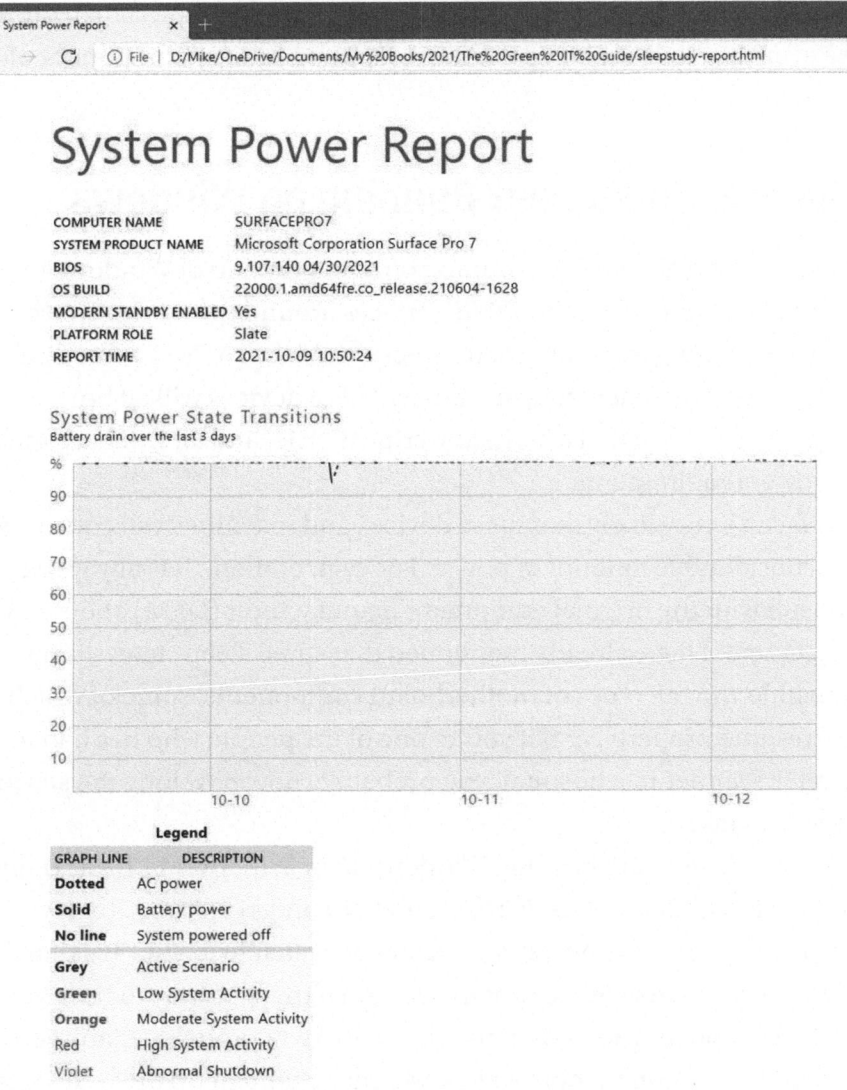

Figure 7-14.   *The sleep study file*

Sleep study is best used to see which, if any, apps are waking the PC from sleep to update themselves. This is a fairly regular occurrence with modern Windows laptops and should only use a very small amount of power, especially considering the PC doesn't switch on the screen during these events, which of course is the most power-hungry component of a laptop.

Industrial Equipment Running on Windows

There are very many devices running on some version of Windows in industry, in business, and in public services around the world. These include everything from automatic teller machines (ATMs) to medical scanners and manufacturing machines. These devices will all be performing what's called a "mission-critical" role, and all will have their own power requirements.

In fact it's very likely that these devices and machines will consume a not inconsiderable amount of power. For each of these, it is always wise to consult with the original equipment manufacturer (OEM) about power management. I have already mentioned that some sleep states aren't compatible with all types of motherboard components, some of which won't resume properly, and if you're one of the people who has had to cold start a CT scanner in a hospital, you probably know how long the startup process can take.

If these devices are running Windows 10 or Windows 11 LTSC (Long-Term Servicing Channel) or IoT (Internet of Things) editions, then you will still have Windows power management available to you. This can be a boon when the devices are not in use, and if there's a way to have your bank's ATMs sleep when not in use, the world will probably thank you. As I already mentioned, however, power management on these devices should be handled with extreme care and with the support and guidance of the OEM.

Caution   Please note that Windows XP and Windows 7 are now completely out of support and as a result can be hugely vulnerable to hacking and malware attacks, usually targeting vulnerabilities in the operating system that have never been patched (usually because nobody found them). These devices should *always* be isolated from the Internet and your own networks to help prevent such attacks from occurring and, as in an example I gave earlier, rendering your CT scanner useless.

Windows Server Systems

As more and more businesses and organizations transition their communications, analytical, and other needs to cloud services such as Microsoft Azure or Amazon Web Services, which I talked about in Chapter 4, there are fewer and fewer servers still in use on company premises.

They're still not completely gone, however, and Microsoft do still sell stand-alone versions of their server operating system products. When it comes to power management, you might be tempted to have the servers online all the time, as you never know when somebody might want to dial in.

I would imagine that if your organization is still using a stand-alone server, it's because it performs a very specific and critical role that you either feel more comfortable managing on your own premises or that it's running something older that either hasn't yet or cannot be successfully transitioned to the cloud.

My best advice here is to look at the usage logs for your server, when people are signing into it, and what processes the server is automatically running in the background such as backup and from this determine a pattern when it is appropriate to put the server into a low-power sleep state. It will no doubt still be possible to do this with your server, even if it will only be appropriate for a few hours each day or on weekends.

Managing Power Consumption in MacOS

Apple's iMac and MacBook computers are designed to be much simpler to configure and use than Windows PCs and, indeed with the newer M-type processors Apple introduced in 2020, are significantly more power-efficient than a PC running on an Intel or AMD processor.

The power management options for a MacOS computer can be found in *System Preferences* by clicking *Energy Saver* (see Figure 7-15).

Figure 7-15. *Energy Saver is where you will find power management in MacOS*

The controls available to you are fairly basic and straightforward and include a slider control for when the display is switched off, preventing the iMac or MacBook from going to sleep at all, putting the hard disks to sleep if possible (though remember this is really only of use for mechanical spinning disks), and allowing the computer to wake on a network access command from a remote PC or server (see Figure 7-16).

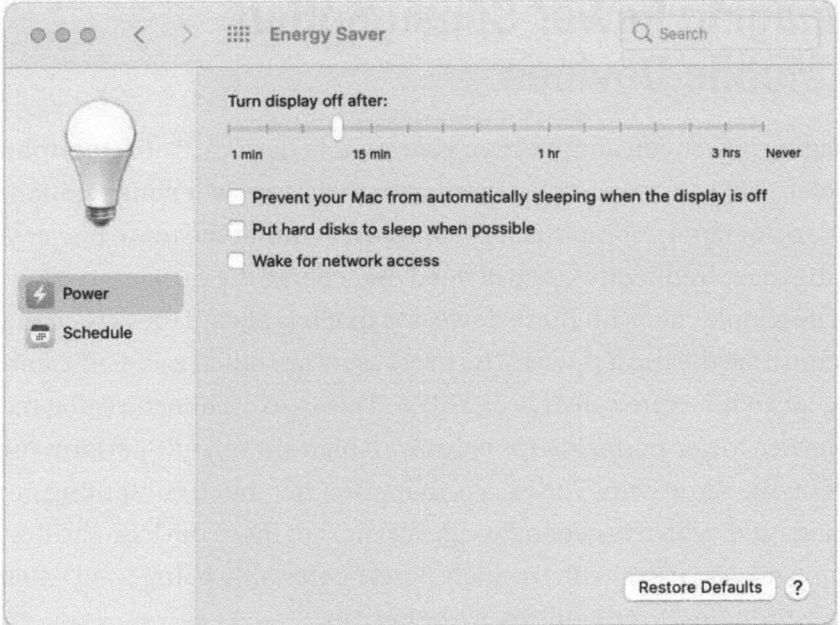

Figure 7-16. *Power management in MacOS is fairly straightforward*

Some Apple iMac and MacBook computers will include additional options, such as *Power Nap*, which will allow the computer to check and update your email, calendar, and a few other services when in sleep, and you can also set a schedule when the computer should automatically go to sleep and wake if you would like. More information (it's not a long list) on the power management features available in MacOS can be found on the Apple website at https://pcs.tv/3ACkOxU.

Managing Power Consumption on Mobile Devices

Managing power consumption on your mobile devices, from smartphones to tablets, isn't any less important than managing power consumption on a desktop or laptop computer. The simple fact is that the more power you use, the more frequently you will need to recharge the device.

The simple rule with these devices is that it is always the screen that will consume the most power. The processors are much more efficient, using an architecture called *big.LITTLE*. This is an architecture that mixes low-power, lower-performance cores with high-power, full-performance cores on the same chip. The idea is that when not much computing power is being used, which is general usage for most of these devices, the low-power cores are used, with the high-power cores only being used when processor-intensive operations are being run.

big.LITTLE is slowly being introduced to desktop computer processors, the first of which being the Apple M1 and with Intel and ARM both working on these chips for Windows PCs at the time of writing. If you can get a big.LITTLE chip for your next PC, it will be well worth it.

Power Management in iOS

Power management in iOS is handled through the device's *Settings* with separate sections for *Battery* management (see Figure 7-17) and *Display & Brightness*. The Battery settings panel can be useful because it informs you about which apps on the device are consuming the most power.

Figure 7-17. *iOS comes with battery and screen management options*

The Display & Brightness settings also include additional functionality such as auto-dimming the screen backlight (which can save quite a fair amount of power) and, on compatible devices, changing the refresh rate of the screen.

It Hertz Your Battery to Be Too Fast

It is common for more and more modern devices to come with screens that refresh at 120 Hz (hertz) or even higher. Traditionally, computer screens ran at 60 Hz (frames per second) as this was widely accepted as the rate at which the human eye could comfortably see the content on screen. Televisions have traditionally run at 30 Hz with online videos such as YouTube running as low as 24 Hz.

The main benefit to 120 Hz and even 240 Hz screens is that movement on screen appears much more smoothly to the human eye. The downside, as you can probably imagine, is that the faster you draw to the screen, the more battery you will consume.

To get around this, device and operating system manufacturers have started to introduce *adaptive frequency technologies*. These raise the screen refresh rate to the maximum, say 120 Hz or 240 Hz, when there's a lot going on, but can reduce it to as little as 1 Hz, refreshing only once per second, when the image is static. This is a technology that can save a lot of battery power, especially when used with dimming the display.

Managing Power Consumption on Android

Google's Android operating system also has *Settings* for *Battery* and *Display*, and these are broadly similar to the ones found in iOS and do all of the same things, from auto-dimming the screen and implementing adaptive frequency features to reporting on individual app usage and battery status when the device is in sleep (see Figure 7-18).

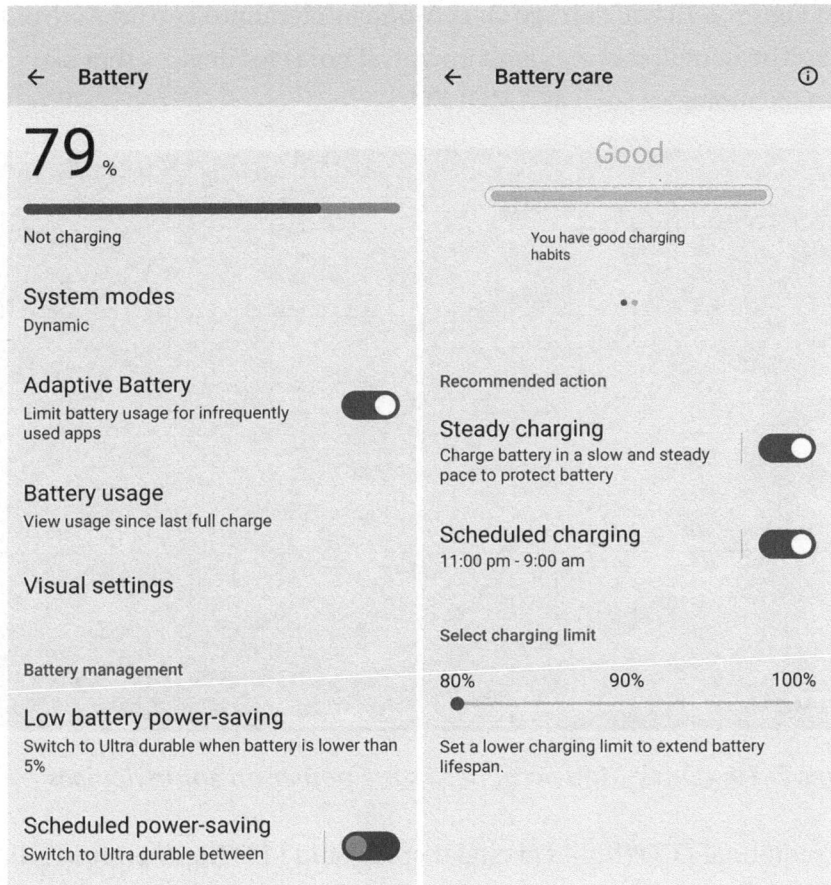

Figure 7-18. *Android's power management features are broadly similar to iOS*

The World Is Going Dark, and We Love It

I want to put in a quick note about *Dark Mode*. This is a feature of all modern operating systems including Windows, MacOS, iOS, and Android, and many people prefer it on their PCs as it can reduce eyestrain. Fortunately Dark Mode also has another benefit, that being reducing power consumption.

In Figure 7-19 you can see Dark Mode implemented on an Android device. The benefit it brings isn't universal but is for devices that use screen technologies such as AMOLED.

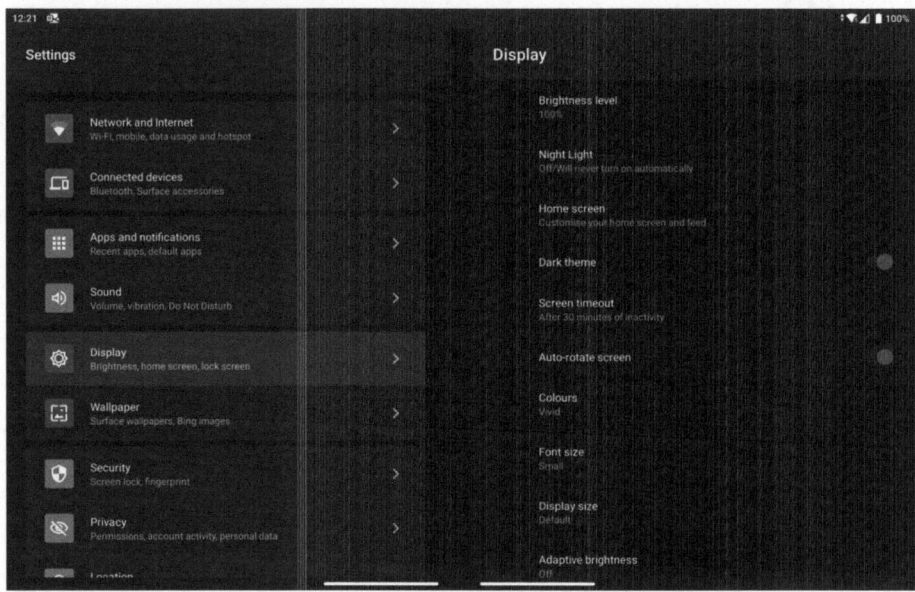

Figure 7-19. *Dark Mode can help save power on some devices*

Traditional LCD (liquid crystal display) and LED (light-emitting diode) displays have a backlight behind the display pixels to illuminate the screen. These backlights are normally separated into "dimming zones," and most screens will have about nine of these zones across the display. In each zone the backlight can be dimmed if the picture in that zone is dark, but if only a very small part of that zone has a dark picture, the zone cannot adjust itself to only black out that one part.

More modern LCD and LED screens are coming with many more local dimming zones, and this is most commonly seen on televisions. OLED (organic light-emitting diode) and AMOLED (active matrix organic light-emitting diode) screen technologies, however, are able to light individual pixels and do away with the screen backlight altogether.

The upshot is that when a pixel on an OLED or AMOLED screen is black, it consumes absolutely no power as it's simply turned off. Originally this technology was developed to make black and dark areas in movies display as the director intended when viewed on your home cinema screen, but it was quickly discovered it could be used to save power as well.

As the price of OLED and, particularly, AMOLED screens has reduced, they are being more commonly seen in smartphones and tablets and at the time of writing are now beginning to appear in laptop and desktop PC screens.

Turning on Dark Mode if you have a compatible screen could save quite a bit of power. In Figure 7-19, you can see that more than half of the total pixels on the screen are black and, thus, inactive and consuming no power at all on my Android-powered Microsoft Surface Duo device. If you don't have a suitable display, however, such as an LCD or LED screen, any power saving will be negligible, if you see any saving at all.

Managing Power Usage for Hybrid Workers

With so many more people now working from home, and also using their own PCs and devices, power management becomes a case of instilling best practice in the workforce. This can be daunting, firstly because people will be using a wide variety of device types and also because you cannot assume that the majority of people will be technically literate and understand what you are trying to tell them.

If somebody doesn't understand what they're being told, the natural reaction is to switch off and ignore it. This is why it is very important to present information in the correct way, and in the next chapter I will show you how to inspire your employees and teach them the information they need in ways that they will understand and engage with.

One thing to note, however, is the sheer volume of operating system versions you will be dealing with. It's fairly straightforward to exampling to an employee that they can't use their Windows 7 PC to access company systems, and indeed this can be blocked from happening by your Mobile Device Management (MDM) settings. It's a different thing altogether though when it comes to Android devices.

Manufacturers want to get people to upgrade to their newest devices, and so they release new versions regularly, sometimes even twice a year as companies like Samsung have been known to do, and they drop support for "older" device all too quickly.

Don't get me wrong. Almost every company does this (Apple being a very notable exception with iOS), and the end result is that there are a huge volume of older, unsupported, and potentially insecure Android devices in use. It will be up to yourselves to determine how and if you want these devices to fit into your own computing ecosystem, but simply telling employees that they have to go out and buy themselves a new phone every year or two will frequently be met with hostility, especially given these people will have their own strains on their finances such as mortgages, children, and the fact your company hasn't given them a pay increase for the last two years.

This then is a subject that needs to be handled with some sensitivity, but for the sake of basic security for your organization, limiting the access for unsupported versions of operating systems of all types, and especially Android, is a wise and sensible precaution.

Summary

As you can see there are a great many things you can do to manage power consumption on everything from a smartphone to a desktop PC, and Microsoft Windows remains every bit as configurable as it always used to be.

With the increase in hybrid workers though, working from home and even using their own PCs and computers to access company systems, and the potential this has to open security holes to malware and hackers to gain access to and even encrypt the sensitive and critical data you store, bringing these workers along for the ride in a safe and secure manner can be very challenging.

This is why in the next chapter we'll look in depth at how you can talk to workers in language they're not intimidated by, encourage them to get involved in saving energy both for your organization and for themselves, and how this can be extended to working with local communities to effect change on a wider scale.

CHAPTER 8

Establishing Policies and Procedures for IT Use

It's one thing to make changes to your personal or professional life or to bring about changes to your business or working practices so that you can reduce your impact on the environment and climate change, but it's another thing altogether to bring other people along with you for the journey.

This can never be done in a high-handed or preachy way as that is ultimately self-defeating as people will switch off from your message. What you have to do is educate, inspire, and make people want to come along on the journey with you.

Throughout this book I've written about the need for education, and this really is at the forefront of bringing about change. The most important question isn't "What?" or "Who?" but always "Why?" This is a founding principle of news journalism and why, since its founding in 1917, the Pulitzer Prize for journalism has always gone to investigative reporters.

Let's explore for a moment why education is so very important to the environment and climate change, and this brings me on to the very founding principle of my own experience as a teacher.

© Mike Halsey 2025
M. Halsey, *The Green IT Guide*, https://doi.org/10.1007/979-8-8688-1233-0_8

Never Make Assumptions

We all come from different backgrounds, from different places, and we all have different experiences. It's crucial therefore that we never make any assumptions about anybody, no matter how well we might think we know them or no matter how well their certain demographic might be understood.

I have traveled the world and seen many different societies and cultures, but for as widely traveled as I would like to think of myself, having gone to the USA, Canada, around Europe, and Scandinavia, I have never traveled to Africa, Asia, the Far East, Australasia, or South America. My closest friend has traveled much more widely than I have, having already visited Canada, Asia, New Zealand, and Kenya and having spent a considerable amount of time in Cambodia in recent years, a place he considers a home from home.

Even he doesn't understand some of the intricacies and complexities of the world, however. To take one example I want to look at my move from the UK to France in 2019. I decided, after 49 years living in and around England, that it was finally time to settle somewhere that was much nicer for my, shall we say, senior years, and so I left the UK behind and moved to the French countryside.

I did this for several reasons. The UK was too overpopulated for my liking, and crime, antisocial behavior, and just plain selfishness had become an enormous problem since the financial crisis of 2008. The cost of living was also soaring, and if I wanted to move to the countryside in the UK, it would have cost me at many more times what it cost me in France. As an example, I purchased a 350-year-old cottage in the middle of deepest-darkest French countryshire in 2020, and an equivalent property in the UK would have cost eight to ten times what I actually paid.

Then came time to apply for residency and to register for the French tax system. Now I already knew that France had one of the highest tax regimes in Europe, with only Sweden coming in with higher taxes. What I never knew until I was embedded in this system was what I would get for it.

Pensions, healthcare, roads, the environment, local services, and all the things I care about the most in my own life were being given the attention and indeed the money that they needed and deserved. While I had heard people over the years describe the UK as a tax haven, I finally realized they were right.

The tax take in the UK at the time I moved was a much less overall than other countries, including the USA, asked people to pay. Indeed the UK is one of only a handful of countries that allow you to amend your business or self-employment income declaration after being told what tax you will pay for that, just in case you made a mistake of course. In the years since the British government haven't handled the economy very well, and the tax take is now roughly equivalent to that of France, the big difference is that you don't see the money being spent wisely or any improvements to public services. The stories are all about the tax raised being used to pay down public debt.

When we directly compare what services people in the UK get for their money, the answer is very little. All of the reasons I chose to leave the UK, such as problems with the levels of policing, litter and fly-tipping on the streets, and a lack of investment in education and healthcare, all came down to the small tax take. This problem is of course compounded by the fact that the British people are also broadly unaware of what happens in France and Sweden and that if you asked them to pay any more tax than they currently do, they would throw their arms in the air and accuse you of being wholly unreasonable.

I then explained all of this to my much more widely traveled friend, and he freely admitted that it had just never occurred to him this might be the case, but that it certainly explained a lot about the state of public services in the UK.

This I feel is a very good, albeit a slightly long-winded, way to demonstrate why you should never make any assumptions about what people know and understand.

Start at the Beginning, but Don't Dumb Down

Part of the process involved in educating people, but without making any assumptions about what they already know or understand, is to find the right way to pitch the subject. The best way normally is to find some way to relate it to their own lives. If people can find something relatable, they'll find it to be much more understandable, and they'll be more inclined to give it their full attention.

Where you start, however, can sometimes be a challenge. There might be a temptation to start with the "Janet and John bit," where the subject is dumbed down to the point that a primary school child would be able to grasp the basics, or to develop far too much context and backstory. A good example of this latter point comes from the movie *Airplane II: The Sequel* (Paramount Pictures, 1982) where an airport official is asked for absolutely everything that's happened up to that point. He hilariously replies, "Well, let's see. First, the earth cooled. And then the dinosaurs came, but they got too big and fat, so they all died and they turned into oil. And then the Arabs came and they bought Mercedes Benzes."

So finding the right place to start the conversation is always important. It's also important that it be a conversation. Again this comes down to not being preachy, patronizing, or condescending, but instead explaining things in terms the listener will be able to understand. If you allow people to ask questions, then they will inevitably become more engaged, so don't fear being interrupted as it can be a good thing.

Let's look at the reason why people ask questions. It's because they don't know what or aren't sure what the answer to that question is, and knowing that answer might fill some gaps in their own knowledge and help them understand the subject better and with a greater understanding of the overall context. Don't assume that just because you understand something that you can explain it in ways that other people will understand. If somebody chips in to ask a question about something you've just said, it's because you either haven't explained it well enough or because you might have missed out something the other person feels should have been included. This brings us neatly onto ...

Context Is King

There is a very common phrase when it comes to education, journalism, and really any profession where the exchange of information is involved, "Context is king," and it's very true when it comes to educating people about climate change and what they can do themselves to reduce their impact on the environment and to help heal the planet we all rely on so heavily to keep us alive.

This all feeds back into making the subject relatable and relevant to the lives of the people you are speaking to. Let's take the subject of deforestation as an example. You'll probably find the people you are speaking to live in a large town or a city, perhaps in the suburbs, where forests are something you have to drive for several hours to visit and the kind of place you go to on a vacation.

Discussing the problems caused by excessive logging in the Amazon rainforest might seem thousands of miles away for some people and out of context for others as they think of the rainforest as being vast, so can't get their heads around how much logging takes place and how even a small amount of it can have a significant impact on the environment.

The World Wildlife Fund (WWF) describes forests as such:

They provide food and shelter for so much of life on Earth – from fungi and insects to tigers and elephants. More than half the world's land-based plants and animals, and three-quarters of all birds, live in and around forests.

Forests have a big influence on rainfall patterns, water and soil quality and flood prevention too. Millions of people rely directly on forests as their home or for making a living. But the risks from deforestation go even wider. Trees absorb and store carbon dioxide. If forests are cleared, or even disturbed, they release carbon dioxide and other greenhouse gases. Forest loss and damage is the cause of around 10% of global warming.

There are two points you can take here that people are better able to relate to their own lives. The first is that stopping deforestation could cut the problems of global warming by up to 10%, but perhaps the most important is the effect it has on animals, birds, and insects.

Many people have heard of the global decline in the number of bees and what effect this can have on crops, harvests, and the food chain, but people also really do care about animals and birds. It tugs on their heartstrings to think their habitats are being destroyed, and the emotional impact of this is something that can have a great effect on them.

Then we look at the use of coal and other fossil fuels. It might not bother the average person too much to think that the power stations producing electricity for their homes and businesses are being powered themselves by fossil fuels such as coal or gas.

There will be people in the room, however, that own electric cars or that have worked hard to reduce their household waste. They might be very happy for their small contribution to the environment, but when it's pointed out that their car is indeed a polluter, because the electricity used to power it in the first instance comes from the burning of fossil fuels, or that electricity they use at home comes from the burning of some of their household waste in local incinerators, all of a sudden, their own contribution might not seem like much of a contribution at all, and that person might become much more involved with the subject matter at hand.

Teaching Methodology

Teaching is a skill like any other. It is though often oversimplified as "importing knowledge or skills to another person, or group of people." As a teacher myself, this infuriates me, and I had strong words for some friends who trained as TEFL ("Teaching English as a Foreign Language") tutors so they could work abroad.

The problem is that teaching is much more than just understanding the subject or having a prior qualification in it. In the case of English, it's so much more than understanding the basic rules of spelling, grammar, and punctuation.

Teaching is a holistic skill that begins with three tenets:

- Assessment

- Observation

- Evaluation

You'll notice that teaching isn't actually mentioned at all in this list, because when you study for a teaching degree, while part of that will require in-service observation by your own tutors, to make sure you understand the principles and are implementing them correctly, you could be in a class with people who teach a broad variety of subjects from child care to law.

I want to spend a little time then examining these three pillars of education, why they're important, and how you can use them effectively in how you train and inspire the people around you.

Step 1 – Assessment

Education begins with assessment. This is used to determine several important things, including how much a student already knows about the subject, if anything, what their ability to learn is and how they like to learn (these are commonly known as learning styles), and what level they are at when it comes to fundamentals that may be required, such as English and math skills.

There are several different ways in which you can assess people. This is most commonly done in education by means of a paper or online questionnaire the student will complete that will test certain skills and knowledge. From this an overall score can be extrapolated, which gives the tutor an idea of where the learner is already at and what their ability to learn might be.

This can also be done, however, by discussion, most usually in a group. The downside of questioning people in the group environment is that you run the risk of making somebody feel self-conscious, either because they don't or feel that they don't know or because they are uncomfortable speaking in a group (remember that not everybody is an extrovert).

It's very straightforward to gather useful information from a group of people though, and these are the stages you can go through to do so:

1. In a group or roundtable discussion, ask people generally what they understand by terms such as "Climate change," "Global warming," "Recycling," "CO_2 emissions," "Fossil fuels," "Greenhouse gas," and "Renewable energy," and allow the subject to flesh out into a conversation if time permits as different people will have different levels of understanding and some people might have never heard specific terms, so the peer group can learn from each other while you use the opportunity to assess the knowledge of each person.

2. Ask specific questions of individuals to flesh out the detail of what it is they know and understand. This can be something of a skill you learn with time, as the trick is to ask questions of people at their own

level of education and understanding, so as not to overwhelm or intimidate that person and while also not making it appear to the group that some people are getting asked simpler things than others. A broad range of questions is normally a good way to achieve this.

3. A short questionnaire on the subjects that have been discussed can help clarify and consolidate information in people's minds while also providing you with more accurate, measurable data on what the individuals in the group understand.

4. Lastly, either a learning styles questionnaire, sometimes known as VARK (I'll come to this in a moment), or a discussion about how people find it easiest to learn can help you determine how best to pitch the actual subject matter you'll cover to the group.

Learning Styles and VARK

There are four recognized learning styles, called VARK. This stands for visual, aural, read–write, and kinesthetic. These learning styles represent how people like to learn and how they find leaning to be easy for them:

- **Visual** learners prefer to watch presentations, videos, or slide decks, and they find that this is a good way for them to absorb information.

- **Aural** learners like listening to people, or audio descriptions of the subject, and find this is how they best take in the information.

- **Read–Write** learners prefer to read books or texts, and then they consolidate what they have learned by rewriting it, usually in note or summary form.

- **Kinesthetic** learners learn best through activities, such as role-play, group research, or making or building something to achieve a goal.

The majority of learners are kinesthetic, which is why early years and primary school education largely revolves around play, creativity, and making or building things. Next comes read–write, where it is very common for people to consolidate what they have learned by writing notes for themselves, and it is always a good idea to encourage this.

Most learners, however, will have a combination of all four learning styles. There are plenty of tests you can find online that people can complete, such as this one at `https://vark-learn.com`. Finding the best way to pitch the subject can really help with education, and a group of employees in an office will probably prefer different ways of learning from a group of PhD students.

Step 2 – Observation

Observation takes place during actual teaching, and this is where the benefits of in-person classroom teaching (or in your own case more likely meeting room) really come to the fore. During the pandemic, many if not most of the world's children were forced to undertake learning over the Internet – that's the ones that were lucky enough to have a computer and an Internet connection – the rest being forced to either learn from paper-based resources and books provided by their school or obtained by their parents or not being able to have any kind of education at all for more than a year and a half.

Perhaps you were a parent of children that had to learn online, or maybe this book has been on the best-seller list now for so many years (wishful thinking – Ed) that you were at school at the time and part of your education had to take place online.

You might be aware then of the difficulties in remote teaching. It might be trendy to teach over the Internet given all the tools available to us nowadays such as group text and video chat, document collaboration, and Microsoft Whiteboard, Zoom Whiteboard, or Google Jamboard, and I fully accept that it's a great way to connect students with the most experienced and expert teachers out there, no matter where in the world they may be. Overall though, remote teaching is, in the mind of this particular practitioner, a completely terrible idea if it's the only way to reach children and not used instead as a supplementary method to enhance a classroom-based experience that already exists.

The reason for this particular little rant is simple. If you teach somebody remotely, or ask them to learn on their own by reading materials, and there is no face-to-face time between the teacher and student at all, it's almost impossible to determine if the student is in fact learning anything, if there's anything they're having difficulty with, or if they just find the whole subject matter hideously complex to begin with. It's also bad for the student as they can't just chip in at any time to ask you a question about something they don't understand. Most of the time they're just stuck, on their own, getting frustrated because the one bit they didn't get just makes everything else that comes afterward more difficult.

Peer-to-Peer

In the world of IT, well, I had to bring it back to computers eventually, peer-to-peer is a technological school of thought that uses a distributed network of computers to share resources between one another. It might be most commonly associated with the illegal downloading of movies and television shows, where different parts of the video file exist on a multitude of different Internet-connected computers that themselves pop on- and offline periodically, but between them a complete copy of the full video can be constituted.

Peer-to-peer is also used for other purposes, however, and you might remember the SETI@home project, which was an application people could install on their computers that enabled individuals to donate some of their processing power and time to sift through huge volumes of data collected from observatories around the world, in the hopes of finding a radio or another signal that could indicate the existence of extraterrestrial life. SETI@home used a form of peer-to-peer technology since its first release way back in 1999.

Note   Back in 2015, a French company ran a trial of Internet-connected home radiators, each containing not a heating element, but a computer server. The servers could run computational software for medical and scientific research, and in return the companies or organizations involved would pay for its electricity usage, while the host household benefitted from the free heating the appliance would generate. This was great for both research and the environment, though sadly the idea never caught on.

In classrooms peer-to-peer has a different, yet not entirely disconnected, meaning. We talk about working with and learning from our peers, which is generally defined by the dictionary as being *a person who has equal standing with another or others, as in rank, class, or age.* When you're at school, your peers are your classmates and the children in other classes; when you're at work, your peers are your colleagues; and when you're out in the big wide world, peers can be used to describe people in a similar social, political, or economic class as yourself.

It is very, very true that we learn from our peers, and I have already mentioned in this chapter how roundtable discussion between a class of people can help them impart their own knowledge between one another, with the role of the teacher there purely to timekeep, keep the conversation on track, and provide accuracy and correction when required.

If you are training people within your company or organization, then it is essential that some form of face-to-face teaching is part of the overall program.

Why We Observe

Observation of students comes with many benefits, not the least of which is that the teacher can tell when everybody has bemused looks on their faces, and they realize they're clearly pitching the subject incorrectly, or that there's been a genuine mix-up and they've just found themselves in the wrong room (it does happen).

As a general rule though, observation of students in a classroom offers the following real-world benefits:

- You can see if anybody is being left out of teaching, either because they don't understand the subject you're teaching them, don't understand the task you have given them, or are in a group activity and are not being included by the other members of that group.

- You can gauge how much people understand about what they're being taught by wandering around and asking seemingly random questions about the subject (they might seem random to the students, but in fact what you're doing is something called "checking learning," or checking that learning is taking place).

- You can encourage peer-to-peer learning. You might, for example, see that one student has finished a task quickly. Checking they have completed it correctly, you can then encourage them to support people who might be struggling and need more help and guidance. This helps not only the student you've asked them to assist but also themselves as they're both consolidating what they know and understand by repeating it to other people, but you're also helping them to better understand how and where other people are having difficulty with that subject, making them better at helping others in the process.

Step 3 – Evaluation

The subject of checking learning brings me neatly onto evaluation. Most people in business will think of evaluation as that pointless, waste-of-time form the trainer asks you to fill out at the end of the session so they can get a nice ego-stroking (a little hint on this: if you give people little stars to rate something, always make it an even number; then they can't arbitrarily pick the one in the middle).

Evaluation, however, is *much* more than just a checkbox, form-filling exercise. It's what you do to "check that learning has taken place." There's no point in teaching a subject for a few hours if half the people in the room will leave none the wiser than when they entered. That helps nobody and will turn people off from education rather than engage them further.

Evaluation then is two-fold:

- You're checking that each person in the room is able to take something valuable away from the lesson, that they have understood at least the main thrust of what you were teaching them (remember not everybody learns at the same level or at the same pace), and that they know what to look for and where to look if they want to learn more.

- You're learning as a practitioner what worked, what didn't work as well, and what you can improve for next time. You might, for example, find that one particular thread of the subject hasn't been understood by the class. This is fine and nothing to be ashamed of, as teachers are also constantly learning and improving their craft.

You can evaluate people in different ways, all of which are good, but the one(s) you choose will be those that best fit your scenario, the group, the context of the training, or time you have available.

- You could go down the academic route and ask people to fill in a quiz, perhaps a multi-choice questionnaire (though people will guess and you'll get less accurate results) on the subject that you taught them.

- You can go around the room and ask everybody one or two questions about what's been taught. You need to remember that this works hand in hand with assessment and observation so that you only ask people questions appropriate to their own level of learning, but it can be a good way to consolidate the subject in the minds of the group.

- You can do it as part of observation by asking people to make notes on the subject you are teaching them, and then while they're engaged on a task, wander around the room and take a sneaky look at all their notes. While not everybody will read their notes afterward, note taking is a good way to help people comprehend and clarify the subject in their own minds.

When it comes to the summary, there are additional things you can do, such as encouraging water-cooler discussions between the students later, if they all work in the same place, or to perhaps suggest they set up a best-practice noticeboard on which they can post notes of suggestions they might have or have been told for helping the environment.

This latter method has additional benefits, as it will also reach people in the workplace that didn't attend the training and hopefully encourage and provoke additional conversations between the students and the wider workforce.

Never Use the Word "Understand"

One thing I really can't emphasize enough though is never, ever, to use the word "understand" when describing students or subjects. They can use the word, but you're simply not allowed to do so. The reason for this is that "understand" is an unquantifiable thingumybob. Nobody can really pin down what it means, as one person's understanding of a subject will likely be at great variance from another person's understanding.

There are other terms you can use, however, that are every bit as good and that in this context mean the same thing anyway. Can the students "demonstrate" something, i.e., can they show, through words or actions, something they have been taught? This is a very good alternative as it is something quantifiable, whereas understanding is not a quantifiable metric.

Another term you can use is "identify" as in, can the students identify something that contributes to climate change? This, again, is something quantifiable and demonstrable.

Inspiring Your Workforce Through Your Actions

While it's all well and good to teach your workforce about what you're doing, why it's important, and what they themselves can do about it, you might not have the knowledge or skills in-house to establish and run training courses. Indeed you're reading this book, so the assumption I make could be that you're starting out on your journey and are still gathering information on what you can do and why it's important. I won't make that assumption though because, let's be honest, I've spent most of this chapter telling you never to make assumptions. Let's just say this chapter might be filling gaps in your own knowledge.

In this case you want to bring your workforce with you by inspiring them with your actions and deeds. Here, rather than it being the content you're focusing on, instead your communication is king (alas, there aren't enough appropriate words that begin or rhyme with the letter Q). When you decide on a new future for the company, perhaps a new product line, new marketing strategy, or a change of direction for the business, you'll have a series of planning meetings between the senior management and related stakeholders and employees. The outcome of these meetings will be a plan is devised and written up so that everybody involved is clear what is going to happen, when, and why.

The difference between a business plan and an environmental plan is that you wouldn't necessarily convey the former to your workforce. This could be because the information is sensitive and you don't want your competitors getting wind of what you're planning, just in case they steal the march on you.

When it comes to your environmental strategy though, this wouldn't matter; if anything, you *want* your competitors to do the same thing at least. Sure, if you adopt the right climate strategies, then you can use the public relations benefits that come with it to build the business and to get ahead of your competitors; you are in business after all.

If they do get wind of what you're doing though, it's not necessarily a bad thing, as word will get out about what you're doing and all publicity, as the saying goes, is good publicity.

So it is with your workforce, you want them to know what it is you're doing but crucially, and this brings me back to the first point I made in this chapter, *why* you are doing it.

Make the Workforce Part of the Solution

This is the point at which you want to bring the workforce with you and make them part of the solution. Just in the way that global climate change can't be tackled without every person and every business and organization doing something to help, it also can't be solved by your business itself unless every member of the workforce plays their part in what you do.

So what does this mean? Well, what it certainly doesn't mean is union-style meetings where employee representatives sit in with senior management and chew the fat over the subject matter at hand. It's *all* the workforce you need to bring with you, and each and every one of them needs to play their part. If you go down the employee representation route, people will end up being told what they must do, instead of what you really need, which is choosing to do so themselves.

Now let's tackle the elephant in the room here. Not every employee will want to get on board with your plans. Some will be skeptical, some will not see the relevance to them, and some might not see climate change as a man-made problem or perhaps even a problem at all. Lastly, some people might be just too damn busy. People might accept that the climate is changing, but feel that it's a natural process rather than something humanity has caused.

To these people I would say this: That belief is fine. We're not going to shame or dismiss somebody for having a belief. It is true though that humanity *can* do something about it, and this is how these people can be encouraged to get on board.

So we come to communication, planning, and inclusion. Take the time to explain to your workforce what you plan to do, but be prepared to listen to them in return. They might, you never know, have ideas that you hadn't considered that could be very helpful and effective or perhaps even expand your plans further. Don't dismiss the dumb ideas, as that will only discourage people from helping. Find a way to make everybody feel involved and valued.

As part of your plans, there will be things that individuals can themselves do. This could be a small thing such as unplugging their phone or laptop charger when they're not using it, as I spoke about in Chapter 2, turning off their PC monitor when they're not using that, or encouraging their own teams to meet others virtually rather than in person.

Keep Everybody Involved

There can be a temptation within business to set teams against one another, so that they compete to be the most productive, to generate the biggest revenue, and to reduce costs. With your climate program, you need every single person and every single team on the same page. It might then be tempting to encourage teams to compete against one another to see who can become the most climate-friendly.

This can have downsides, however. Remember you are trying to bring *everybody* on board, and that means that everybody is equally valuable and one team is not, and can never be, better or more valuable than any other. No person is more equal than any other person.

So whatever it is you decide to do, find a way to keep everybody involved. Earlier in this chapter I said you could have a suggestions board on which people could pin their top sustainability tips, things they know themselves or have heard or read about from others. You might want to encourage people to submit articles they've read online or stories from themselves or others that can be compiled into an email newsletter or a section on the company intranet that they can all read. You never know, you might learn something yourself that you didn't know before.

Inspiring the Workforce

It's through this inclusion and making everybody in the business or organization feel valuable and involved that you can inspire the workforce. Let's take one possible scenario. The project starts small with teams deciding what they can do with their own small part of the business to reduce their impact on the environment.

You might have one department look at the amount of printer paper they're using and decide that much of it can be done by saving files as PDFs instead that are sent to people by email or collaboration tools such as Microsoft Teams. Another team might also look at the volume they print but, deciding that it really is necessary to print in large volumes, source more sustainable paper instead and switch to a bamboo supplier. They could also decide that everything should be printed in monochrome and at draft quality to save on toner.

Another team comes to you and asks for recycling bins to be fitted around the company, not just general recycling, but separating all the different types of product that can be recycled. You contact your local waste management company, and they tell you they indeed take food scraps, glass, and even items employees bring in from home such as unwanted clothing, batteries, and small electronic items for recycling. Around your premises then, you can install recycling for paper, metal, plastic, glass, and food scraps, with the waste management company adding additional recycling facilities onsite or nearby in cooperation with your local town or city council.

Another team within the business decides that, as everybody in the business works regular hours, they can start to car-share. This brings unexpected benefits as journey times are reduced when they're then allowed to use the carpool lanes or diamond lanes and the fuel costs for employees come down too. Rotas are devised to help facilitate journeys into work and back, with flexibility included to allow for people having appointments and sick days.

Then the facilities management department come up with a great idea. They'd been planning an upgrade to the office for some time and had already spoken with contractors about the feasibility of installing equipment like inverters, which I spoke about in Chapter 2. They've been looking around the office at the equipment they'll be replacing, which is most of the desks, tables, and chairs. There's a lot there, and so they've contacted the city council, who have in turn put them in touch with some local community groups.

Several of these groups have quite literally bitten their arm off for a few tables and chairs, and more have asked for desks. The facilities manager reckons that 60% of the furniture that's being replaced can go to a good home locally, and they've begun looking around the business at other things that will be replaced during the refit.

Getting the Ball Rolling

Each department is invited to share their best-practice stories and ideas with the rest of the business, and this gives each department ideas in turn. Some will also roll out the same plans as others; the business as a whole might encourage a company-wide carpool scheme so as to get the best effect from it or to ask the local transportation company if they'd consider placing a bus or a tram stop nearby, so that employees who normally drive to work every day can instead be encouraged to take public transport.

Each employee begins to get in on the project, not because they're forced to, but because they can start to see small steps building into a greater whole. They begin to tell their friends, family, and colleagues from suppliers and customers what you're all doing, and the ball starts rolling.

It doesn't take long before people in the local community and even further afield are beginning to hear about what it is your business is doing, and the marketing department decides to issue a press release and set aside a place on the company website where all of your environmental plans can be promoted.

Working with Local Communities

I have suggested a little while ago one way in which your business or organization can work with your local community to help tackle climate change and reduce waste. This type of thing is actually fairly common and has been for years, but not every business adopts it, and premises refits can all too frequently come with large skips outside the building filled with a combination of furniture, carpet, computers, and appliances.

You have several avenues available to you to feed into the local community and community and charitable groups. The first is through the town or city council if they have coordinators that provide support to these external voluntary groups; this might be managed centrally or through your local library. You can also contact your local paper or television station and ask if they will write a story about what it is you're doing and what it is you can offer to the local community if anything is going spare.

Contacting local sports clubs and teams is also a great way to reach the community, and they might place posters and information around their stadium or club premises for a while telling people how they can contact you.

There's also the possibility of setting up a web page where all your to-be-discarded goods can be "purchased," either for free or, in the case of more valuable items, for a fee. This is fairly common in business especially for restaurants and factories that close, where the equipment they own can be very expensive.

The most important people though are the people already working for your company. If you let these people know what you can do for the community, what you have available, and how you want to work more widely with them, then you will quickly find that your employees are heavily involved in everything from childcare centers, to sports venues, to the local book club. Word will quickly spread about your work, and you can designate a department or person within the business for them to contact.

It's not just about giving away the furniture and technology you no longer need either. You may decide there are other ways to contribute to the community and where they can help you in return. This could involve donating excess food and drink from the company canteen to a local food bank, working with a local community or pressure group to push for better public transport links, offering your car park one Sunday a month for a car boot sale where people can resell things they might otherwise be tempted to simply throw away (one person's garbage is another person's treasure after all), or just helping get the message about your environmental shakeup out into the community by sponsoring a floral display on a city roundabout.

In turn you might then find local community organizations that can do things for you. Perhaps a group sells and delivers locally grown organic fruit and vegetables, and you can place a regular order for your staff canteen and kitchens.

Locally Sourced

Maybe there are other local businesses that can supply products to your business? You are already a part of your local community simply by virtue of being there, and you're plugged into the best resource you can possibly hope for, for information about that community and what they do and can provide. This information source is, of course, yourself and your workforce.

In exactly the same way as I mentioned, you should have a single point of contact within your company for external groups and organizations to use; that single point of contact can also be the person that people within your company can go to with ideas and suggestions of who in the local or the wider community might be good for you to contact.

Take my own example. I live in the middle of a huge farming community. There's everything grown here from wheat to vegetables, and there's also a large amount of cattle and sheep farming. Now I know we should be reducing cattle farming as it's bad for the environment in many ways, from the cow burp of death polluting the atmosphere and destroying the ozone layer to the welfare of the animals. Without getting into a protracted debate on the benefits of vegetarianism and veganism, for as long as people are consuming meat, is it not better for the environment to have that meat come from a local source?

Where do you purchase your food, fruits, and vegetables? I'm willing to bet it'll be from the local supermarket. These businesses offer choice, convenience, and variety. They're open up to 24 hours a day and have absolutely everything you need under one roof, and therefore what's not to like?

We need to ask ourselves where all these products are coming from. Sure, certain fruits and vegetables are seasonal, and out of season will come from around the world where they're still being grown at that time of year. As for the rest of it though, we're looking at products shipped around the country and around the world in massive trucks and shipping containers.

These use huge volumes of oil to fuel them, fossil fuels that we're supposed to be using much less of. It makes sense then to take a little more time over your shopping as you could find that the local butcher and fruit and vegetable store sell locally sourced products. In addition to not using huge volumes of oil to ship them around, they'll likely be much fresher and tastier than the supermarket-stocked equivalents and last considerably longer as well.

Local markets and especially farmer's markets are great sources of environmentally sustainable foodstuffs, too, if you have them in your area. There are additional benefits to shopping at smaller, independent businesses too. Now I hate memes (those pictures with pithy messages we see all the time on social media), but recently one caught my eye:

> *In line, the cashier tells an elderly woman: "Madam, you should bring your own shopping bags because these plastic bags are not eco-friendly!"*

The elderly lady apologizes and replies: "In my day there was no such green wave."

"That's our problem today, ma'am. Your generation did not care enough about the environment."

"You're right," the elderly lady replied. "Our generation did not care for the environment adequately. Back in the shop, glass bottles of milk, carbonated drinks, and beer were returned. The shop was taking them back to the factory where they were washed and sterilized before they used them again and again. We really didn't care about the environment in our time. Even the baby diapers were washed because there were no disposable ones. We dried them ourselves, not in electric dryers. These diapers were dried outdoors using wind and solar energy.

In our time, we really weren't worried about the environmental status. We only had one TV and one radio at home, not one TV for each room. And the TV had a 14-inch screen, not the size of a stadium, which when it broke down will be thrown away unknown where. In the kitchen we had to do everything with our hands because there were no electrical appliances to do everything for us. When we sent something fragile in the mail, to pack it we used old newspapers, not plastic bubbles and Styrofoam balls that took 500 years to degrade.

We didn't use gasoline mowers to mow the grass in our time, they were mechanical, and we used our muscles to get them moving. Exercises were amazing and we didn't have to go to the gym to keep fit.

You're right. We weren't worried about the environment at our time. We drank water straight from the tap, not from platinum bottles and cups that are now filling the oceans.

In fact, there was no green wave in our time. Then we all got on the tram or bus. The boys used bikes or walked to go to school instead of using their parents as a 24-hour taxi service.

So isn't it amazing that the current generation talks so much about the 'environment' but doesn't want to give up anything and doesn't think about living a little more like we did in my day?"

There are then, very clearly, benefits to shopping locally, and you never know what you might find. It's definitely worth a look as if you *can* procure at least some of the products and services you need from local suppliers that in itself will do wonders for helping you achieve your sustainability goals, and I spoke at length in Chapter 1 about the things I've been able to do in my own life.

Plastics and Packaging

I want to wrap this chapter up though with a discussion about packaging. I am making a very conscious effort to reduce the amount of packaging I use from the products I purchase. Getting my fruit and vegetables from the local farmer's markets goes some way toward this, but I was pretty appalled recently when I bought some filled pasta from the supermarket for lunch, only to find that within its plastic bag was another plastic bag containing the food.

If we look at how recyclable different products are, then plastics definitely come at the bottom of the list. Plastics can only be recycled a few times before they're of such low quality they have to go to landfill or they end up killing wildlife in the planet's oceans.

Paper and cardboard are slightly better, but they, too, can only be recycled a few times before they have to be burned or destroyed. By far the two best materials you can use for packaging are metal and glass, both of which can be recycled ad infinitum. I have changed my own purchasing habits now to reflect this, using paper bags for fruits and vegetables rather than plastic ones and purchasing foodstuffs such as pasta in carboard boxes rather than the ones sold in plastic wrapping.

Additionally I have completely stopped buying wine by the box (convenient if I only wanted one or two glasses a night) in favor of buying it by the bottle, because these are made of glass. Soups and other products I'll buy in metal tins rather than plastic tubs and so on.

Consider buying goods "en vrac," too (no idea how to say in English, sorry): rice, pastas, sugar ... More and more goods can be bought like this.

All of this is much easier when buying products on a local level because it's the big manufacturers and supermarkets that are the primary users of plastic, and this is because they need to keep things fresh for longer as they are shipped much further and for far longer than locally sold products.

This might also be something to consider if your own company manufactures goods. Can you use a cardboard wrapping instead of plastic, for example?

Summary

Your local environmental policies can only be a win-win. You'll inspire the people that work for you, they'll tell their friends and families, you'll get more goodwill from the local community, and in return you'll become a more desirable company to work for.

That goodwill will stretch outward to your suppliers, stakeholders, and customers, be they local, national, or global, and you'll inspire them as they'll look at what you're doing and look to see if they can do something similar themselves, as will your employees and their families and friends.

You don't have to do these things on your own, but starting that way can really get the ball rolling. Before you know it, a small idea from the accounts team in their own office has become something that other people and businesses have adopted ...from little acorns and all that!

While coming up with inventive and collaborative ways to reduce your business' impact on the environment is laudable, some things your business needs to do because they're mandated by regulation. In the next chapter we'll look at what regulations exist around the world that can dictate how your business responds to the climate and the ecology of the planet.

CHAPTER 9

Regulation and Compliance

Every year, the United Nations holds a Conference of the Parties (COP) summit somewhere in the world. At these conferences, international climate policy, treaties, and agreements are presented, discussed, and agreed and …occasionally, even kept to. By the time this book is in editing, we'll be seeing pictures from COP 29 in Baku, Azerbaijan. You can read more about the COP conferences on the UN website at pcs.tv/3MBNQeC.

Now I say that agreements are occasionally kept to because in November 2020, President Donald Trump pulled the USA out of the much-talked-about Paris agreement. The Paris agreement was signed at COP 21 by world leaders in 2015 and was a legally binding international treaty that committed nations to try and prevent global temperatures rising by more than 1.5 degrees Celsius (2.7 degrees Fahrenheit). It was hailed at the time as a highly significant step forward and was signed by 194 countries including China and Russia, commonly seen as some of the least cooperative nations and also the biggest polluters.

You can read more about the Paris agreement at pcs.tv/4cZSptI, and a full list of signatories can be found online at pcs.tv/3XvRltg.

After this, the COP agreements lost a lot of their credibility, with the COP 28 summit in Dubai coming under intense scrutiny when the conference president-designate was announced as Dr Sultan-al-Jaber, the head of the state-owned Abu Dhabi National Oil Company (ADNOC).

© Mike Halsey 2025
M. Halsey, *The Green IT Guide*, https://doi.org/10.1007/979-8-8688-1233-0_9

It not only emerged that the UAE had planned to use the climate conference to strike oil deals with other nations, but the deal obtained by the end of the conference to phase out the use of fossil fuels was called "weak" by experts. COP 29 in a similar fashion, as I mentioned already, is being held in Azerbaijan, which is also a major oil-producing nation.

It's clear then that getting nations to agree on international climate policy is very difficult, which results in great risk to countries including Sri Lanka, Japan, Fiji, and other nations that are considered most at risk from the effects of climate change. You can read more about the most at-risk nations and how they could be affected at pcs.tv/3XeOaon.

This leaves individual countries to legislate where they can, but this in turn leads to political arguments in those nations about cost and the burden such legislation puts on the people of that nation and their financial well-being, given that "We're only one country, nobody else is doing this, so why should we bother as it's not going to make any difference anyway except for pushing up everybody's bills?"

This of course is the entire point of this book and something I'll talk more about in Chapter 11 when we discuss how ineffectual governments can be. All they can really do is legislate rules and guidance for businesses, organizations, and individuals to follow and adhere to, so you might as well get on with it anyway.

The Current State of Climate Regulations

It may not come as any surprise to you, then, that currently there are very few actual laws and regulations that your business or organization needs to follow and adhere to. The vast majority of regulations apply to manufacturing and recycling, so if you're a purchaser of IT equipment, any rules that need to be followed will have already been done, and nothing else will apply until you dispose of that equipment at the end of its life.

As an example, here in France, there can be fines levied against anybody or any business for not disposing of electrical and electronic equipment in the correct way and at the correct place.

Environmental and Social Governance

Probably the closest we have so far are the environmental and social governance (ESG) rules that have been adopted by the USA, UK, and European Union. These rules are a set of standards used to measure the social and environmental impact of an organization, and they vary slightly across the world.

In the USA, for example, the rules require organizations to disclose

- Climate-related risks and their actual or likely material impacts on the registrant's business, strategy, and outlook

- The registrant's governance of climate-related risks and relevant risk management processes

- The registrant's greenhouse gas (GHG) emissions, which, for accelerated and large accelerated filers and with respect to certain emissions, would be subject to assurance

- Certain climate-related financial statement metrics and related disclosures in a note to its audited financial statements

- Information about climate-related targets and goals and transition plan, if any

These rules apply to larger organizations only. The US states that only businesses with a public float of more than $75 million are bound by them. In the EU and the UK, the rules are more strict, as you might imagine as the

EU always tends to move further and more quickly on such matters. The EU considers their rules should apply to any business with a net turnover of more than €40 million. The UK by comparison sets the bar at 500 employees or a turnover of £500 million.

You can read more about ESG and how it might apply to your business or organization at pcs.tv/3XyX55A, and your government will provide their own information on compliance. A search for environmental and social governance on the US.gov website reveals a long list of useful documents, reports, and links.

The Most Important Substance in Existence

Back in Chapter 1 I wrote that in July 2021, six US states, California, Colorado, Hawaii, Oregon, Vermont, and Washington, all banned the sale of PCs that consume more than a maximum amount of kWh/yr (kilowatt hours per year) of electricity.

This effectively banned the powerful PCs used by PC gamers (though they can still purchase the high-power components and build a PC themselves), but I can also imagine that Pixar, Industrial Light & Magic, and businesses and charities involved in engineering and medicine would have been having conversations at the time with their state governor about the policy, as it also banned many of the computers they need and use.

There are no additional bans elsewhere in the world, at least none that I could find, but the ban is ultimately self-defeating. To demonstrate why I'll use the example of making a cup of coffee, something we can probably all agree is the single most important substance in existence when it comes to business productivity.

In your workplace you will have a kitchen, or at least a kitchenette. In this kitchen you will have a kettle, and that kettle will be used to boil the water you need to make your cup of coffee. Now, just as I did in Chapter 2, I'm going to get into some math, which is always exciting.

Let's say that you have 1 liter of water in your kettle. It takes the same amount of energy to boil water, no matter how it's done. For an electric kettle, this is approximately 0.116 kWh to boil 1 l of water; this is a constant regardless of the power rating for your kettle because it's defined by the laws of thermodynamics and the properties of water itself. Some years ago, the European Union banned the sale of high-power kettles and other electrical devices including vacuum cleaners.

This means that the kettle you're using might not be as powerful as your previous kettle. It might just be 1,200 watts instead of 1,500 watts. If then it takes a set amount of energy to boil 1 l of water, it will take longer to boil that water in the lower-power kettle than it would in the high-power kettle. Regardless of the time taken, however, exactly the same amount of power is consumed by each kettle to do that job.

While you can't make exactly the same argument for a vacuum cleaner or a computer, it's easy to see that some parallels can be made and similar conclusions drawn. If we go back to Pixar, we have here a company that creates and renders computer-animated movies, one of my favorites being *WALL-E* (Walt Disney Pictures, 2008). This movie is entirely animation and has a running time of 97 minutes.

It stands to reason that time is money, these animation companies are very busy, these movies are very expensive, and so the faster their computers can render scenes, the cheaper the movie will be to produce, and the more money can be made from that production when the movie eventually hits theaters.

So the logical assumption is that the rendering is done to the full capacity of the computers and servers used. This will result in a fixed kWh cost for each second or minute of footage. If that rendering is performed by a less powerful computer or server, it's clear that the rendering would take longer. This is because, if the more powerful computer was running to its maximum capacity, a lower-power computer also running to its maximum capacity would take longer to render the same scene.

The upshot of this is that the kWh cost for rendering that scene will be the same for both computers, and perhaps even higher for the less powerful computer, depending on the power efficiency of the components used, something I'll come to shortly.

The same will apply in the field of medicine. Let's say that in one of these US states there is a scientific or medical charity or organization that is trying to find a cure for cancer. Now obviously this is a highly significant and important task. They will have huge volumes of data to chug through to try and determine if X works or what effect Y will have on Z. Thus, it is also safe to assume the computers and servers they use will also be running at their maximum capacity. After all, we don't want to delay the discovery of a cure just to save a little on the electricity bill.

Buy Powerful?

Now we'll look at everybody else, including those hard done by PC gamers. I have a very powerful PC in my office. It's fairly new as well, with an AMD Ryzen 7 8700G processor running at 4.2 GHz, 96 GB of RAM, 4 TB of storage spread across two M.2 drives, and an AMD Radeon RX 7900 XTX graphics card. I use this PC for work, both written and producing video, but also for gaming (I'm an *Elite Dangerous* player, so send me a friend request to Cmdr. Travers if you are as well, and o7 Cmdr.).

Using the estimates provided by AMD and the manufacturers of the other components in the PC, I can estimate that when running at maximum capacity, this PC will consume somewhere around 700–800 watts of electricity. The processor consumes a maximum of 65 W, and the graphics card specifications recommend using an 850 W power supply (PSU), which means they'll be allowing for some headroom.

Currently I'm using this PC to write this book using Microsoft Word, and I have a music player app also open so I can listen to some music in the background, in this case Jean-Michel Jarre. Is this PC running to its maximum capacity? Well, I'd certainly hope not given how much money it cost me, but we can assume it's only consuming a very small amount of the power it would if running to its maximum potential.

Then we come to gaming. When I'm out exploring the galaxy in my Krait Phantom or pootling around the main star systems, which are known as "the bubble" in my Cobra Mk IV, I'm using more power than just typing in Word, but still not the maximum capacity of the PC because at this point *Elite* is a ten-year-old game.

Only if I were to buy one of the very latest AAA games, and a monitor that can handle high frame rates, like 240 Hz, and tried to run that game at its maximum graphics performance and at that high frame rate would I hit the maximum power consumption for the PC. For everything else the PC chugs away using much less power.

So why did I buy a PC that's so much more powerful than I need, you ask. There are several reasons for this, and they're considerations that many people might or could have when making a purchasing decision about computers. The first reason is that sometimes I do need to hit or get close to that maximum potential. When I'm recording video courseware for Pluralsight, I have to render the videos. Just as happens with Pixar when they produce a movie, if I render video using this PC, that process will go much more quickly than it would on a less powerful or my previous computer (which has been moved to my spare bedroom as a gaming PC for a friend when he comes to visit me – the old gaming PC that was in use there was sold to my electrician so he can do gaming, all something I'll come back to).

The next reason is that because this PC is more powerful than I need, it will inevitably last for longer. The software and games we use and play are getting more complex all the time, and each generation requires more powerful hardware than the last generation. If you try running a recent AAA game on a PC from a few years ago, then you'll be lucky if you get playable frame rates on screen at high-quality settings, and you'll have to reduce all the graphics settings downward or to their minimum. Similarly, if you want to render video on that old PC, you'll either have to do so at a much lower resolution than full HD, or it'll just take considerably longer.

This leads back to my electrician (hi, Paul) and the repurposing and sale of older PCs, which are still perfectly good and can perform their given tasks for some years to come. The longer you can use hardware for, the less will go to recycling and landfill, and you'll remember from the beginning of this book just how large the e-waste pile is already.

So in spending more money and buying myself a PC that's more powerful than I need, I'm not only helping the environment but also saving myself money in the long term (any way you want to sell it to yourself – Ed). In the present though, the PC isn't using any more electricity than my old one; in fact it's probably using less as the newer components are more power-efficient, and the fact this new PC can complete some tasks more quickly means a lower power draw overall.

I took the same route with my laptop, buying a Microsoft Surface Laptop Studio that came with an Intel Core i7-11370H processor running at 3.3 GHz, 32 GB RAM, 2 TB M.2 storage, and both the Intel Iris Xe graphics provided on the processor and an Nvidia GeForce RTX 3050 Ti GPU. This laptop only uses the Nvidia GPU when it needs to, using the low-power Intel graphics almost all of the time.

You might ask why I bought a laptop with a much older Intel processor, 11th generation (released in March 2021) when the current (as I write this) generation is 14, with the company's 15th-generation chips set to be announced later this year (2024). The answer is that this laptop was purchased back in February 2022, two years and seven months ago at the time of writing. You would never know this was an almost three-year-old laptop, however, as it keeps pace with everything new to the market today and will continue to run quickly and smoothly for a good few years yet. I love this laptop and have no plans to replace it.

So What Kind of WALL-E Created the Ban?

Companies like Pixar will face the same questions when they buy new workstation PCs and server hardware. Do you comply with the regulations and only buy PCs that comply with state laws, or do you buy from out of state and get the most powerful PCs you can, knowing that they'll last longer by sheer virtue of being more powerful, and thus save money overall while not consuming any more power in general tasks than the PCs that it's legal for them to buy in that state? I say "companies like" because I'm pretty sure that Pixar will always purchase the highest-end kit anyway.

This is a clear example, to this observer anyway, that this law runs counter to the actual desire to reduce the impact computing has on the planet, and this is probably the reason why nobody else has adopted it.

There's also the not insignificant fact that, as I mentioned with my own new desktop PC, the modern components it uses are more power-efficient than previous generations anyway and so will consume less electricity overall than an older computer would, rather making the high-power PC ban look as pointless as the EU's earlier ban on high-power kettles.

What Other Laws and Regulations Exist

As I mentioned at the beginning of this chapter, this really is the current limit of the laws and regulations that affect the use of computers and IT equipment in businesses and organizations. All the other laws and regulations that affect you will be about making sure the equipment is regularly tested and is safe to use and what happens when you eventually retire equipment for being too old or after it breaks and doesn't work anymore. All of these have been around for years already and are very well known, although in Chapter 6 I went into some detail about how you can most effectively recycle and repurpose older IT equipment and computers.

The only other laws and regulations will apply to the manufacturers of the hardware and devices you purchase and mostly revolve around recycling and reducing pollution, with everything else being voluntary, such as the EPEAT Registry I talked about in Chapter 3, which allows technology manufacturers to have their products rated for their overall sustainability, including everything from the use of recycled plastics and metals, to the carbon footprint of the construction and shipping, to the sustainability of the packaging used.

How Regulations Might Change and How to Stay Ahead of the Changes

So how might regulations change into the future, and how can we all stay ahead of those regulations? In order to predict what might happen, we'll need to get out the crystal ball, but some fairly logical assumptions and conclusions can be drawn based on what we know of the current state of regulation and where public and world opinion is heading.

What We Know Now

About 25 years ago, a few companies making shower gel started selling new products that included "microbeads." These are solid polyethylene plastic particles that are less than 1 mm across. The idea was they would help invigorate the skin when showering, add a new and different feel to showering, and, of course, make huge wads of cash for the manufacturers.

I began purchasing these shower gels, considering them different and interesting, because like everybody else I was unaware of the effect and impact they would have on the environment. Some years after they went on sale, it was discovered that these tiny plastic beads were causing water pollution, and they were being discovered in the stomachs of small fish and other amphibians, and even turtles, birds, and some larger mammals.

This in turn was toxic for those creatures, so in 2017 the USA and South Korea became the first nations to ban them. Within two years, many more countries around the world had banned the manufacture and use of microbeads.

Microbeads are just one example of the "what we know now" scenario, and plastic is a good place to start because people are becoming more and more aware of the dangers posed to the environment, fish, and other aquatic and avian life by plastic that finds its way into the world's rivers and oceans.

According to the US National Ocean Service (pcs.tv/3XwEYgl) quoting data from *Science* magazine, "*While it's tough to say exactly how much plastic is in the ocean, scientists think about 8 million metric tons of plastic entered the ocean in 2010. That's the weight of nearly 90 aircraft carriers, and the problem continues to grow.*" These plastics come in many forms, from food wrappers, drinking straws, beverage bottles, and grocery bags to takeout containers and plastic knives and forks.

According to the journal *Nature*, plastic pollution is becoming trapped in and causing damage to at least 84 shallow and 25 deep coral reefs around the world in the Pacific, Atlantic, and Indian oceans. Their research found plastic debris in 77 out of the 84 reefs they surveyed (pcs.tv/4d3BYgg).

These types of discoveries can often lead to changes in behavior by business, but also to government regulation. Many governments around the world have banned single-use plastic items like grocery bags, plastic knives and forks, plastic takeout food trays, and other items such as plastic drinking straws. The result is that we're seeing many businesses, including fast-food and retail companies such as McDonald's and Starbucks, switching to paper alternatives for takeouts and reusable containers for people that choose to eat in.

Are these regulations a bad thing? Initially, and especially with the plastic bag and plastic straw bans, there was pushback from the general public. As the ban set in, however, people got used to new ways of doing things, and as the level of public awareness grew on the problems waste plastic was causing to the environment, so too did support for these and other bans around the world.

Repairability

So given what we know now, what types of regulation can we expect to come in the future? Probably the most likely is regulation on the repairability of electrical and electronic devices. In Chapter 1 I detailed the "Right to Repair" movement, and in Chapter 3 I told how France had introduced a mandatory "repairability score" icon to be visible on new products so that purchasers could make better-informed decisions.

More and more manufacturers are now focusing on making their products more repairable. About three years ago, I was having coffee with a vice president on the Surface Team at Microsoft. He told me it was very difficult to make devices repairable, but I knew that Microsoft as with every other electronics manufacturer around the world was stuck in a cycle of "Our customers want thin and light, all our competitors are making thin and light, so in order to compete we must also continue to make thin and light."

Consumer awareness of repairability has grown in recent years though, and electronics manufacturers have been feeling increasing pressure from customers, governments, and the media to put more effort into making products repairable and to also use more recycled materials (plastics, metals, and cardboard) in their products and packaging.

We're now beginning to see this come to fruition because, let's be honest, it's much easier when all of your competitors are doing it too, as that takes a lot of the pressure off to focus purely on thin and light devices that are glued together. It's also encouraged manufacturers to innovate more, as they know people still want thin and light where possible.

This all began with some companies, including Microsoft to be clear that I'm not disparaging them, saying they were starting to release repairable electronics. In truth, many of these might have included a few screws to open the base, but nothing else was replaceable except for the storage. The media and product reviewers hit on companies for this, and behaviors have continued to change, especially with laptops.

A good example of this is Apple, which always insisted that only they could repair iPhones, iPads, and iMacs because, let's face it, they wanted everything thin, light, and held together with strong glue. Eventually Apple announced a scheme whereby third-party repairers could get hold of repair kits and parts, but the company made this so incredibly difficult and expensive, with vetting checks and high prices for equipment and parts, that hardly anybody signed up. This of course was the whole point. Apple made money from the repairs and didn't want to share that revenue.

Eventually customers forced Apple to be more willing to allow third parties to repair their products, and while there's still a way to go, the movement is at least in the right direction.

Now we're seeing voluntary schemes such as the EPEAT Registry scheme I detailed in Chapter 3, where manufacturers can get a gold, silver, or bronze rating for their products for their overall environmentability (is that a word? – Ed).

Taking this to its logical conclusion, it's pretty clear that other countries will mandate schemes in the way the French have, and we'll in the future see standardization of these schemes in the way energy rating schemes for products' electricity usage happened a decade or so ago and property sales had to come with an energy efficiency certificate for the buyer.

This won't affect you as a business, unless you manufacture electronics, but it will come as a plus for you when making purchasing decisions, as you will be able to be much better informed about the products you buy and the companies you buy them from.

Bumboo

If I told you the toilet paper I use in my house was bamboo, then you would probably wince and wonder how I'm able to sit at my desk long enough to write this book. It's very true though that bamboo is becoming more and more popular for replacing paper in toilet paper, kitchen roll, and other paper products including tissues and facial wipes. I'm still looking out for bamboo printer paper, but haven't found any yet, so I'm still ordering recycled paper for now.

Bamboo paper is different from ordinary paper in that it grows considerably faster than trees. It's in fact the world's fastest-growing plant and can be harvested after just five years, compared with about 100 years or more for a tree. Bamboo also grows very densely, in just about any habitat and environment, enabling large amounts to be grown in smaller areas or very large amounts to be grown on the same piece of land you would use for a much smaller number of trees.

Bamboo is also not a plant in which birds and animals will nest, making it safer for wildlife when you're harvesting it. Bamboo is also very common in some of the less economically developed parts of the world, enabling those countries and communities to develop this new industry and reap the profits of doing so.

Most importantly though, in usage, you would never know the difference between paper made from bamboo and paper made from wood. The tissue and toilet paper is still extremely soft and durable. Where I live in the French countryside, we don't have a sewer nearby, so every house needs to have a *fosse septique* (septic tank). Without going into too much detail about how I discovered this, you can't use three-ply toilet tissue with a septic tank as it won't break down well enough – it's too thick. Three-ply bamboo toilet tissue though does not have the same problem, and that's just a win in my book! (eeuugh! – Ed)

As part of the drive toward sustainability, I personally believe that over the coming years as more and more businesses discover the benefits of using bamboo for their paper products (cups, lids, food trays, boxes and packaging materials, etc.), governments will also try to incentivize companies to make the switch.

It'll probably take a decade or so, but there's a very real chance that bamboo will be mandated for certain types of product in the future, with the use of wood to make paper eventually banned and plastic packaging and packing materials banned where a bamboo alternative exists.

Electricity Consumption

The next place where I think we'll have new regulation is in electricity consumption. Back in Chapter 5 I detailed the problems caused to electricity grids and power generation by the huge data centers being used to power AI tools for businesses and consumers. I said that for a data center with one million of Nvidia's new NPU processors, the equivalent of *two* nuclear power stations would be required to power it.

Power consumption by data centers and by tools such as AI is definitely going to change in the coming years. The newest generations of computer processors are able to handle smaller AI workloads locally on the device, which means that for individual workers wanting to use the tools on their own files, documents, contacts, and data, they can do so using only their laptop or desktop PC, with no cloud processing required. It also means that companies can apply these SLMs (Small Language Models) locally or in their own cloud with the contents of the files, documents, and data they store and use for normal business operations.

There is also a big push within the technology industry for more power-efficient chips. This comes in part from using smaller and smaller fabrication methods, but also from increasing efficiencies elsewhere in the circuit designs.

We're going to probably hit a ceiling in the coming decade though with the fabrication process, as the new AMD processor in my own desktop PC uses a 4 nm (nanometer) fabrication process, and what is probably the world's biggest and best-known chip maker, TSMC in Taiwan, is well into planning its 2 nm fabrication process (pcs.tv/4dOKDUT) and is laying the groundwork for 1 nm chips in the future (pcs.tv/3AVtcDC).

One nanometer is absolutely miniscule. A single gold atom is one third of a nanometer thick (if you can even use the word thick in this context), and a sheet of paper is a whopping 100,000 nanometers thick. We're also talking about a manufacturing process that's smaller than the building blocks of life, with a strand of DNA being 2.5 nanometers in diameter.

Where we go from there seems impossible to predict unless scientists make quantum computers viable, which operate using particles smaller than a single atom, and when you consider that an atom is made from a combination of particles like protons, neutrons, and electrons that rotate around them, that's pretty damn small. So it's safe to assume that the power consumption of our computers and data centers is definitely going to reduce eventually.

In the meantime though, the world is facing a power generation problem, and there's still no clear way to see how it will be solved. There are several possibilities at this point:

- Mandating that all new buildings must have solar panels installed during construction is just about guaranteed to happen in the coming years.

- Ripping up planning laws that are preventing solar and wind farms from being built due to complaints and protests from local residents is possible, but far less likely except in countries like China where planning consent isn't really a thing.

- Working harder to make tidal energy viable, which to me seems like the obvious first step.

- Imposing higher tariffs on energy usage for the biggest users, either domestic or commercial.

This last option to me seems the most likely. Personally I would like to see a world in which every household receives a set amount of electricity for free. This amount would be set as the amount an elderly couple, with a light usage of electricity for cooking, heating, and entertainment, would use.

Above that I would place different cost tiers with the first tier being a small charge per unit for electricity that would affect working parents with several children and a price level above that for heavy users (people such as myself) who use far more electricity than a normal household.

The benefits to the environment could also be good if a tiered approach was taken for business, as it might encourage more businesses to allow their workforce to be flexible and work from home more. It would need to be carefully considered though not to unfairly penalize certain business types, such as cafes and launderettes, which would use more electricity than a small office with lighting, heating, and a few PCs, and done in such a way that those cafes and other retail outlets wouldn't end up closing because of a sharp drop-off in footfall.

This is, of course, just one way that it could be done. It's my idea so naturally I think it's a good one, but I'm not an economist. My father was, and I learned a lot from him, but it's not for me to say how policies such as this would play out across an entire economy.

Whatever the outcome, I believe that it's entirely possible that regulation of energy usage and consumption will be brought in, in the coming years, if for no other reason than to encourage (perhaps even force) businesses and consumers to install solar panels, wind turbines, heat pumps, and other types of renewable electricity generation where they can be of use and where they make practical sense.

Electric Vehicles

Back at the beginning of this chapter, I wrote about the problems associated with recent COP climate summits, with oil companies and oil-producing nations trying to water down agreements and use the summits as a way to sell the world more of their oil.

Countries around the world, and especially across Europe, have already set rapidly approaching deadlines for the phasing out of the sales of new petrol and diesel cars, meaning that within ten years all new car sales should be electric.

This in itself presents significant problems. Many of these nations – UK, I'm looking at you – are *way* behind in their rollout of charging infrastructure, with some housing completely or almost completely unsuitable for the fitting of safe-to-use charging points such as terraced housing and large apartment blocks. If I were the British government, I'd have been installing electric vehicle chargers on street lampposts several years ago.

There are also the problems caused by mining and shipping of those mined materials around the world to make batteries and other essential components and the effect this can have and the damage it can do to the environment. There is a huge volume of metals and minerals required to meet the demand for electric vehicles. Much of this, such as metals like lithium, can only be found in a few countries in the world, with Australia, Chile, and China being the largest producers, with Argentina, Brazil, Zimbabwe, the USA, and Portugal making up most of the rest. There is also, let's face it, a finite amount of these materials and questions over whether enough of it can be mined and quickly enough to meet the demand.

Some of these large producers have been known to be, shall we say, controversial in world politics, and there are problems in other countries, too, such as a huge 700-ton deposit of lithium being discovered in Maine (USA) though nobody wants to give permission to mine it (pcs. tv/3Xiz9C9).

For as cheap as it is to charge electric vehicles at the moment, especially when you're able to do so at home, we can be absolutely certain those taxes will rise considerably when governments know we no longer have the possibility of purchasing anything *other* than an electric car.

There are other problems though that directly face business. I was listening to an interview with a professional gardener and arborist recently who works with farmers and on large tracts of countryside land. She drives a 4 × 4 vehicle and said that an electric vehicle would never be able to cope with the terrain she encounters each day.

Then there are the problems faced by businesses that need to transport goods so they can be sold. The technology for electric cars is well established, but the technology needed to run fleets of electric trucks is still in its infancy.

The most viable solution will be to encourage more and more people to ditch their cars in favor of public transport and home delivery. This would reduce the overall amount of vehicles on the road, possibly considerably, and many people, especially younger people in cities, have abandoned their cars already.

It's safe to say though that while electric cars might still be seen by some as "the next big thing," they will bring problems with them, and further taxes and regulation will follow as sure as night follows day.

Artificial Intelligence

No discussion about future regulations would be complete without mentioning artificial intelligence. Now back in Chapter 5 I wrote about AI and about how while it's certainly artificial, it's definitely *not* intelligent. So while nations are discussing regulations to cover AI, both internally and supranationally, those regulations cover what AI is *used for* and not what it can do on its own.

The reason for this is that we're living in an increasingly dangerous world, certainly when it comes to information, or rather *misinformation*. AI tools such as ChatGPT have been used to create deepfake imagery and video of politicians, celebrities, business leaders, and world events that either skew the truth and the message so as to misrepresent it or that deliberately create a completely false message in order to try and achieve a different outcome.

While there's no publicly available evidence to support this, it's widely known that "state actors," another way of saying different national governments, are involved directly or indirectly with creating this material. This in itself creates a whole new problem. Let's say that the US government and the European Union create laws that ban AI tools from being used to create "deliberately false or misleading" content, the most likely term to be used in any legislation. This doesn't mean that AI tools used in other countries, such as China or Russia, will be bound by those rules.

The only way those rules would be in force in third countries would be if the processing for requests from those countries took place on AI tools based and located in the USA or the EU. Any tools based outside those nations wouldn't be covered.

So we can imagine China creating messages that support its political positions on Hong Kong and Taiwan and that Russia might want to use the tools to destabilize elections in the West.

Whatever happens with regulations covering AI, we know they will fall into two groups, both of which have the potential to impact their use in business.

The first, as I've just mentioned, is the use of AI to create false or misleading content. The fines for this would probably be fairly high, and it would be all too easy for somebody using these tools within a business to create that content completely accidentally, because they either don't understand the tool or they don't understand the regulation.

The second area where regulation will inevitably come is in the use of copyrighted material, or at least material not already in the public domain or already owned by the creator, to be used to train LLMs (Large Language Models), SLMs (Small Language Models), and GMs (Generative Models). I detailed in Chapter 5 that there have already been lawsuits from creators such as the *New York Times* and US comedian Sarah Silverman.

It will be down to individual businesses and organizations to decide how they want to approach these subjects, probably ahead of any regulation I would recommend, to raise awareness across the business of what is and is not acceptable use and why these rules are important.

Staying Ahead of Regulatory Changes

At the beginning of this section, I posed the question of how business can stay ahead of coming regulatory changes, especially when we're really just making educated guesses about what those changes might be.

Perhaps the beginning of this is, should your business or organization be able to justify the costs involved, the appointment of a regulation and compliance officer. You may already have one of these in your business because of what it is you make or produce. If you're in the food or drinks industry, for example, then you'll inevitably have a team of people already working on this.

These are people who know and understand how and where to look for coming regulatory changes. They're experts who can advise on what's coming and inform what can and must be done to comply and where those regulations might change or impact your existing business operation.

There are also business organizations that can advise and that will have their own experts watching regulation and predicting where they think it might go next. These business organizations might work on a local, regional, state (county), or national level, and it's well worth hooking into them so they can keep you up to date on what's likely to happen in the future and what you need to prepare for now.

The other option is to keep your eye on the news and your ear to the ground. Public opinion is usually a good indicator of where legislation will go next. Right at the moment in the UK, there are huge discussions about the big water companies polluting rivers and the sea because they're not investing appropriately on upgrading and repairing infrastructure, when instead they're paying huge dividends to their shareholders. Where the public lead on this case, the government is following, and new regulations look to soon be introduced.

Similar discussions are being had in bars and across water coolers around the world about energy creation, renewables, nuclear power, and both the cost of electricity and gas and where the gas and coal being used to power countries is coming from. This is, in turn, influencing the policies of governments from the USA to Germany. Even China, traditionally the biggest user of coal power stations in the world, is taking the matter seriously at the highest levels of government.

Where all of this will affect business and how that might impact you is, as I mentioned before, something that can only currently be seen with a crystal ball, but it's not always that difficult to predict when you understand the signs and the language being used.

Making Your Business Regulation Compliant: What You Need to Know

Regulatory compliance can be a nightmare, or at least appear to be a nightmare. There are so many rules and regulations to follow in all aspects of business, some of which will make perfect sense, while others might seem completely implausible that it can be daunting, especially in a smaller business.

As an example, some years ago now when I was teaching, I was placed in charge of health and safety compliance for the training center I worked in. This was important because we had students, both teenage and adult, in the center five days a week, and being able to demonstrate we were taking the health and safety of those people seriously was a condition for gaining the contracts we needed in order to be able to operate.

One of the regulations I had to comply with was called COSHH. The Control of Substances Hazardous to Heath regulations became law in the UK in 2002. The UK government website defines COSHH as *"The law requires you to adequately control exposure to materials in the workplace that cause ill health."*

The upshot of this was that where there were substances that could cause ill-health if used improperly, I had to write a risk assessment for each substance and update that risk assessment every year or earlier should something change.

Perfectly fine you think, and it would be, were those risk assessments not to include boiling water in kettles for making tea and coffee and the detergent used to wash coffee cups and mugs afterward. COSHH very quickly became a chore and one I didn't enjoy having to comply with.

Make Compliance a Priority

Whatever our personal feelings about regulations, they're there for a reason, and we all have a legal responsibility to comply with them. It's therefore very important that your business or organization treats regulation seriously and makes compliance a priority.

If you do not already have a compliance department, team, or designated professional working within the business, then it's a good idea to assign that task to appropriate people. Alternatively, there are consultancy firms that you can designate some or all of this responsibility to.

Understand Current Regulations

Being able to comply with regulations means you need to know what those regulations are that affect your business and a good understanding of each, so there can be no misinterpretation of them that could lead to noncompliance.

As I mentioned earlier in this chapter, there are business organizations that will be able to advise you about current regulations, and again there are consultancy firms that you will be able to turn to that can also advise on compliance.

Get Things Right from the Start

Partial compliance is the same thing as noncompliance. It's therefore very important to make sure that, as the saying goes, all your ducks are in a row and you are fully compliant right from the start. Quite apart from the fact that this is important anyway, it will also make continuing compliance much easier and simpler to maintain later on. Staff and management will be much more aware of what's required, and maintaining something is always much less work than having to create something from scratch, especially when you're doing so in a retrograde way.

Keep Yourself Informed

I spent a large part of this chapter talking about the possible changes to regulation we could expect to see in coming years. These regulations cover subjects as diverse as the use of artificial intelligence tools to the use of electricity and bamboo replacement paper.

Business groups and consultancy firms can help you stay informed of what's happening with regulation, but also trade journals and business television and print news are also a good place to stay up to date.

Stay Flexible

When change comes you need to be able to adapt to it. Having structures and processes within the business that are too strict and inflexible will act as a barrier to compliance. It is therefore important that at all levels of the business, processes and policies are either flexible enough to adapt to changes, or procedures exist and are in place that allow for those processes and policies to be changed and updated quickly to reflect the requirements for new and changing regulation.

Get Involved Locally

Regulatory changes don't always come from national governments. In some countries, especially the USA, states and individual counties can make their own decisions about what regulation is good for their areas. A good example of this I mentioned in Chapter 1 is the bans placed on the sale of high-power computers by six US states.

Maintaining a community presence in local and state government then can be a useful way to stay up to date with compliance, and you can normally achieve this by working with public and charitable sector organizations. These will be local business and special-interest groups (climate groups as an example) that will be able to keep you better informed of what you need to do on a local and state level.

Even nationally there will be individual changes. For companies operating with the European Union, you will have both EU and national regulation to comply with, but also the possibility of subnational regulation as well. This will vary from one country to another, so making sure you are compliant at a local level can still be important.

Summary

While there are almost no regulations currently that affect the use of computers and IT in business, it's clear that might change into the future, especially as businesses make greater use of LLM and SLM tools to boost productivity and make sense of the huge amounts of data that accumulates on company servers.

We've spent a lot of time looking at both national and supranational regulation and structures, so in the next chapter we'll take this to the next step and examine how interconnected these structures are and why and how that can affect your role in business.

CHAPTER 10

Understanding the Interconnected World of Business and IT

Everything is connected to everything else, so the saying goes, and if anything the coronavirus pandemic showed us just how interconnected we all are and how we rely so heavily on each other. Part of this is down to the "just in time" approach modern businesses take for their supply chains. There's no point in sitting on a bunch of components, where you have to pay for storage and insurance, and doubly so if you're not entirely certain of the demand for the product you'd make with them anyway.

However, things go much, much deeper than just in time, so let's have a brief reminder of recent history. During the pandemic there were a series of component shortages for IT systems. Some of these were the result of the pandemic, and others would likely have happened in some form anyway but were either hastened or made worse by the pandemic.

© Mike Halsey 2025
M. Halsey, *The Green IT Guide*, https://doi.org/10.1007/979-8-8688-1233-0_10

The Interconnectedness of the World

If any world leader ever stands up in front of their people and assures them that their country is self-sufficient and able to stand entirely on their own, they are either (a) deluded, (b) lying, or (c) simply unaware of the actual situation in their country, as it's impossible in these modern times.

If we go back several hundred years, then you'll probably find that individual countries were indeed able to support themselves. They would have had farming and natural resources such as steel and iron to pull out of the ground, these metals and other minerals being common enough to be found just about everywhere.

These countries could also mine for coal or gas and heat and power their homes and businesses. All was good with the world. Then global trade started, and by the mid-twentieth century, everything had changed. Some countries didn't want to mine specific metals or materials any more, sometimes for ecological reasons, sometimes because of local or national protests, sometimes because it was simply cheaper to purchase these things from abroad.

As consumers became more aware of the world around them, they also wanted to buy things that could simply not be grown or made in their own countries, such as certain types of fruit. Demand grew and global supply chains started to grow with it with massive container ships starting to appear in ports around the world in the mid-twentieth century.

Countries then stopped producing certain types of good or products altogether. Again this was often down to it being much more cost-effective to purchase them from abroad instead.

Some industries with too much pollution have been moved to other countries – chemical factories, medicine, steel – because European standards for environment and security were too expensive here.

Industry began to speak out against this, and by the turn of the century, some countries had realized the importance of having, as an example, their own steel industry if for no other reason than if there was another war they might not have enough to make all the tanks, bombs, and planes they'd need.

By this point though it was largely too late. While some industries such as steel either continued or were resurrected, it was always on a *much* smaller scale than before, and most countries around the world relied more and more heavily on oil- and gas-producing nations as Saudi Arabia and Russia.

This all worked fairly well despite the odd political skirmish, and the world continued to run fairly smoothly. All of this changed, however, at the end of 2019 when the World Health Organization received word of an outbreak of a new and potentially deadly virus that had escaped from a virology laboratory in Wuhan in central China.

The Effect of Bitcoin

Whether you use bitcoin or other digital currencies yourself, you'll certainly have heard about them. During the pandemic there was a global shortage of gaming and other high-performance graphics cards, caused in no small part by bitcoin mining.

These virtual currencies are created in giant server farms, using vast amounts of electricity I might add, to create (the official term is mining) more currency. These currencies are set up in such a way so as to prevent there being more and more currency created at exponential rates that would, just as with any currency, devalue it.

Thus, the systems created make it more difficult for new virtual currency to be created as time goes on. In order for one server to make a single bitcoin (and I'm using this as an umbrella term for all virtual currencies), it might have taken one month of work. As more currency was created, however, this would eventually stretch to two months, three months, and so on.

Because the people who were mining bitcoin wanted to create more and more of it, they needed more computing power, and that required larger and larger server farms, each more powerful than the one that came before it. To do the mining they needed the right type of parallel processing capability, something it turns out graphics cards are especially good at.

It is estimated that the energy consumption needed to mine a single bitcoin is between 86,000 kWh and 286,000 kWh, with the industry consuming more than 128 GWh (gigawatt hours) of energy per day. One gigawatt is the same energy produced by more than three million solar panels or 360 wind turbines, or 128 GWh, and it's enough to power almost 93,000 homes.

And so these people began buying up the global stock of graphics cards. This led to a shortage, prices rose, and just one upshot was that when Microsoft and Sony launched their new game consoles at the end of 2020, it was about two more years before they could actually ship any to eager customers, with things only beginning to ease when China, where the bulk of bitcoin mining was taking place, declared all virtual currencies illegal during 2021.

The Other Type of Mining

It wasn't these bitcoin farms, however, that caused the global graphics card shortage on their own; there was a problem being caused by a different type of mining as well. This was that the coronavirus and worldwide lockdowns were having a serious impact on the metals, minerals, and other materials that we needed to pull out of the ground to create the components needed for the graphics cards in the first place.

This in turn led to certain types of components not reaching factories in time for the assembly of computer parts, and thus the whole system began to fall apart. This is when you consider that one graphics card will be made up of around a thousand components that come from many different manufacturing sources and are all made from different materials that may or may not have been available in enough quantities at the time.

Older Processor Shortages

One other problem that hit the production and availability of technology was a sudden reduction in the amount of older processors that were available. Again this was partly due to lockdowns, with factories in Asia and the Far East being closed for long periods of time and workforces being affected by coronavirus infections, vaccination rates, and social distancing rules.

This was just something that exacerbated the problem, however, as it had initially been caused by processor manufacturers retooling their factories so they could produce the newest and latest generations of processors. These new chips were sold in great volumes and with much higher profit margins, to be used in ever more powerful smartphones and other latest-generation devices for the consumer.

These chips had components on them that were sometimes just 4 nm (nanometers) across, and so that same equipment couldn't be used to create chips that were based on older 10 nm or 12 nm technology.

Now in normal times there would have still been more than enough capacity to manufacture the older processors that industry still needed to purchase, but the pandemic created a major problem, and it was particularly bad for the automobile industry, as it was these older chips that effectively ran the world for us. Everything from cars, to smart speakers, to industrial and medical equipment, to wind farms, and to engineering and farm equipment runs on these older chips. Why? Simply put, because all these types of equipment simply don't need the level of processing power in the latest generations of smartphones, and having more powerful processors would only push up the prices anyway.

Pandemic Pressures

All of this came at the same time as other pressures placed on worldwide supply chains, including a global shortage of long-distance truck drivers. This resulted in backlogs of cargo containers building up at ports around the world, container ships unable to even get into some ports because there was nowhere to offload them, and goods having to be diverted, sometimes even to other countries, where again cargo containers were piling up because of the truck driver shortage.

Ultimately this fed back into the pressures facing those businesses and consumers needing to purchase everything from graphics cards to SoC (System on a Chip) processors for their new car line. Some factories had to close part-time because they couldn't get parts, orders for other parts therefore had to be canceled so as to avoid huge stockpiles being built up at factories that had nowhere to put them, the manufacturers of those parts were therefore affected, and the whole global supply chain began to break down. Everything is, indeed, connected to everything else!

The Interconnectedness of Business

It's much the same with businesses of any type. If you're a manufacturing business, then what I have described about just in time manufacturing and global supply chains will be nothing new to you. If you're a service industry or a financial business, then you will also be able to relate to the globalized marketplace, either because you have placed some of your offices elsewhere in the world to make them more cost effective or because that's where the best particular skills you need can be found or because a competitor has done that already and you've suffered a loss as a result.

Global Reach Is Not Equal to Global Presence

This subject of specialized skills and education being available in certain countries in the world is actually a good example of some of the globalization problems facing the IT industry. Let's take the big tech firms as an example, Microsoft, Intel, Google, Apple, Nvidia, OpenAI, and Amazon.

All of these firms, which provide the backbone for the IT and most other industries around the world, are all US companies that are still based in the USA, either California or Seattle. Only ARM sits apart in this regard being a British company still based in Cambridge, UK.

When the microprocessor race first began in the 1960s, there was huge excitement. This was, however, long before transatlantic business flights were even affordable, let alone commonplace, and decades before the Internet made worldwide communication easy.

These companies were exciting, and the people with all the relevant skills or those that wanted to learn those skills headed to where these companies were. What happened next became a type of co-dependency race, as people moved to what would become Silicon Valley as that was where the jobs were and new businesses either based themselves in Silicon Valley or moved to the area both because they wanted to partner with and learn from the businesses that were already there and because that was where all the people with the skills were now based.

By the time the rest of the world realized they wanted in on the act, it was far too late, and incentives from governments around the world to nurture and create their own tech hubs, in London, Paris, or wherever on the planet, largely failed.

There are a few major tech hubs outside of the USA, most notable Cambridge in the UK, which is a huge hub for the development of artificial intelligence systems and also for medical research. Boston in the USA is also a huge tech hub, helped by the presence of Harvard University, the Massachusetts Institute of Technology, and, consequently, robotics company Boston Dynamics. In parts of the Far East in China, Japan, and Taiwan, you will also find large tech hubs, though these also exist in part because of differences in languages and culture and people there being generally unwilling to move to Western nations.

All Tech Is Run Out of the USofA

These days we just accept that all tech is run from just a handful of megacorporations in the USA, these being Microsoft, Intel, AMD, Google, Apple, Nvidia, OpenAI, and Amazon, among a few others such as Oracle and IBM. Indeed at the time of writing this, eight of the world's top 15 biggest tech firms are based in the USA, with three being based in Japan (Sony, Hitachi, and Panasonic), three in China (Huawei, Tencent, and Lenovo (which is also in part based in the USA)), Foxconn being based in Taiwan, and Samsung being based in South Korea where it's so large it occupies about 20% of South Korea's GDP (Gross Domestic Product) being a company with fingers in just about every type of pie from ship building to insurance; the company even used to make tanks and other military hardware before handing that part of the business over to the South Korean government at the turn of the twenty-first century.

If anybody tries to start a business now to compete with the likes of Microsoft, Google, or Amazon, especially for something like cloud services, they're doomed to fail – not because these massive corporations would muscle them out, but just because these firms have such a stranglehold on their respective markets that business and industry around the world just doesn't want to move away from using them.

The Interconnectedness of Nations

I've already written in this chapter about how nations are tied to one another and dependent on each other for materials, fuel, and even protection from other nations. Huge political and trading blocks exist such as the European

Union (EU) in which many countries have formed a monetary union in addition to a political one. Indeed the EU is a good case in point, as not only do all 27 member states share common regulations and rules, 26 of those states share a common travel area known as Schengen, where the peoples of each country can freely cross into others to visit, live, and even work, without needing to show a passport or apply for a visa.

Nineteen of the EU countries also share a single currency, the euro. This means that many of their financial systems and rules are run by the European Central Bank, such as the setting of interest rates.

The EU is unique among international treaty organizations, though there are many other examples of close trading blocks around the world such as the European Free Trade Association (EFTA), which in addition to EU countries also includes Liechtenstein, Norway, and Switzerland; the North American Free Trade Agreement (NAFTA) between Canada, the USA, and Mexico; the Mercado Comun del Cono Sur (MERCOSUR) or Southern Common Market, which includes ten South American nations; the ASEAN Economic Community (AEC), which includes 11 countries in Asia, including Singapore, Vietnam, and Brunei; and the Asia-Pacific Economic Cooperation (APEC) organization with a huge 21 member states including Australia, Russia, and China.

Some of these groups' members cross over into other trading blocks as well, though some including the European Economic Area (EEA) are exclusive. Indeed these trading blocks are far from rare, as a great many of them exist from Africa to Asia and a great many countries around the world are members. The move toward free trading blocks is also a growing trend, and more countries are joining these blocks every few years.

The DisUnited Nations?

There is a tendency to think of the United Nations as the ultimate coming together of countries around the world, with 193 countries being members, though there are 215 countries in the world, a figure sometimes disputed by politicians and academics who argue that some don't fit the definition of self-governing or are not recognized as nations by the UN.

Some of the countries that are not UN members are fairly significant, such as Taiwan, which is recognized by 16 member states as a nation, but has always been claimed by The People's Republic of China as being part of their own nation. Taiwan is a country I mentioned earlier as it is one of the world's largest exporters of semiconductors and electronic components.

Even some of the world's most secretive and controversial nations are members of the UN, such as Turkmenistan and North Korea, while other "nations" are yet to be officially recognized or join for political or religious reasons, such as Somaliland, Kosovo, Northern Cyprus, and Palestine.

So with the UN encompassing countries as diverse as the USA, Russia, China, North Korea, every European country, and Turkmenistan (which is by far the most secretive nation on the planet, even by North Korean standards), you would think that reaching international agreements over subjects as important as climate change would be fairly straightforward. After all, all these countries want to work together, right?

When we delve into the history of the UN though, you might see that perhaps the organization's stated aim isn't quite as all-encompassing as it appears. It was first formed in June 1945 as a way to try and bring some kind of unity to the world after the horrors of the Second World War and the complete failure of the League of Nations, the forebear of the UN that itself was created after the First World War, to prevent worldwide conflict from ever occurring again. The League of Nations was therefore formally dissolved in June 1946.

The United Nations and Climate Change

There are many issues on which countries at the United Nations broadly or even almost unanimously agree, such as human rights violations, world trade, and the sanctity and importance of places such as the polar regions and the space above our planet. This is why proliferation of arms at the South Pole is banned by International Law, and nations that you might never consider would ever cooperate on anything work together both there and on the International Space Station to conduct research into many subjects, including climate change.

When it comes to the floor of the United Nations Assembly, however, things are very different. Each country has their own view on climate change, and that view is almost always led by governmental, not by national, interests.

Take China as an example. They have built a reputation for constructing huge numbers of coal-fired power stations to power their ever-expanding economy and the needs of the population. While China is also a leader in nuclear power, and is really now beginning to set strong targets for becoming carbon neutral, they are only prepared to go so far, so quickly, because of the power requirements of their nation and the difficulty in weaning themselves off coal.

Smaller countries are not all that different, with the UK still very reliant on gas-powered stations. The problem the UK faces is different as they want to move to nuclear power, but the country is quite small, and there are many protests on the ground from people whose rights and views must be respected by law, which can hold everything up practically indefinitely.

Then we come to some of the smallest or less-developed countries, and these are right across the planet from the Caribbean to Scandinavia to Asia that continually press the UN for action on climate change because they face an existential threat that they simply would not be able to cope with or defend against on their own. Some of these nations are indeed very much at peril such as the Philippines, Fiji, and Madagascar.

When I wrote the first edition of this book, a story broke about a leak of documents revealing that several countries had signed a letter to the UN asking them to "play down" the need to move rapidly away from fossil fuels. You might have been unsurprised to see Saudi Arabia's name on the list given that oil exports are a major part of their economy. What came as a greater shock, however, was to see that Japan had signed the letter. It doesn't take a long search online to see that Japan is one of the countries *most* at risk from the effects of climate change.

Short-Term Political Interest vs. Business Sense

If anything, all of this proves that short-term political interests will always rule at the UN and at global climate summits and that the smaller the nation is, the more their voices will simply be drowned out by the largest economies, as it's clearly just all about money and political inaction.

In the UK there was a hugely popular political sitcom in the early 1980s called *Yes Minister*, and one of the leading characters, a senior civil service chief called Sir Humphrey Appleby, once famously said, "Diplomacy is about surviving into the next century; politics is about surviving until Friday afternoon!" I couldn't agree with him more.

So if climate change is effectively a game played for short-term political interest, and not something that nation states want to act on seriously, what can be done? This is where business has already picked up the baton and started running with it.

Business is not waiting around for their respective governments to do something about climate change, and they've decided to get on with it themselves. The main reason for doing so is that they know that the wider public, which includes their customers, stakeholders, and shareholders, *do* consider climate change to be an existential and immediate threat.

So they choose to act on climate change both because they know it's good PR and also because they don't want to lose customers to a competitor that beats them to it. Of course they also know it's the right thing to do, but we're looking purely at business motivations here and being cynical for a minute.

The Interconnectedness of Climate Action

This ultimately brings everything together and our globalized world becomes a global stage, in which globalized organizations and businesses work globally, to fix a global problem facing the whole ...erm ...globe (drinking game? – Ed).

To look at a few examples, wind farm technology is being pioneered in the UK, Scotland is pioneering tidal technology and other technologies to produce hydrogen, nuclear fusion is being actively developed by a company in Canada, the USA has many companies involved in the development of sustainable meat substitutes, and Google is actively involved in the development of smarter cities that can help reduce their own climate emissions. Even Microsoft has got on board testing a data center on the bottom of the ocean and has been talking about placing one in orbit of the planet. That project been canceled now.

The Back Bone and Why You Have One

Every single person on the planet either contributes to climate change or can do something about climate change. The latter is definitely true as there's plenty we can all do, individually and collectively, on our own and through our businesses to act, inspire, and effect change on our planet.

We are, after all, one species, despite what some people might tell you. The human race is everywhere; every color, every gender, every creed, every point of view is just part of the overall human condition and the thing that makes us all so fantastic, an infinite variety and diversity in how we think and operate.

With climate change this becomes the biggest benefit we could imagine, with new ideas emerging all the time from just about everywhere on the planet. However, it can still sometimes be difficult to see what we ourselves can do.

It's probably appropriate at this point that I tell you some of my own views, as it might put context into the importance of individual and business action on climate change. There are two things I firmly believe don't work; the first of these is direct climate action, from groups such as Extinction Rebellion in the UK and France. These people block roads and try to bring major cities to a grinding halt to raise awareness of their cause.

I would argue that these people don't need to raise awareness of their cause and their actions will be completely ignored. Governments won't suddenly decide they need to change their course of action and become much more proactive on climate change just because a major road has been closed for a few hours due to people glueing themselves to it, and the general populace know what needs to be done anyway and don't need to be reminded by people that are actively preventing them from getting to the places they need to be.

The other, and hear me out on this one, is Greta Thunberg. Here we have an incredibly articulate and intelligent young woman, but who, for all the high-quality information she can impart, sadly lacks any amount of authority or influence. She is, alas, the type of person who is invited to polite dinner parties or to business and political conferences so that powerful people can make it look like they've had a good telling off.

The people with genuine influence are the people being interviewed by the world's media, the BBCs and CNNs of the world. These people include environmentalists such as Sir David Attenborough and King Charles and his son Prince William, the Prince of Wales of the UK and the Commonwealth. These people have genuine authority and people *do* listen to them. This is because they are outside of politics and business and are not the types of people to have an ulterior motive for what they say, when, and why.

One Person Can Make a Difference

When it comes to being a leader on climate change, we all can start with baby steps, one foot at a time. I'm sure you recycle, as I do. I worry though if I'm recycling enough and am really starting to look seriously at the materials I dispose of and wishing more of them came with clearer labeling as to whether they're recyclable or not.

I must be doing something right however as, while my local municipal council send a truck every fortnight to empty my rubbish bin, I only need to put it out once every month, sometimes two months, because there's hardly anything in it. Conversely, my own recycle bin needs emptying every fortnight as it's always full.

So let's look at this more and take for example that green tape that comes wrapped around some of your packages from Amazon. It looks like plastic, but kind of also doesn't look like plastic? Is it recyclable? As it turns out, absolutely all of the internal and external packaging used by Amazon worldwide is 100% fully recyclable, but I had to search online to find this information as while the company is doing a great job of helping reduce its impact on climate change, it's not advertising this information very well.

What are the other things we can all do? We're told that abstaining from eating meat once a week can make a difference, and to be honest this is something I'll generally do once or twice a week anyway without even thinking about it, such as cooking a pasta dish (which I'll be having for my lunch today) or when I have a pizza in the evening (without ham or pepperoni, obviously).

Even when it comes to our own entertainment, we can make sensible choices about how to purchase services that are environmentally sustainable, and you can find links to some of the bigger worldwide entertainment providers' sustainability polices here:

Netflix – `https://about.netflix.com/sustainability`

Disney+ – `https://thewaltdisneycompany.com/environmental-sustainability/`

Apple – `www.apple.com/environment/`

Spotify – `www.lifeatspotify.com/diversity-equity-impact/climate-action`

In fact there are a great many things we can do as individuals to help reduce our own impact on the environment and without having to compromise our own lifestyles in the process. These include

- Taking our own bottles and cups when we fill up on juice or get a morning coffee.

- Setting our home thermostats to be two degrees lower, which in itself can save between 3% and 5% of our energy costs.

- Walking or riding a bike for a short journey that we'd normally drive for, such as to the local shop in the morning to buy some milk and bread.

- Reducing food waste by reusing leftovers or, in my own case, feeding leftovers from larger meals to my dogs as part of their own diet or turning them into a curry (not the dogs, I hope! – Ed).

- Replacing inefficient lightbulbs with low-power LEDs, something I highlighted (if you'll excuse the pun) in Chapter 2.

- Planting a new tree or two in your back gardens or, if you don't have a garden, helping a local community group or school to plant some trees.

- Reducing your plastic use, by looking for alternatives such as metal or paper products and purchasing products in carboard packaging rather than plastic.

- Avoiding single-use products, which ties into the last point, and trying to purchase products that can be used more than once. This also includes avoiding fresh goods in supermarkets that are packed in plastic unnecessarily when non-packaged options are available and avoiding products that come with too much packaging, which is common with ready meals.

- Choosing slower shipping options for products. Expedited shipping tends to result in more traffic on our roads, whereas slower shipping options tend to result in fewer, more effectively used, and fuller vans and lorries.

- Unplugging things when they're not in use or when you go away. There's a case to be made for keeping your television plugged in, but your smartphone or laptop charger doesn't need to be plugged in all the time.

- Saving water by using water-saving heads for your taps and showers that can often come free or inexpensively from your water utility provider and using water for more than one task, such as using old washing up or bathwater for watering the plants in your home.

- Adding a water butt or two to your garden if you have one, so you're recycling rainwater for watering plants and lawns, rather than relying on mains water.

- Washing your hands and clothes in cool water. It's been scientifically known for years now that washing clothes and hands at just 20 degrees Celsius (68 degrees Fahrenheit) can produce results every bit as good as washing at 40 degrees Celsius (100 degrees Fahrenheit) or 65 degrees Celsius (150 degrees Fahrenheit), and even washing your hands in cold water with soap will clean germs effectively

These are all common-sense things that we all know, but the issue comes when you wonder what good it's going to do to climate change if you change your own personal behaviors in this way. Let's look at the bigger picture then and scale this up to a billion people or two billion people or 2.7 billion people, which is roughly how many currently live in developed countries.

Scale this up to the almost nine billion people who live across the whole planet, and, while this would take time and not everybody will live in circumstances where it's all possible, then you have made an enormous contribution to eliminating climate change.

One Business Can Make a Difference

You might think of your business helping to reduce the impact of climate change and to become more sustainable as fitting a wind turbine in the car park, moving to a more heat-efficient premises, and conducting meetings over Teams or Zoom rather than flying people around the world. Sure, this is all part of it, but let's look at the interconnectedness of things and the place your business has in the wider world.

We've already looked at the things you can do as an individual, that you're inevitably doing at least some of already, and that most if not all of your colleagues are also already doing. This has a knock-on effect, both for their friends and family and for their colleagues.

It's no different for your business. In Chapter 8 we looked at how you can use training and education to inspire the people in your employ and others into better behaviors. This is an important way of affecting change, and you might be surprised at just how quickly that change can spread when you set the right example.

So setting aside the wind turbine and the heat-efficient premises for a moment, let's look at the everyday practice of conducting business. There is absolutely no substitute sometimes for meeting people face to face, but do we need to be flying around the world to conduct business? This is something I've personally been saying since long before climate change was a "thing." When the pandemic struck, people and businesses were forced to change their behaviors.

It was a very happy coincidence that this happened just after companies including Microsoft had finished rolling out cloud infrastructure that allowed people to properly work either at home or remotely for the first time, effectively, and in constant communication with the mothership (as it were).

Remember that Microsoft Teams only launched in March 2017, just two years before lockdowns struck. If a global pandemic had hit before that time, things would have been very different, and it would have been extremely difficult if not nigh on impossible for some businesses to continue to function. SharePoint, after all, only gets you so far.

So over the pandemic period, you would have been forced to conduct meetings over the Internet, Teams, or Zoom. You might even have grown to like this and have a firm plan in place to continue it into the longer term. This action in itself sets an example that others would then be tempted to follow.

Let's take one example. You are having meetings with a couple of stakeholders, and you decide that the meeting should be virtual. One of the stakeholders doesn't like the idea and asks you to fly someone out to their office as it's more personable.

You explain that having the meeting over the Internet actually provides more benefits, and you list some of them:

- You can be more productive because you're not spending many hours outside of the office traveling and waiting at airports.

- If any additional documentation or advice from a colleague is required, then it's available right there, rather than having to table some subjects for discussion later.

- The costs for your business are reduced as you're not paying for hotels, taxis, and business-class flights.

...and so on. Eventually, and probably not before too long, the stakeholders will understand that if they change their own behaviors, then they can save money as a business, and that money can be invested instead in other areas. This is quite apart from the benefit of not losing many days of productivity over the course of each year with people traveling from A to B.

This, in turn, can help set off a chain reaction of businesses doing little things, perhaps just changing one or two behaviors that, just as it happens with individuals, collectively makes an enormous global impact.

Mental Health and Well-Being

I did mention though that there are occasions where there is simply no substitute for meeting people face to face. Sometimes you just need to look someone in the eye to see how genuine they are being or to reassure them about a new project or about taking something in a different direction. Perhaps you need to show them a prototype product or see a proposed location for a new project.

These are important reasons for sure, but face-to-face meetings also serve an important psychological purpose. When we were all working from home during lockdown, many of us, quite possibly yourself, suffered from cabin fever, perhaps because of being trapped in an apartment somewhere, possibly even without a balcony to step out onto. Perhaps you were stuck at home with young children that needed constant attention and stimulation. Maybe you're just not very good at being stuck indoors for long periods of time – not many people are.

I would add the point that often meetings in international companies are not in the native language for people, so easier to manage on premises than on virtual.

I didn't want anybody to feel sorry for me during lockdown, as I was in a decent-sized house in the middle of the French countryside with seven acres to stretch out in. I was extraordinarily lucky as the year before I'd been in a small, three-bedroom, semi-detached house on a housing estate that only had a small garden and far too much local noise. So I get it, because despite having all that space around me, I still got cabin fever as I wasn't allowed to get out and about or travel.

I don't see this as being any different from the way people feel in the workplace. There are huge benefits to having people in the office rather than working at home, some of the time at least, but workers can still suffer from cabin fever if they're not allowed to explore and roam.

This, I feel, is where conferences and expos come in handy. You can take some fairly extreme examples such as the Consumer Electronics Show (CES) every January in Las Vegas where it's well known every attendee tends to leave with a dose of the flu, but conferences and expos are something that many people feel are valuable.

They're valuable for meeting people, they're valuable for people's state of mind and sense of well-being, and they're places at which you can discover and learn things that you might not expect. They're also places for sharing best-practice tips and advice over a cocktail or an evening meal …if you take my drift.

Bringing Everything Together

If there are lessons to pull from all of this, I'd say it's two things. Firstly, any business needs to be prepared for the unexpected as the worst things can happen at any time. That's why it's called the unexpected after all. So having contingencies in place for supplies and finances is crucial, though I'm sure I don't need to tell you that.

The other lesson is that rather than wait around for your government to show guidance and issue advice on what to do and how to behave when it comes to climate change, just expand on what you're already doing and run with it. People pick up on these things, people feel inspired, and when your stakeholders and even your competitors see what you're doing, they'll follow suit, not wanting to be left behind.

You will no doubt then see something another company is doing and want to adopt that too. Nobody should be afraid of being accused of copying, because every action we take helps reduce the impact of climate change, and after all …imitation is the most sincere form of flattery.

Summary

So this is the baton we're now going to run with, and in the next chapter we'll look more into the world of business and how business leaders are shining a light and leading the way already. We'll look at how companies are setting their own bold targets to become carbon neutral.

One good example of this is Google, which has ambitious targets to become completely carbon neutral by 2030, a whole 20 years ahead of the targets of most countries. You might look at Google and think, *Well, they're a massive company with huge resources, so it should be easy for them.*

But here we're dealing with economies of scale. Yes, they have the money, but they also have massive offices, spread all over the planet, and huge volumes of employees. They might have the money to spend on these projects, but all they're doing is scaling up from your own budgets and your own challenges.

The lesson then is to not be intimidated by the nature and the scale of the task ahead of you, as inspiration and support is much, much closer than you might think.

CHAPTER 11

Placing Your Environmental Policies in the Wider World

In Chapter 9 we looked at where countries and politicians sit on the world stage and what the problems are with getting governments to adopt more stringent environmental policies. Take Japan as an example. This country is considered by many to be the country that is *most* vulnerable to the effects of climate change after the heavy rain, heat waves, the Osaka earthquake, and Jebi typhoon all hit the country in 2018. The government of Japan know that they have to do more and that they need to switch to renewables and nuclear, but the Fukushima Daiichi nuclear disaster in 2011 has meant the Japanese government and the Japanese people all now view nuclear with a healthy skepticism. As a result, when the COP 26 climate conference came around in 2021, Japan opposed measures to have countries pledge to stop the burning of coal, and the country remains one of the world's largest polluters in the use of coal-fired power stations.

Convincing the people of a country and its politicians that they need to do more about climate change then can be a tough sell. Saudi Arabia has made huge amounts of money from oil over the years, and it's not running

© Mike Halsey 2025
M. Halsey, *The Green IT Guide*, https://doi.org/10.1007/979-8-8688-1233-0_11

out yet. While the country might be trying to wean itself off the black gold, knowing that eventually their economy will have to move to a different type of export as it's predicted the oil may run dry sometime around 2030, convincing the people of that country who are enjoying a high quality of life, and politicians and business leaders who have become rich off the back of oil, is far from easy.

How Business Leaders Are Changing the World

Elsewhere in the world though, it's business leaders that are facing the climate change challenge head on. In 2017, President Donald Trump announced that he was pulling the USA out of the Paris climate agreement that had been signed only two years earlier by his predecessor, Barack Obama. In response to this, the CEOs of 80 US companies including Apple (Tim Cook), Microsoft (Satya Nadella), Tesla and SpaceX (Elon Musk), Google (Sundar Pichai) along with the CEOs of companies including Adobe, Salesforce, HP, IBM, Verizon, and Corning all signed a statement that they were still committed to the Paris agreement and would abide by it.

Tim Cook went further in 2019, saying on Twitter (now X) that "Humanity has never faced a greater or more urgent threat than climate change." See Figure 11-1.

Tim Cook ✓
@tim_cook

Humanity has never faced a greater or more urgent threat than climate change — and it's one we must face together. Apple will continue our work to leave the planet better than we found it and to make the tools that encourage others to do the same.

unitedforparisagreement.com
United For The Paris Agreement

4:33 PM · Dec 2, 2019 · Twitter for Mac

689 Retweets   **93** Quote Tweets   **4,052** Likes

Figure 11-1. *Tim Cook is one of many CEOs who support climate change action*

They don't always get it right though as Bill Gates found out in 2021 when he celebrated his 66th birthday on a private yacht off the coast of Turkey with 50 guests including Amazon and Blue Origin founder, Jeff Bezos. Gates and many of the guests flew to the country using private jets, and Gates then flew them to the yacht by helicopter. It was estimated the jet fuel used just by the helicopter emitted more than 21,000 pounds of carbon per gallon of fuel burned, with the helicopter itself only able to travel 10.75 miles on one gallon.

Bezos was said at the time to have made a 120-mile round trip to the yacht by helicopter, and the charter yacht, which cost Gates $2 million per week, emitted more than 7,000 tons of carbon dioxide per year, or 19 tons each and every day.

Then, while the COP 26 climate conference was still going on in Glasgow, Scotland, Bezos announced plans for Blue Origin (you know, the company that makes rockets that look quite a lot like a man's thingy) to build a tourism space station that would host up to ten guests at a time. The space station, which would also house research laboratories, would cost $10 billion, and many criticized Bezos for spending the money on such a vanity project when there were still so many problems that needed sorting on Earth. In response, Bezos said that he was investing even more money in solving climate change projects through his Bezos Earth Fund and that when it comes to space travel and tackling climate change, *"...we need to do both."*

However, not just on the very day I'm writing this chapter, but literally down to the minute, a SpaceX flight, privately funded by US billionaire Jared Isaacman, is undertaking the world's first civilian spacewalk. If there were ever to be a definition of the phrase "vanity project," then I think it's happening right now.

The Projects Led by Business Leaders

The Bezos Earth Fund (`www.bezosearthfund.org`) is interesting as it's both a huge project to tackle the effects of climate change and one that most people have never heard of, making it of little wonder that he came under so much fire for his space tourism business.

Founded in 2020, it was set up to support climate science and technologies to reduce the effects of climate change, and Bezos himself, one of the world's richest men, donated $10 billion to it. He said of the fund:

> *Climate change is the biggest threat to our planet. I want to work with others to both expand known avenues and explore new ways to combat the devastating effects of climate change*

on this planet we all share. This global initiative will fund scientists, activists and NGOs – any effort that offers a real opportunity to contribute to the conservation and protection of the natural world. We can save the earth. It will require collective action by large corporations, small firms, nation states, global organizations and individuals.

Bill Gates, also one of the world's richest men, runs the Bill & Melinda Gates Foundation with his ex-wife, Melinda (www.gatesfoundation.org). This foundation also invests considerable sums in tackling the problems of climate change.

Elon Musk (Tesla, SpaceX, and X, which was formerly Twitter) also has a foundation that seems to work much more quietly and in the background; it doesn't even have a working website as I write this, though you might eventually find one at www.muskfoundation.org. This foundation donates money to renewable energy research among other climate projects.

Not wishing to be left out, as every billionaire needs a foundation (I thought that was hollowed-out volcano? – Ed), Mark Zuckerberg and his wife, Priscilla Chan, set up the Chan Zuckerberg Initiative in 2015 (www.chanzuckerberg.com). This organization is funded from the profits from Zuckerberg's company, Meta, to fund a wide variety of projects including those related to climate change.

The billionaire founder of investment firm Berkshire Hathaway, Warren Buffett, however, might have already given away tens of billions of dollars for charitable work, much of it to the Bill & Melinda Gates Foundation, but when it comes to climate change and his own company, he takes a harsher line. In 2015 he talked about his company's commitment to using renewable energy, but went on to say:

When you are thinking only as a shareholder of a major insurer, climate change should not be on your list of worries.

Oracle founder Larry Ellison shut down his own charitable foundation in 2020, telling *Forbes* magazine:

> *Philanthropy is the definition of not sustainable. Business is the definition of sustainable.*

Google's founders, Larry Page and Sergey Brin, don't run their own foundations in the way other billionaires do, but they have both worked on and supported projects aimed at tackling climate change, and the pair garnered headlines in 2014 when they walked away from membership of the free market lobbying group, American Legislative Exchange Council, over its links to climate change denial.

The People Providing the Solutions Could Also Be Causing the Problems

To be completely fair and even-handed though, the story earlier about Bill Gates' birthday celebrations in 2021 is indicative of a bigger problem. It has been estimated that the world's wealthiest 1%, through all their personal, professional, and business activities, produce double the combined carbon emissions of the world's poorest 50% and, according to research by Oxfam, are expected to contribute 16% of global carbon emissions by 2030.

This resulted in calls by the Oxfam report's authors for governments to *"constrain luxury carbon consumption like mega yachts, private jets and space travel."* So far though there's no indication that any action has been or will be taken, especially when you consider the private spacewalk taking place literally as I write this.

Research undertaken in 2018 showed that in the year prior, Bill Gates took 59 flights covering a distance of more than 340,000 km (213,000 miles), which is equivalent to circumnavigating the world eight times. These flights alone generated more than 1,600 tons of greenhouse gases, around the same as the annual emissions from 105 Americans (insert fart jokes here – Ed) according to the report's authors.

Then in 2021, the Cambridge Sustainability Commission (www.cambridge.org) undertook research showing that the wealthiest 5% of people contributed 37% of global carbon emissions and that nearly half of the recent growth in emissions was created by the wealthiest 10% of people.

Peter Newell, a professor at Sussex University and the lead author of the report, told the BBC:

> *We have got to cut over-consumption and the best place to start is over-consumption among the polluting elites who contribute by far more than their share of carbon emissions.*

How Big Is the Problem Caused by Businesses and the Rich?

While all of the details above make for interesting headlines, it's safe to say that things are changing. I heard a great story a few years ago about a billionaire from Monaco who had to fly somewhere further away than they normally flew, so they couldn't take their own private jet. Instead they flew on a commercial airliner, and the billionaire's son asked, "Daddy, why are all these people on our airplane?"

International pop superstar Taylor Swift caused controversy in 2024 when it emerged that she not only flew about 178,000 miles (286,463 kilometers) by private jet, of which she owns two, in 2023, but that she flew from Tokyo where she was appearing for her Eras Tour all the way to New Orleans where her boyfriend, Travis Kelce, was playing in the Super Bowl. She then flew back to Japan to continue her shows, again by private jet.

It's easy to justify the use of private jets for the rich and for businesses, as time is money and we've all suffered the 2-hour wander around an airport lounge buying things we don't need from shops we don't like, but people are now beginning to realize this can't be how things are done going forward.

In part the global pandemic helped with this (at least something positive came out of it – Ed) as national lockdowns cleared the skies of smog normally caused by aircraft and cars and people resorted to holding meetings over the Internet using Zoom or Teams.

Suddenly people could enjoy the skylines of cities like Mumbai and Beijing, which were normally clouded by a dense and quite toxic haze, and wandering around streets and parks wasn't accompanied by the constant roar of traffic.

The bad press the richest individuals and some businesses receive is also changing behaviors. You can be clear that investors in Berkshire Hathaway will listen carefully to what Warren Buffett says about climate change and to how seriously he takes the subject. They'll make their investment decisions based on that, and, in a way, it's the wider public and organizations bringing pressure to bear.

How Business Is Changing Post-pandemic

The way business is conducted therefore is changing, and the coronavirus pandemic has done a lot to bring about this change. These changes are also helping lessen the impact of climate change (at least in the short term) and changing the behaviors of everybody from the person on the street to the executives in the boardroom.

Let's look at the travel example I mentioned a little while ago. Nobody wants to spend 2 hours wandering up and down the halls of an airport departure lounge, but this is only going to get worse. There are pressures being brought on the airline industry to reduce the overall number of flights they make (estimated at 176,000 per day in 2019).

With less people traveling, because more business is being conducted online, it's an easy pill for the airline industry to swallow, and so the waits for a business person to travel might be longer. Additionally, some countries such as France and the UK are talking about reopening long-closed regional railways and banning internal flights on routes where a rail alternative exists, though France hasn't done this yet and there are protests where I live to try and get the local regional railway open again before it deteriorates too much.

All of this adds up to a lot more wasted time for business travelers, and if there are fewer flights, this will inevitably result in people taking longer trips away resulting in more productivity lost and greater costs for business. Conducting meetings online has never looked so attractive.

Then there are the changes being made to companies that own fleets of cars. These are very rapidly being switched over to all-electric or hybrid vehicles, largely taking advantage of government schemes to help fund the increased costs of the cars.

Even this isn't all good news though as a report issued in 2022, and broadcast on British television channel, Channel 4's *Dispatches* program, showed that some hybrid vehicles were producing more harmful emissions than some diesel cars.

The city of Paris decided to multiply three times the price for parking for heavy cars (more than 1.6 tons), thus leading to rechargeable hybrid cars impossible to use in Paris.

How You and Your Business Fit into the Bigger Picture

So where does this leave you, and where do you fit into the bigger picture? You've probably been reading this chapter feeling an ever-heightened state of anxiety and that your head is about to explode, especially if you're a Taylor Swift fan, so it's probably wise that we bring things back down to Earth gently, much like Jeff Bezos does with his Blue Origin rockets.

The world of climate science is changing, and the world of technology is changing ever more quickly. Take the example I mentioned earlier about research into hybrid vehicles. Nobody would have expected this or seen it coming, and it might leave you thinking that you should only buy electric, until you read another piece of research indicating that the parts for the batteries have to be shipped from mines on completely opposite sides of the planet and that the carbon footprint of producing the batteries in the first place is so high that it effectively negates the benefit in having an electric car in the first instance.

All you can do is your best. You have to use your best judgment, take a leap of faith, and make your best guess. Take advice, listen to the people around you, and read up on the subject just as you're doing here, as you can guarantee that some of the things that are taken for granted when it comes to climate science and how we tackle climate change would have changed between my starting to write this book and the day it was published.

Nobody is going to get things completely right, as you can see from the actions of people such as Bill Gates. Do we think Gates wants to make climate change worse? No, of course not, but neither can he or anybody else lock themselves away in a small house powered entirely by mushrooms, writing letters on paper from the local bamboo farm and eating grubs and insects (though these are a very nutritious food for your pet cat or dog – they're very high in protein, and my dogs eat them every day).

It's the same with you, as not everything you do in your own life or in your business or organization will be completely right. You might see the benefit to replacing the Range Rover with a Tesla, but when your partner wants that vacation in the Caribbean they've always longed for, it's still perfectly okay to say yes.

Getting on the Right Side of Customers and Stakeholders

Having an environmental policy for your business or organization is, we have probably established, not always enough. You can put out a press release to say you are now completely carbon neutral, but should your customers and stakeholders realize you're achieving this entirely through the purchase of carbon credits and just offsetting your emissions by buying into tree planting, solar, and wind projects, then the whole thing is very likely to come back and bite you on the arse.

This isn't the only consideration to make, however, when deciding on what and when you should communicate to customers, stakeholders, and the wider world, and you should first ask yourself these questions.

Is What We're Doing Enough?

This is a question you can likely give yourself a little slack with, as other people will very likely be prepared to forgive you for taking baby steps. If a sustainability policy is something that's new to your business, then you have to start somewhere, and it's likely to be with something fairly minor.

You don't need to worry that people will view you as negligent because you've already been recycling for years and ought by now to be doing more, as everybody recycles and it's a legal requirement in a lot of countries. Recycling therefore isn't something that most people will factor into a sustainability policy.

If you are starting small though, perhaps by installing solar panels to reduce your energy consumption, then it could be a good idea to frame your actions either as part of a plan or with an aim to achieve certain targets.

You don't need to have set-in-stone targets like Google and Microsoft do, of using only renewable energy by such and such a year. These companies are vast, have huge teams dedicated to just sustainability itself, and can afford the consultancy costs of the brightest experts in the business. Thus, for a company of their size, it's a fairly straightforward mathematical exercise to calculate the overall energy needs of the business and work out how many solar panels and wind turbines you need to install at each premises to provide the energy they need.

You, I would imagine, don't have an army of mathematicians at your disposal or at least don't have mathematicians that aren't otherwise engaged in fruitful work earning money for the business. Your goals will need to be realistic, but also flexible.

Setting overall *aims* then is likely the best way for you to progress – not to say you'll be using completely renewable energy, but to declare it as a goal you will aim to meet as early as conditions allow.

This means you can deliver positive news, even on a small start, that will reassure customers and stakeholders that this is only the beginning and there's more to come.

Still though, you might feel that what you're doing *isn't* enough to warrant a press release and some fanfare. If this is the case, and you'll probably know instinctively if people are going to go "Meh!" when you tell them, then it's perfectly fine to hold off, even if your competitors are ahead of you.

Instead then, the best response will be that your business *is putting together a sustainability plan and already taking steps to reduce your carbon emissions*. Then go on to say that *a full announcement will be made when there's something substantive to say*. This doesn't say you're not doing anything, and makes it clear that you are, but just says you don't want to waste anybody's time with a minor announcement at this stage.

Is This the Right Time to Be Announcing Anything?

It's not always a good idea to just release a statement to your customers and stakeholders for the sake of it. If you're a small- to medium-sized enterprise, then it's not really something that people would pay too much notice, too, anyway. You're more likely to get the occasional, individual query that you can respond to at the time.

If you're a larger enterprise, then it's likely you will have shareholders. With this come regulatory controls about what you need to announce and when, such as when you need to hold your annual general meeting and release your annual or quarterly financial reports. Is this the right time to announce a sustainability plan?

This is something that will be determined by your own financials. Let's say you've had a horrible quarter or profits in the last couple of years have dropped by a few percentage points. You might decide that this isn't the time to announce you're buying some very expensive wind turbines for the land behind your offices and fitting solar panels on the roof, when the payback from that investment will take a good number of years.

Conversely, you don't want to have a great year and then announce to your shareholders that they're not getting as large a dividend as they expected, as you're planning to spend most of it. So it can be tricky deciding what to announce and when, but how you announce things could soften the blow somewhat.

What Is the Right Way to Make the Announcement?

So what is the right way to make an announcement about sustainability policies for your company or organization? Sticking with corporate enterprises for a moment, your annual report after a good year might be the perfect place to announce a sustainability plan that will move forward over the next few years.

This annual report will be showcasing the business and all that you do, highlighting your past and recent successes, and detailing some of the projects you'll be moving forward with in the coming years so as to get the prospective shareholders excited enough to purchase more shares and push up the value of the company.

You'll find though that most companies, even the biggest ones on the planet such as Microsoft, Google, and Apple, will announce their own sustainability plans via a blog. Microsoft in fact announce pretty much everything in blog form, and they've got so many of them, right across the business, that it can be difficult to keep track.

Making announcements via a blog though can bring enormous advantages. The first of which is that the people who watch your company, if it's a large enterprise, only need to read the specific blogs that relate to them. You might have a financials blog, an innovation blog, a blog talking about customer and after-sales support, and a blog intended to keep stakeholders engaged, and alongside these you can add an environmental and sustainability blog.

For a smaller business, just having a single blog will suffice. Putting the information out in this format fills two important roles:

- It keeps the information visible and accessible in perpetuity. Not everybody will catch the news the first time around, and you don't want them thinking you're not doing anything just because they missed the initial press release.

- It provides a narrative story you can expand on over time. This is useful for keeping people up to date with your policies and practices, and you can highlight successes as you go, where you might have achieved a target early or where you're making changes or improvements to the current plan.

Creating a Narrative

Indeed it's important to create a narrative when you're discussing your sustainability policies and the changes you're making to the business. This is something unlike any other part of the business structure, where you will be keeping your research and development work secret, as it's commercially sensitive, or secretive over your financial affairs as (unless you have shareholders) it's nobody's business but your own anyway.

Sustainability is everybody's business, and it's also something that we all know never happens all at once. Nobody, no business, no organization, indeed no government has been or will ever be able to announce a sustainability policy that will suddenly change things overnight. When you decide on a policy, there will be a period, whatever the policy might be, where things need to be put in place, changes need to be implemented, and plans and further plans need to be drawn up, amended, examined, reviewed, amended again, and then expanded upon later.

Again this is where a blog can come in very useful. You can have a sustainability page or series of pages on your own website to make it easy for people to find your broad overarching strategy and policies, but as a part of that, the blog demonstrates that you've not forgotten about it, you're always working on it, and your plans are working and being expanded upon over time.

Considering the Things Outside of Your Control

As with anything in life, there will always be things that are partly or completely outside of your control – how your government generates power for the electricity network being a big one, weather and dramatic weather events being another. Additionally, the business or organization might have to contend with a crisis somewhere along the lines, and these are always of the "unexpected" variety by their very nature.

This could hit your plans for the business as a whole, not just sustainability, in different ways. It could create negative publicity, it could hit the company's immediate financials, or it could mean your financials will be affected over time.

When you're discussing your sustainability story narrative then with the public, customers, stakeholders, and whoever else it is that is reading your blog (such as prospective employees who will likely want to know what you're doing), you should be careful of setting too much in stone.

This brings me back to the *aims* I mentioned you should have a little while ago. If you set in stone that you will definitely do A within five years or B within seven years and then your circumstances change, you might end up looking foolish for having to scale back your plans or perhaps even having to scrap some of those plans altogether.

To look at two specific examples from the billionaires I wrote about earlier, both Jeff Bezos, who founded Amazon, and Mark Zuckerberg of Meta have had to see off huge challenges in negative publicity. For the former it was taking William Shatner (Captain James T. Kirk from *Star Trek*) into space at the very same time an absolutely crucial global climate summit was taking place in Glasgow, Scotland.

While nobody was criticizing William Shatner for becoming the oldest person to go into space, Bezos himself had to deal with a huge backlash from the press and media about how wasteful the whole project was when there was so much to do here on Earth and about the huge carbon emissions involved in sending four "tourists" into space in the first place.

Some newspapers did report though that "Blue Origin's rockets are powered by a mix of liquid hydrogen and liquid oxygen. The propellants are much cleaner than conventional rocket fuel," but they also said that people are asking questions about the effect these rockets have on global warming and that "ultimately, calculating the overall effect of each of these rocket launches on the planet and its atmosphere will require further, detailed studies."

All of this put Bezos, Blue Origin, and, by association, Amazon under a huge microscope that the man and the people involved in running those companies would have very likely preferred had not happened. All this of course could have perhaps been avoided if such a high-profile passenger hadn't been traveling at the same time the COP 26 summit was taking place.

Mark Zuckerberg on the other hand had a much more down-to-Earth set of problems to contend with when a whistleblower gave documents to the press showing that Facebook and Instagram knew their platforms were damaging to the mental health of teenage girls, but allowed the practice to continue because it made them money.

This was just one of a number of major Facebook and Instagram controversies that occurred all at the same time the company announced it was changing its name to Meta, much in the way Google had rebranded to Alphabet a couple of years earlier.

The rebranding made perfect sense commercially; WhatsApp, Instagram, Oculus, and the web analytics and messaging services Onavo and Beluga are all owned and operated by Facebook. Google conversely also owned the home automation firm Nest, DoubleClick, Looker, Waze, Fitbit, and of course YouTube.

With Facebook and Google being their own brands and their own product, it made complete sense for these to also be moved under umbrella companies. Facebook and Google were also massive publicly listed companies, meaning that plans for these rebrands and reorganizations would have had to start a couple of years earlier and the dates for delivery and changeover would have to be set in stone as there would be so many people, companies, and departments and regulators involved.

None of this looked good for Facebook, Instagram, and Zuckerberg, however, who was widely seen by the public of trying to bury the bad news and change the company name just to try and distract from it.

Staying Agile and Keeping Plans Flexible

This then means you should always try and keep whatever plans you have for sustainability flexible and adaptable as and when a change is required or when circumstances come along that force a change of policy or a change of direction.

This brings us back to your *aims*. You can have aims for the business across several areas. These, just as an example, might include

- Switching to entirely renewable electricity sources or generating your own power

- Moving your manufacturing or purchasing away from nonrecyclable materials or single-use plastics

- Providing new means of transportation for employees to get to and from your offices

- Stopping national and international travel wherever possible and conducting business with partners and customers and within the company entirely online

Some of these are easier to do than others, such as moving meetings online to Teams and Zoom, while others will throw up their own challenges, both from within your business and also from elsewhere. These might be, to give a few examples, the availability and pricing of appropriate manufacturing materials, the cost of energy efficiency technology and equipment, your plans to move or refurbish your existing premises, your expansion plans around the country or around the world, or new products you are planning to bring to market.

Again this brings us back to where an ongoing dialogue with the world is a great approach. This enables you to be flexible while never having to scale back or completely cancel any project, because you're just reacting to the circumstances in which you find yourselves, and where those circumstances might on occasion require taking a more modest approach, others might allow you to progress more quickly than you might otherwise have imagined.

Summary

Communication is clearly the best and most effective way to engage with customers, stakeholders, shareholders, the general public, and the press and with the wider world, and blogs are one of the best ways to achieve this. You don't need to give this role to a specific person either, as many other people in your business will on occasion have something important or relevant to contribute.

It might be that a specific department has been able to become fully sustainable ahead of time; perhaps manufacturing have found a supplier of recycled plastic that's come entirely from the ocean. This is the type of thing that's great news, and the people directly involved in that work and decision making will likely make a far better job of explaining it in an engaging way than a PR person.

Ocean plastic is a great example of how manufacturing is changing, but there are also many new innovations and future ideas being brought to the table, and we'll look at some of these later in this book.

In the next chapter though, we'll examine in more detail some of the unexpected changes and events that can affect your business and its sustainability plans. The post-truth world is becoming an increasingly unstable and unpredictable place, so we'll examine how this all affects supply chains, investment plans, and government and business policies.

CHAPTER 12

The Post-truth Planet

I remember back in the mid- to even late 1990s looking at friends using the Internet and thinking that this didn't look very useful and wouldn't be of much interest to me. If you grew up around the same time, you might have thought the same thing. *This Internet's just for the young*, you might have thought. Conversely you might have known nothing else other than growing up with Internet access, and the thought that the entire world didn't have it for centuries before makes you wonder how anybody was able to achieve anything at all.

Around the turn of the century, online shopping and banking services began to appear, and this of course was what caused the Internet revolution to start. People were regularly using email and messaging services such as MSN, AOL, and ICQ, and the world discovered that we could near instantly communicate with friends, family, and colleagues anywhere in the world.

Naturally this led some people to wonder where these communication technologies could be taken, and the first social networks began to appear in the form of Friendster and Myspace in 2003. Facebook and Twitter appeared in 2004 and 2006, respectively, but it was the launch of the second iPhone, the iPhone 3G, from Apple in 2008 that started the trend of everybody staring constantly at a social media feed on their smartphone. The original 2007 iPhone didn't have an app store, something the company quickly corrected.

© Mike Halsey 2025
M. Halsey, *The Green IT Guide*, https://doi.org/10.1007/979-8-8688-1233-0_12

By the time 2015 came around, we were beginning to get used to being deceived and lied to, even by politicians. The techniques used by oppressive regimes including China, Venezuela, Afghanistan, and Syria were starting to be used by Western governments. They realized that if a lie was said often enough and repeated often enough on social media, the public would believe it. This was most pronounced in my own life by the Brexit referendum in 2016, when the UK voted narrowly to leave the European Union.

There were many lies fed to the British people by the politicians leading the vote leave campaign, including that the country would save £58 million every day that could all be spent on the National Health Service (NHS). Not only was this figure completely untrue, but the use it was to be put to was not the NHS. 2016 also saw the election of Donald Trump, who took office in the White House in January 2017. Donald Trump has been widely known to lie directly to the American people, with the latest as I write this being a story about Haitian immigrants eating the cats and dogs of the local people in Cleveland, Ohio. Even Trump's running mate, JD Vance, repeated the story, hilariously claiming that the immigrants were from "Haitia" and not Haiti as he should have said.

This claim, which has been said is completely untrue by everybody in the state from local police to the state governor, has led to problems locally with Haitian residents, and far-right extremist groups such as the Proud Boys have been spotted in the city.

While listening to the radio this morning over coffee, there was a story about how Russia, China, and Iran were going to use misinformation to interfere with the US presidential election. This of course is something that also happened in the USA in 2015 and 2020 as well as being noticed in other elections around the world including Germany, France, and the UK.

Then the Covid 19 pandemic struck the world, and with it came a raft of misinformation and conspiracy theories, from the virus being deliberately released to the vaccine causing harm and even about how Bill Gates was using the vaccine to implant tracking chips in the population.

So we're now living in what has been termed the "post-truth world," and traditional media, such as newspapers and television, are having to produce special "fact-checking" pieces where they can debunk untrue claims and provide their readers and audience with the real truth.

Post-truth and the Climate

Back when climate change first came to the public attention around the mid-2000s and people such as former US Vice President Al Gore produced his documentary *An Inconvenient Truth* (Paramount, 2006), there were people claiming that climate change wasn't a thing being caused by mankind. These people were called climate deniers. Over the years there were arguments back and forth about climate change, with some people out and out lying about the facts and others trying to defend the truth.

In all honestly there's evidence that backs up the claims of both sides, and as I said at the very beginning of this book, I'm not here to be all preachy and tell you that climate change is definitely a man-made thing. It's widely accepted now though that, whatever is causing it, the climate is changing, and some of the practices and behaviors of human beings aren't helping.

Perhaps because of this wide acceptance, there isn't a lot of misinformation about climate change, outside of some in the scientific and political communities giving the occasional interview or talk in which they state that there's nothing to see here and we should all just move along and get on with our day. I don't believe that, and you clearly don't believe it either; otherwise, you wouldn't be reading this book.

Conspiracy Theories Aren't True ... Or Are They?

I mentioned a little while ago about conspiracy theories that sprung up about the Covid 19 pandemic and the vaccine rollouts that happened around the world. The post-truth world has also given rise to a sharp increase in conspiracy theories including in 2020 when many believed that the rollout of 5G mobile telephony services was causing health problems, with some even vandalizing and setting fire to new 5G base stations and towers.

Other prominent conspiracy theories have led to a rise in antisemitism and anti-Islamism, and these days it's possible that anything can really be a "conspiracy" with the recent, as I write this, assassination attempts on US presidential candidate Donald Trump being "orchestrated by the Democrat left" and "staged by the Republicans."

The QAnon movement in the USA has been around for a few years now and is a far-right conspiracy theory–led political organization that led the uprising at the US Capitol building on January 6, 2021. They are one of a great many such groups around the world on both the far left and the far right of politics.

Climate change is not immune to conspiracies, and these include climate change being used as a mechanism to force people to stop driving cars, that commercial jets were deliberately spraying chemicals into the atmosphere for governments to cause climate problems, that it's really the Chinese government behind the entire thing so as to make US manufacturing noncompetitive, and that post-Covid it's a plan by powerful political, business, and religious leaders, including the Pope, to create a new world order.

My personal favorite though is the theory that lit up social media in 2023 that Oprah Winfrey deliberately started wildfires in Maui (Hawaii) using space lasers, with people producing "evidence" in the form of doctored photos showing powerful laser beams hitting the ground.

Birds Aren't Real

In 2018 a conspiracy emerged in the USA called "Birds Aren't Real" that claimed that all the birds in the USA had been exterminated by the government between 1959 and 1971 and current birds were really lookalike drones operated by the US government to spy on the population.

The theory went that the birds contained cameras and microphones, and the reason birds sat on electricity lines was so they could recharge their batteries.

The man responsible for the conspiracy theory, Peter McIndoe, gave many television and press interviews and toured the USA handing out leaflets, encouraging people to "wake up" to the reality they were being spied on by their own government. By 2021 the Birds Aren't Real movement had thousands of members, all of whom were promoting the theory and all of whom were secretly in on the joke.

In May 2022, McIndoe gave an interview to *60 Minutes* in which he came clean for the reason for making it all up. He told the program, "So it's taking this concept of misinformation and almost building a little safe space to come together within it and laugh at it, rather than be scared by it. And accept the lunacy of it all and be a bird truther for a moment in time when everything's so crazy."

World War 3 and Me

Conspiracy theories and especially misinformation have led to a sharp rise in conflicts in recent years, with states including Russia using misinformation as a justification for military action and invasion. When Russia rolled into Ukraine in 2022, following their previous annexation of Crimea in 2014, Russian President Vladimir Putin told the Russian people that the Ukrainian government had been taken over by Nazis and that the Ukrainian president was planning to attack Russia.

In October 2023, the far-right Islamist group Hamas conducted a series of attacks on Israel, killing more than 1,000 Israelis and foreign nationals and kidnapping more than 250 men, women, and children. This quickly led to the Israeli government invading the Gaza Strip, which was run and policed by Hamas, and the killing of more than 40,000 people by Israeli forces.

Israel repeatedly claimed that Hamas had fighters embedded in civilian groups and hospitals around the Gaza Strip and used this unprovable information as justification for the wholesale destruction of the area, forcibly displacing more than two million Palestinian people.

Some people have said that what Israeli Prime Minister Benjamin Netanyahu claims is all true, but others see it as an excuse for the widespread extermination of the Palestinian people, something the International Criminal Court (ICC) based in the Hague (Netherlands) must have partly agreed with when it issued arrest warrants for both the leadership of Hamas and Netanyahu in May 2024.

This conflict has since spread to neighboring Lebanon with Israel attempting to neutralize the Iran-backed Hezbollah militia based there through everything from rocket attacks and assassinations to using pagers and walkie-talkies as explosives.

As the USA and other countries try and prevent the shooting from turning into an all-out regional war, dragging Iran and other countries into the conflict, some people believe we have already entered the Third World War, but that we've not recognized it yet because it's not turned out the way we would normally have expected. Vladimir Putin has threated to use nuclear weapons on several occasions as a way to prevent the USA and European countries including the UK, France, and Germany from directly intervening in Ukraine, but it's also been reported that President Xi Jinping of China and India's Prime Minister Narendra Modi, two of Putin's best allies, have told him personally that under no circumstances is he ever to use nuclear weapons.

This of course makes a complete mockery of the nuclear deterrent. We had all been told for decades that no nuclear power would attack because we also had nuclear weapons we would use to retaliate against them with. Clearly nobody expected Putin to use his nuclear weapon threat to prevent other nations from assisting a country he was invading.

Nuclear misinformation isn't a new thing. For several decades the US government was telling its people about the threat posed by the then Soviet Union (USSR) also having nuclear weapons, when the truth was that the Soviet economy was practically on its knees and the government there was having difficulty feeding the people. This ultimately led to the fall of the Soviet Union and its dissolution in December 1991. Glasnost (meaning openness and transparency) and the good relations between the new Russian Federation President Mikhail Gorbachev and US President George Bush came out of necessity to try and get the Russian economy moving again.

Iran is also on its way to become a nuclear power and has no love for Israel, which is why Western governments are so concerned about the prospect of the Israel–Hamas war spreading across the Middle East. Hopefully by the time you read this, all these conflicts will have been peacefully resolved, and the world will begin talking about global nuclear disarmament. At the time I write this though, it's still not looking good in the short to medium term.

How an Unstable World Affects Supply Chains

Earlier in this book I wrote about how the advent of the container ship changed global supply chains, but also acted as a disincentive for individual countries to be self-sufficient. Because anything could be shipped around the world, some countries gave up on manufacturing essential products like steel.

This all worked well for decades when the planet was at a time of relative peace. However, that's just not the case anymore. At the beginning of this chapter, I documented how global and national politics is becoming more and more fractured and unpredictable and how politicians in countries as diverse as the UK and Venezuela are openly lying to the public in order to achieve their aims.

This has made the process of international diplomacy extremely difficult, but let's be honest, diplomacy is about surviving into the next century, but politics is just about surviving until Friday afternoon.

When we examine then how global supply chains can be and are being affected by world politics, it's good to start with Russia's invasion of Ukraine in 2022. This is because both countries are major suppliers to the world of essential products.

Ukraine is one of the world's largest suppliers of sunflower oil, which is used for everything from food preparation and cooking to farming and cosmetics. Russia by comparison is a major producer of many of the minerals and metals used by the renewables industry, including aluminum, nickel, graphite, and palladium. The country is also one of the world's largest suppliers of natural gas. When the invasion of Ukraine began, the world suffered huge rises in demand of, and shortages of, both natural gas and sunflower oil.

China by comparison is the biggest mining country in the world, including many minerals and metals essential for technology and the renewables industry such as graphite, gold, silicon, cobalt, and lithium. The USA, the world's second-largest mining country by comparison, is more limited to iron ore, copper, and gold.

In fact much of the Western world is resource poor when it comes to mining with none of the minerals and metals required for technology found there. The upshot of this is that the state of international diplomacy can sometimes mean resources needed can become more difficult to obtain, pushing up prices and limiting the use they can be put to.

Cloud Services and International Relations

Cloud services are not excluded from international diplomacy and politics. There are countries in the world where it can be considered *risky* to store your cloud data. These include China, Saudi Arabia, Malaysia, India, Thailand, and Russia. This is either because these countries have laws that force cloud and other data providers to provide unfettered access to data, such as with China and Saudi Arabia, or where data protection laws are either weak or nonexistent.

By comparison, the countries with the strongest data protection laws in the world are the European Union, Iceland, Norway, Japan, and Switzerland. Data protection laws in the USA are more fractured than in other countries, either covering just specific industries or operating on a per-state level.

When you use cloud services, you will sometimes be offered a choice by your provider of which country(ies) you wish to store your business data in, Microsoft being one of these companies. The choice for consumers is much less available. It's common for businesses, organizations, and governments to store their data either in their own country or, where this isn't possible or practicable, in a third country that has strong data protection regulations.

It's also important to consider that you're often not just storing your own data, but that of your customers, which can include personal and sensitive information such as addresses, dates of birth, and banking and credit card details.

This all means that when it comes to the storage of data, careful consideration must be given not just to the current state of data protection regulation, but also to the current and projected state of world politics and where might and might not be considered a safe country in the future.

How World Politics Affects Compliance and Sustainability

While it can sometimes be difficult to obtain the materials needed for components and manufacturing, when it comes to compliance, things will always be much simpler. This is because the industry and governance rules set for you will be the same, not just for all of the other businesses and organizations in your country, but also for your government, and no government is going to hold people to compliance rules that it's extremely difficult or perhaps even impossible to keep, especially when they also have to comply with those rules themselves.

The same goes for sustainability. There are safe and reliable countries that are major producers of sustainability products, such as the UK, which is a major producer of wind turbines, and the USA is a large producer of solar panels. Sustainability is a huge growth industry, so it's only sensible that the largest economies want to invest in it and encourage businesses in their country to become producers.

Building Resilience into Sustainability Planning

Everything I've detailed in this chapter about the current state of world politics and conflict is just a snapshot of where the world is at, at the time of writing this book. When I wrote the first edition of this book back in 2021 and 2022, things were very different. Back then I did mention the Russian invasion of Ukraine as it had just begun, but that was the only major conflict happening in the world.

Back then, there was no indication there would be war in the Middle East, and the biggest problem China had to worry about was the huge amount of bitcoin mining taking place in the country. Even Serbia, which looks right now as though it could erupt into civil war, and the USA, which is also going through very turbulent political times that could end very violently if not properly managed, were happy and safe countries to be in.

So when you're building resilience into any part of your business that involves third countries, and the possibility of events that might be or are completely out of your control, it's always a good idea to have a backup.

Contracts can often be difficult and take a long time to sign, especially for procurement where, should a major world event happen and a shortage of one or more components occur, there will be more competition from other companies and your competitors to obtain those components. This is something we saw during the pandemic when many of the mines around the world producing minerals and metals used in technology had to temporarily shut down.

The pandemic though has taught the world a lot, and I have no doubt that it also taught you and your business much as well. With the coronavirus now a distant memory, however, it's always wise never to forget the lessons we learned in those two years. A global event, political or driven by climate change, could affect supply chains, or perhaps even another pandemic will hit the world. Nothing can be predicted when it comes to world events, and it's always a good idea to remember this when building a resilience plan for your business.

Agility is the name of the game, and this applies as much to cloud services and data as it does to the procurement of raw materials and IT and sustainability equipment.

Sanctions and Tariffs

Another consideration that cannot just affect the agility and performance of your business, but that can do so with very little or even no warning, is the prickly subject of sanctions and tariffs.

When the Russian invasion of Ukraine began, a series of sanctions were placed on Russia. These sanctions, which were imposed by many countries and trading blocks including the USA and European Union, both included bans on trade and limits on the types of technology sold such as a ban on the newest microprocessors.

In 2022, the US government placed legal bans on the purchase of components from some Chinese companies Huawei and ZTE, citing an "unacceptable risk" of equipment being used for spying by the Chinese government. You might have your own opinion on this. I personally think the risk was considerably overinflated, but then you only have to look at Israel's use of pagers and walkie-talkies, which were manufactured in Hungary, a country and a people most of us would consider safe and respectable.

Countries are not above protectionism either. In mid-July 2024 the European Union, wanting to protect jobs in its car market, announced a tariff of up to 37.6% would be imposed on electric vehicles coming from China. This also included some Western brands, such as Volvo, Volkswagen, BMW, and Tesla who got caught up in the tariffs where some of their manufacturing took place in China.

The reason for imposing the tariffs came from the sales of Chinese EVs jumping from 3.9% of the market in 2020 to 25% by 2023, a rise that spooked EU officials, but that to be honest probably doesn't properly take account of the general rise in the sales of electric vehicles overall.

Again with data there are countries in the world with specific bans on where data can be stored. Some countries ban the transfer of data to other nations that do not meet minimum standards for data privacy and protection. These bans can affect all data or just specific types of data such as tax and financial records.

Sometimes the imposition of sanctions and especially tariffs can lead to what's called a "tit for tat" war, where tariffs are imposed going the other way. Let's say, for example, that country A imposes tariffs on country B for specific products where they're trying to protect their own industries; then country B could impose tariffs on something that country A is a major exporter of. There's no way to predict this. We just have to deal with these problems when they arise.

Can We Predict the Future of IT Tariffs and Sanctions?

There is one area where we can predict sanctions and tariffs will affect entire nations and the businesses operating in them, and that is the nation of Taiwan. Tensions over Taiwan have risen greatly in recent years. China has always seen Taiwan as part of their domain, and as such Taiwan still doesn't have a presence at the United Nations. Taiwan, by contrast, wants very much to remain an independent nation, and it's protected in the South China Sea by navies from around the world, predominantly being the USA.

China occasionally deliberately provokes the American and Taiwanese governments, with air force flyovers into Taiwanese airspace or Chinese naval ships moving into Taiwanese waters or attempting to block the passage of US naval vessels.

Despite the efforts of the West to deter China from invading Taiwan, the Chinese government has remained utterly resolute, and it is possible that an invasion of Taiwan might occur sometime in the future, leading to a direct conflict between the USA and China in the South China Sea.

While there is considerable doubt this would ever spill over into a larger war, as *fortunately* nobody seems to want that anymore, sanctions, tariffs, and supply shortages are definitely a strong possibility.

For this reason, the US government has been encouraging companies like Intel to produce more chips and components in the USA and has been investing heavily in US-based fabrication plants as a result. The European Union and countries including the UK have so far been less quick to encourage local manufacturing of technology components, though programs such as the European Processor Initiative (EPI) do exist to encourage the design and manufacture of low-power processors in Europe.

It is very likely however that the costs for some technology, if not all technology, including that required for renewables and sustainability, will rise sharply in the coming years as tariffs and shortages become more common. Taiwan is, of course, the world's largest producer of microprocessors, with the world's largest chip manufacturer TSMC being based there.

Summary

People often refer to "the state of world politics," but rarely has the word "state" been so appropriate, as that's clearly what it's in. With even Western leaders engaging openly in misinformation, there's no indication it'll improve any time in the foreseeable future.

Some governments including the UK are currently investigating new laws that prevent lying in public office, but such new laws are being held up with discussions on how you implement them. The best lie is one planted inside a truth is something often said, so what would be a lie and if there was a lie, how could you conclusively prove it and differentiate it from that person's opinion. People have a nasty habit of finding their way around laws, and this would certainly be one of them.

We'll look more optimistically at the world though in the next chapter and at some of the innovative and exciting new sustainability technologies in development and coming in the future, from energy made from coffee (I get a lot of energy from coffee – Ed) to container ships that can capture up to 95% of their own carbon emissions.

CHAPTER 13

Assessing Future Technologies

It's safe to say that while technology can bring enormous benefits in the battle against climate change, it's also fair to say that technology is not always the solution to the problem. Take the steam engine for example. This is a technology that completely changed the world after it was invented in 1698. Rather than being something that could have been used to make the planet a healthier place, it's widely accepted that the steam engine is the cause of not just climate change, but also smog and centuries of health problems, rather than being a part of the solution.

When it comes to your own solutions, retiring that old steam engine that's powering the factory might not be the first thing that springs to mind, unless you really do have a steam engine still in operation that is, in which case please send me a photo.

Throughout this book I've talked about many things you can do to make your own business or organization more environmentally friendly and sustainable. Many of these are free, such as changing power settings on computers or asking people to not leave their laptop chargers plugged in all the time. Others are fairly obvious, such as fitting new double-glazed windows when you refit your premises or fitting some solar panels on the roof to generate some of your electricity.

Beyond these, however, it can be difficult to ascertain what you can do, what you're supposed to do, and what you indeed *should* do, as not all sustainability technologies are created equal.

The Solar Effect

Let's take solar panels as an example as this is a good indicator that "you get what you pay for." Solar panels have been around for a long time, but they vary greatly in cost and efficiency. There are many different designs for solar panels, too, some more suitable for specific use cases, like providing power to charge an electric car or for heating water in your home. Then you have battery storage to consider too. All of this can be very confusing, which is why so many businesses and consumers sign up to schemes run by their electricity provider.

These schemes allow the installation of panels for a very small cost, perhaps as low as $1, but there are problems. The first is that you don't own the panels, and some people, especially when they have fitted solar panels on a "rental" scheme such as this, encounter legal obstacles when they want to sell the house, as the incoming owners have to agree to take on the contract.

Then you find that you don't own the electricity they generate. Your electricity supplier will allow you use *some* of the power the panels generate, but you'll still be paying for the bulk of your electricity at the provider's set rate, and there's no guarantee that the energy you're using is coming from a renewable source either.

Lastly there's the efficiency of the panels to consider, and this will vary wildly from one provider to another. Let's take the example of a major electricity company, such as EDF here in France. These companies have an incentive to provide high-efficiency panels, as they're meeting strict targets set by their government and by the company's board for power generation. It is for this reason that the contract period for these panels can be very long, upward of 20 years, as the initial cost of the panels is high and the company has to recoup their investment.

If on the other hand you are having panels fitted by a local installer, perhaps as part of a grant scheme run by your local, state, or national government, there can be an incentive to prioritize profit over power generation. These companies are possibly more likely to fit older, cheaper, low-efficiency panels, as that way they'll make their money back quickly before moving on to the next installation.

When it comes to solar panels then, it's essential to shop around, seek advice from several sources, and assess the efficiency of the panels you are buying into. As I write this the most energy-efficient panels operate at a maximum efficiency of around 30%, and this improves iteratively with every new generation of panels. Some older panels, however, might have an efficiency of about 20% or even in the low teens, and your return on investment won't be anywhere near as high as you would wish it to be, even if the panels were inexpensive or free to install.

Being Generally Efficient

It's not all about solar panels either. Other current sustainability technologies such as wind turbines will have their own power efficiency ratings, and these will vary from one product to another. You might find, overall, that the difference in efficiency isn't matched by the difference in price, and a system that costs three times the cheapest model will likely not be three times as efficient.

This is where you need to do research again, and it's something people are already used to doing with electric vehicles. When people buy an automobile, there's always an emotional decision in there somewhere. This is why the advertisements you see on TV try and present their vehicles as sexy or desirable, in addition to being practical and efficient.

With electric vehicles though there are other considerations. How far will it go on a single charge? What is the charge time from flat? What type of charger does the vehicle use? With my own electric car, the Aixam eCoupe, which I spoke about in Chapter 2, it uses a standard domestic two-pin plug. I do have a Type-2 charger adapter for it, but it's incapable of charging at Type-2 speeds. This will always equate to slow charging, and from flat the battery will take almost 5 hours to fully charge. Add this to a maximum range of 62 miles (100 km) (45 miles on a typical trip) and a top speed of only 28 miles per hour (45 km/h) that equates to around 12 miles (19 km) range per hour of charge.

Compare this with a Tesla (which incidentally is around eight to ten times the cost of the Aixam, even though you're getting considerably more for your money), which will give you 44 miles per hour of charge with a fast home charger and up to 200 miles for just 15 minutes spent connected to a Tesla supercharger. While the initial outlay for the Tesla is considerable, it is clearly a far more power-efficient vehicle (with the benefit it does come with a few niceties that the Aixam doesn't).

So choosing the most power-efficient products for yourself, your home, and your business is therefore hugely important, and advisors, energy efficiency websites, and local, state, and governmental organizations will always be available to provide advice and support.

Leading the Charge

This brings us neatly onto the subject of what's next with power efficiency and with technological advancements in the generation of clean energy. As we've been talking about electric vehicles, batteries seem like a good place to start. Modern lithium-ion batteries, which are found in just about everything these days, are significantly more efficient than they ever used to be. You might remember some old batteries had a "memory" and stopped charging past a certain point after a while.

Lithium-ion batteries do require chemicals that have to be mined, and some of these chemicals can be toxic to people and very harmful to the environment. In 2020 the Institute of Energy Research (www.instituteforenergyresearch.org) released a report that said in 2016 a toxic chemical leak from a lithium mine in Tibet poisoned a river that runs from Tibet into China, killing livestock and fish along the route.

There are new battery technologies being developed by scientists around the world, and some are hugely exciting.

The Lithium-Sulfur Battery

Researchers at Monash University in Melbourne, Australia, have developed a lithium-sulfur (spelt "sulphur" in some parts of the world) battery that can outperform standard lithium-ion batteries by a factor of five, leading to batteries that can power a typical smartphone for a week or give an electric vehicle a range of hundreds of miles more than is currently possible.

The Seawater Battery

IBM Research, however, is trialing a new battery technology that is completely free from harmful chemicals such as nickel and cobalt and that could also outperform lithium-ion. IBM's battery, which is partially sourced from seawater, charges faster and lasts longer than current battery technologies while coming in at a lower overall cost.

The Sand Battery

While we're on the subject of the ocean, researchers at the University of California Riverside have developed a battery made from silicon (common sand), which is purified and powdered, before being mixed with other minerals to create pure silicon.

This battery technology has the potential to achieve three times the performance of current batteries while also being cheaper to manufacture.

Graphene and Carbon Nanotubes

By far the most interesting and promising technologies, however, come from graphene. This substance is fairly new and is a one-atom-layer thick arrangement of carbon atoms that is 200 times stronger than steel and is also an excellent conductor of heat and electricity.

Researchers at Chalmers University of Technology in Gothenburg, Sweden, have been investigating ways to make graphene batteries that are also a structural component for electric vehicles. This could ultimately result in superlight electric vehicles that are, as you would imagine for such a product, highly energy-efficient.

Carbon nanotubes are cylinders of carbon atoms with a diameter of less than 1 nm (nanometer). They have practical applications in everything from cardiac surgery to creating aircraft that can change the shape of their wings mid-flight.

It's with batteries and the environment, however, that some of the most interesting potential can be found. Researchers at North Carolina State University have demonstrated silicon-coated carbon nanotubes for lithium-ion batteries that can increase the capacity of the battery by a factor of ten, while researchers at Los Alamos National Laboratory in New Mexico are developing lithium-air batteries, which will also have this superhigh capacity.

In addition to the capacity benefits, batteries based on carbon nanotubes could be charged in as little as 2 minutes and last for 20 or more years. This of course is a huge leap over existing battery technology.

Graphene and the Environment

The benefits of graphene and carbon nanotubes don't end with batteries, however. There are significant environmental benefits to be gained from using them as well. These include technology based on carbon nanotubes to clean up oil spills by creating nanotubes that can absorb many times their own weight in oil.

Carbon nanotubes have also been demonstrated to be useful with water desalination, being more efficient than current technologies and requiring much less power. This has led to development on small, inexpensive water desalination and purification devices that can be used in developing countries and disaster zones.

Sensors made from nanotubes, which are effectively paint-sprayed to create them, can detect and bind to bacteria in water, trapping it and helping clean the water. All in all it is an amazing technology that will change everybody's life in the twenty-first century and beyond.

The Most Interesting Future Environmental Technologies

Graphene isn't the only technology coming across the horizon to help us save the planet. There are a whole host of amazing technologies, some of which are already here and others of which are so inventively clever you might wonder how we ever lived without them.

Coffee Power

One very close to my own heart, as every day is spent with a few cups to get my own engine started, is coffee power. UK-based startup Bio-bean (www.bio-bean.com) recycles coffee grounds, turning them into biofuels for heating buildings and powering transport networks. They are the world's largest recycler of waste coffee products and collect them from businesses across London and the UK.

Fighting Fire with Noise

As our climate changes, the world is facing more problems with wildfires in forested areas, and California has been hit especially badly in recent years. Technology is being developed, however, to use low-frequency sound waves to put out fires, with the sound waves disrupting the air surrounding a fire, cutting off its supply of oxygen.

Laboratory-Grown Meat and Dairy

One technology that you will have definitely heard of is laboratory-grown meat products. These are getting much better and much cheaper than they have been in the past, with companies across the world from the USA to Hong Kong, Israel, Spain, Japan, the Netherlands, and Singapore all creating everything from burgers and steaks to dog food.

Other companies are using the technology, however, to create laboratory-grown dairy products like milk, ice cream, cheese, and even eggs. The dairy industry is estimated to be responsible for 4% of global carbon emissions, which is more than air travel and shipping combined, and so development of lab-grown dairy products is bringing tangible benefits to the environment.

I'm Not a Celebrity – Feed Me Insects!

Speaking of dog food, I always feed my border collies, Evan, Robbie, and Téo (see Figure 13-1), the best and most nutritious food available and use ratings websites to inform me of what's best for their health and diet.

Figure 13-1. *Evan, Robbie, and Téo always have the best diet*

Not only are the biscuits I feed them insect-based, but they are produced by a small company, local to France where I live, helping not only reduce their impact on the environment but also keep money in the country and their local community.

There has been extensive research into insect-based diets, especially for cats and dogs, and it has been found that insect-based foods can be healthier and better for a dog than a piece of prime steak (mmm, prime steak – Ed), in addition to being far better for the environment.

Let's face it, there's no shortage of insects in the world (though bees are becoming a major issue), and there are exciting prospects ahead for insect-based diets in our own lives, rather than them just being consumed on TV shows like *I'm a Celebrity...Get Me Out of Here!* as they are high in protein.

The Carbon-Capture Tree

Way back in the first chapter of this book, I enthused about a carbon-capture tree that was capable of extracting carbon dioxide from the atmosphere 1,000 times more efficiently than a regular tree. This technology takes the form of a tall structure that sits by a roadside or perhaps around the parking lot at your business premises, and it draws carbon from the air and stores it.

They actually don't look anything like trees, but given trees are the best natural way to remove carbon from the air, they're named fairly appropriately. They use a technology called "direct air capture" to chemically scrub CO_2 from the ambient air and then store it in specially designed panels that can later be appropriately cleaned or disposed of safely.

We can label this technology as "one to watch" as it's still extremely expensive, but to be able to invest in a technology for your premises that can scrub CO_2 from the air passively, 24 hours a day, every day of the year, using little or no power in the process, is exciting indeed and we can expect carbon-capture trees to receive much more publicity in the coming years.

Kinetic Energy–Generating Flooring

What is definitely cheaper is technology that generates power from movement. This is actually a much more prevalent and cheaper way to be environmentally sustainable. The idea behind smart buildings and cities is that floor tiles or outdoor paving is replaced with special tiles that generate electricity from the kinetic movement of people who walk on them.

Some larger corporations have already fitted these floor tiles along busier corridors to help generate power for the building, and they have also been used at various outdoor locations and events including London's Heathrow Airport and the Soccer World Cup. There was even a nightclub owner who had fitted these on his dance floor to help reduce his electricity usage.

While these tiles don't generate much electricity in themselves, they are designed and intended to compliment other energy generation methods and to be used in high-traffic areas.

In the coming years we can expect kinetic energy generators to start finding their way into everything from the desks we use at work to home appliances such as washing machines, where the spinning of the drum will generate a small amount of power that will then be stored in batteries to be used next time the machine is operated.

Floating Farms

The United Nations has estimated that by the year 2050 the world will be facing a 70% increase in demand for food over what we produce today. Farming is a problem around the world, caused in no small part by climate change, and drought and other extreme weather effects often damage and destroy complete harvests.

Some scientists therefore are suggesting that floating farms can be created on the top of lakes and other waterways, including in urban conurbations. These ideas include a multi-tiered structure that generates its own power through solar collection and uses nutrients from the water to fertilize vegetables, with some of those nutrients and vegetable matter falling back into the water where it can feed fish.

Solar Roof Tiles

Elon Musk is one of the people behind solar roof tiles. These really are exactly what you might think but give the added advantage of covering an entire roof with solar collectors, rather than just the proportion of the roof you would get with solar panels. Because they are actual roof tiles, too, they're easier to fit as planning permission is generally not required.

Living Buildings

One thing you might have seen with new buildings, and the French are especially good at it, is creating living buildings. This started some years ago with moss and other plant materials being placed on roofs as insulation and grew (if you'll excuse the pun) into buildings where a whole or part of the outside was covered in plant life.

Primarily found in cities, these serve several functions from absorbing carbon dioxide to providing insulation for those people inside the building, reducing the cost of heating the building. They can also capture and store rainwater, which can then be reused in restrooms and some other parts of the building.

Positive energy houses are a model of optimization, too, adding layers of insulation and central ventilation system with heat recovery.

Thorium Reactors

One of the biggest problems associated with green energy is the use of nuclear power as an alternative to coal and gas. We're not at the stage yet where renewables alone can generate enough reliable energy for a developed nation, as you're at the mercy of cloud and wind. Nuclear however is fraught with problems, and the refined uranium used to power the reactors can take thousands of years to decay, and there's no storage solution yet found other than sticking it in barrels filled with concrete and piling it up underground or inside a mountain somewhere.

This is where thorium could help. Thorium is a material that could be used instead of uranium in specially modified reactors. It is much more abundant in the Earth's crust than uranium, which is difficult to mine, produces more power when harnessed as it has a half-life in the billions of years, and also produces much less waste. The technology is still theoretical but could become cost-effective in the future.

Electricity Generation from Wastewater

Back in the days before the steam engine was invented, it was common for mills to generate the power needed to operate their machinery by harnessing the power in running water. This of course is still used today, and tidal energy generation, while sadly not common yet, is developing all the time.

Researchers at Oregon State University in the USA however have created a generator that generates power from wastewater. This system has the potential to not only provide the power needed to clean the water for reuse but also feed a significant amount of power back into the main grid.

Biofuels

This wouldn't be a complete list of all the exciting sustainability technologies out there without making a mention of biofuels. We have already seen how coffee grounds (mmm, coffee – Ed) can be used to make biofuels, but just about anything can be turned into a biofuel from paper and grass to used wood. The biofuels created can then be used to power everything from machinery to cars. Unfortunately this results in competition for using cultivable land either for food or biofuels.

Hydrogen Vehicles

Let's finish this section with a look at hydrogen-powered vehicles. These have actually been around for a while and you'll no doubt have heard about them. The idea is that you fill your tank with liquid hydrogen, which is then mixed in the engine with oxygen to generate power.

This isn't a new idea either as if you're of a certain age you might remember the TV series *Knight Rider* (Universal Television, 1982) where the star of the show – sorry, David Hasselhoff – was a technologically advanced Pontiac Trans-Am that was powered by hydrogen.

The biggest advantage of hydrogen of course is that's it's not a pollutant. Your vehicle would still need a tailpipe, but the only thing it would emit would be small amounts of water.

Sadly, while the technology to create hydrogen-powered vehicles is well understood and companies including Toyota even make them today, the process of manufacturing the hydrogen itself is complex, expensive, and difficult. This can definitely be marked though as another technology to keep an eye on. Another problem is the yield of that energy, far from electricity engines.

Hydrogen Aircraft

Some aviation companies around the world are currently developing planes that are powered by hydrogen. One such company is Airbus with its ZEROe program (https://pcs.tv/3BkddPx). Their goal is to produce the world's first commercial hydrogen-powered jet by 2035. Given there are around 100,000 jets in the skies worldwide every single day, this technology could be a game changer for climate change.

Carbon-Capture Shipping

Another major transportation system that's often criticized for its carbon emissions is container shipping. One UK startup, Seabound (www. seabound.co), is developing a carbon-capture technology that could allow container and other large ships to capture up to 95% of their emissions. However, unlike hydrogen planes, which would need to be all new models based around the technology, Seabound's system can be retrofitted to existing ships.

So the Future's Bright?

We're living in interesting but perilous times. Nobody's doubting that the climate is changing, and the effect of this, from melting ice caps to wildfires, drought, increased rainfall, and hurricanes is being felt across the world. There might be some argument of whether it's being caused by humanity, and as I mentioned right at the beginning of this book, I'm not here to preach or to stand in judgment over anybody. It is clear though that becoming more sustainable and using renewable energies can improve the planet we live on drastically.

As an example of this, you only need to look at before and after pandemic photos of the Indian capital Delhi, which are available on a quick online search, to see that the smog generated by traffic in the city made the air almost too thick to see through, but cleared completely when the country went into lockdown and the volume of traffic fell to a tiny fraction of what it had been before.

The same thing happened to the skies of Europe after the (I'm not pronouncing it) Eyjafjallajökull volcano in Iceland erupted in 2010, pushing a massive plume of smoke and debris into the atmosphere. While this itself wouldn't be good for the planet, per se, it did clear the skies of northern and western Europe of aircraft for some weeks. By the end of that time, it was clear (again if you'll excuse the pun) that the skies were noticeably bluer than they had been before.

We're not at the stage of an extinction-level event yet, such as the eruption of the super-volcano underneath the Yellowstone National Park in the USA or where climate change would become irreversible, so there's reason to hope for the future.

In a large way, the covid pandemic has shown us what that future can look like, and people around the world have enjoyed the clear blue skies and clean air that came with repeated lockdowns. Now the pressure is on to capitalize on that and to create and perfect technologies we can all use to live a more sustainable lifestyle.

What Can We Do Today?

While some of these technologies are some way off development or are just too expensive or difficult to produce in the present, there are still things you can do today. Perhaps the first step is to calculate your own carbon footprint, and many online resources exist to help you with this task.

It's important to be honest with these calculators, as it's not like your doctor asking if you drink too much, in which case you're almost never going to tell them the real truth and they know it. These calculators can tell you how much carbon you and your business or organization emit in a year, and they can also give you advice on how to reduce it.

Organizations and websites such as `www.carbonfootprint.com` and `www.carbontrust.com` can help you determine your carbon footprint. There is also help and support from governments with both the Environmental Protection Agency in the USA (`www3.epa.gov/carbon-footprint-calculator`) and the British government in the UK (`www.gov.uk/guidance/carbon-calculator`) offering carbon calculators.

Even for companies operating fleets of vehicles, calculators are available such as this one from CommercialFleet.org (`https://pcs.tv/3BklB1u`). Even major tech companies are providing help and support, with IBM offering their own carbon calculator service online for businesses, which you can find at `https://pcs.tv/4euxale`.

Government Help and Support

For some businesses and organizations, however, there are things they want to do and things they can do, but often the finance acts as a barrier. In 2021 the BBC reported that many businesses in the UK were calling on the British government to provide support in the form of grants, to help them achieve their and the government's net-zero targets.

This is where business groups and organizations can come into their own. These organizations act as a bridge between business and local, state, and national governments. They're able to lobby government authorities on behalf of businesses and inform business of what help and support is available to them.

Plugging into these business groups then is a crucial thing for your business or organization to do. We've covered a lot in this book about the things you can do, from increasing recycling to using advanced architectural techniques and new technologies, but that's not the end of the story.

There are, as we have already seen in this chapter, new technologies and options becoming available to us all the time. Either as a large corporation or as an individual householder, the amount of work, effort, and innovation being put into sustainability is impossible to keep up with.

Indeed, I would imagine that you might have gone into reading this book thinking it was 90% about installing solar panels and wind farms, when in fact there are *so* many more options available. There are experts out there, they don't need to cost any money or at least any more money than you're already paying them, and they can very often hold the answers you seek.

It's a Marathon, Not a Sprint

While it's very clear that we need to act imminently then to avoid a climate disaster, and climate change becoming irreversible, it's also clear that this is a marathon and not a sprint. We're in this for the long haul and there are costs involved.

I'm fairly certain that you don't have the thousands or millions of dollars just lying around that's needed to make your business or organization completely carbon neutral or even carbon negative. If you do, these things take time. Even the major technology companies such as Microsoft, Google, and Apple have figured that out.

You can't slap up wind turbines overnight, and if you want to create a new, environmentally sustainable headquarters for your company as Apple did with their Apple Park, it can be a slow process. This circular building is covered in solar panels, generates its own electricity, and has features to reduce and recycle water. What it isn't though was quick to produce. Steve Jobs first announced the project to Cupertino city council in April 2006, ground wasn't broken until 2013, and it was April 2017, 11 years after the first plan was submitted, that employees started moving in.

New Microsoft buildings, recently made on Microsoft campus, are also collecting rainwater (and there is a lot in Seattle) and use it for toilets and air conditioners.

Building sustainability for your business then should be considered a bit like many other aspects of life, little and often. You do what you can, you plan, you invest, you roll it out, and then you evaluate and start planning for the next thing, exactly as you would do in your daily life with your business, your home, or indeed your family.

Pulling Together

This is where the point of everybody being more sustainable comes into sharp focus. There are around seven billion people on the planet, around 55% of whom live in urban areas, with this expected to rise to 68% by 2050 according to the United Nations. Everybody doing something, even if it's something small, all helps create a much bigger impact overall.

It might be that somebody's personal or business circumstances mean they can't do much. It could be they only recycle, which might be mandatory for them anyway, or a business can set more efficient power settings on their PCs and computers. The effect might appear miniscule to them or even to you, but it's when everybody does it that things begin to change.

We are all in the same boat, but as the saying goes, we are not all up the same creek without a paddle. We can act individually or collectively, we can lobby governments at every level, we can make changes in our processes and in how we live and work, and we can innovate, something I'm pretty certain you've been used to doing in your own line of work.

Summary

While there are exciting technologies coming along definitely and potentially, which can help reduce the impact of climate change and even reverse climate change in some ways while also helping improve people's health and reduce pollution in the environment, what else might we see into the future that, so far anyway, is so distant as to be difficult to predict?

That's where we'll go in the final chapter of this book, to look into our crystal ball and try to predict where the world might be in 20, 50, or 100 years' time. You never know, there might even be a flying car in it!

CHAPTER 14

IT and the Future

On December 17, 1903, two brothers, Orville and Wilbur Wright, made their first controlled, sustained flight of their engine-powered aircraft, the Wright Flyer. They flew it for 6 km south of Kitty Hawk, South Carolina. Shortly afterward, Wilbur said, "Not within a thousand years will man ever fly." Today, just over 100 years later, roughly 100,000 flights take off and land each day around the world.

In 1945, working at the US Army Ballistic Research Laboratory, two men, John Mauchly and J. Presper Eckert, created ENIAC, the world's first programmable, electronic, general-purpose digital computer. ENIAC contained 18,000 vacuum tubes and 5,000,000 hand-soldered joints; was 2 m (8 ft) tall, 1 m (3 ft) deep, and 30 m (100 ft) long; took up 28 m² (300 sq. ft.) of space; and consumed 150 kW of electricity. ENIAC was programmed using punched cards and could perform around 500 floating-point operations per second (FLOPS).

Just 13 years later, on September 12, 1958, engineer Jack Kilby working for Texas Instruments demonstrated the world's first integrated circuit, and by 1971 a process had been developed to squeeze all of the processor technology needed for a computer central processing unit (CPU) onto a single chip – a huge leap from a room-sized computer to one that fits in the palm of your hand in just over 25 years.

The Intel 4004, released in 1971, was the first commercially available microprocessor. It had a 4-bit data bus and used a 10-micrometer (μm) manufacturing process. It had a clock rate of 1 MHz and could perform approximately 92,000 operations per second.

© Mike Halsey 2025
M. Halsey, *The Green IT Guide*, https://doi.org/10.1007/979-8-8688-1233-0_14

Today, we have processors capable of multiple GHz operations, and they are an order of magnitude faster and more advanced than their older brethren. Modern Intel, AMD, and Qualcomm processors can perform around 350 billion operations per second, and instead of having a manufacturing process measured in micrometers, they have a manufacturing process of 4 nanometers (nm), a thousand times as small. Research is also underway to produce 2 nm and 1 nm manufacturing processes, and to compare, a strand of DNA is 2.5 nm in diameter.

To put all this into context, the oldest known fossils of *Homo sapiens*, our own species as there were other species of human that came before, are around 315,000 years old, with *Homo antecessor* being around 1.2 million years old. Given that we went from the first flight to space travel in around 50 years and from calculating using abacuses to advanced computers in the same time period, this shows the pace of technological advancement for the human race has occurred in the vary last, and smallest, tiny fraction of our time spent on Earth.

So if advances have been made so quickly, and in such a short space of time, what can and will the future hold for technology and its place in our societies?

Predicting the Pace of Change

Moore's Law is the standard by which we have judged the pace of technological change. Gordon Moore was the co-founder of Intel, and in 1965 he proposed that the number of transistors in an integrated circuit would double roughly every two years. This has largely proven to be accurate, though as we push further and further downward in scale, we inevitably begin to hit barriers, such as the physical barrier of what happens when you produce transistors 2 nm in size or smaller.

Given that a single gold atom is one third of a nanometer in diameter, it's easy to see that we might soon hit a ceiling of what's possible with modern electronics.

Then we look at the development of the software designed to run on those circuits and processors. The first commercially available spreadsheet for modern desktop computers was VisiCalc, released for the Apple II in 1979. Lotus 1-2-3 was the first spreadsheet released for the IBM PC in 1982. These programs were tiny by comparison with modern computers, having to fit on a 5 1/4-inch floppy disk, which at the time had a typical capacity of 360 KB (kilobytes) and then 1.2 MB. Today, Microsoft Excel is a multi-gigabyte download and capable of far more calculations and operations than were possible 40 years before.

One of the earliest computer graphics packages was SuperPaint, first designed in 1972 at Xerox PARC and later released for the Apple Macintosh in 1986. Adobe Photoshop was first released in 1990, but now we're using AI in the form of Large Language Models (LLMs) and General Models (GMs) to have the computer on our desk, in our hand, or in the cloud create images for us. All we have to do is describe them to the machine.

I wrote a lot about AI in Chapter 5, especially about how it's not current AI, but it's come so far in such a very short space of time that it's difficult not to ask what it will be capable of in a few more years.

The Future Is Quantum

Much of our computing has moved to the cloud in the last ten years. This has taken many different forms, from services that analyze enormous data sets to web apps that handle email. More and more people are living entirely within a browser on their computers, with everything they do taking place in the cloud.

I wrote earlier in this book about quantum computing, that next big thing that's so complex and so completely different from what we've become used to that it's difficult to get our heads around it. I have decades of experience in high-power computing, but the concept of a quantum bit (qubit) that can exist in both positive and negative states simultaneously and how quantum entanglement can be used to perform calculations in ways that are vastly different from the methods we use now is enough to make an average person's head explode, and to me, just looking at the math is enough to give me a serious headache.

However, to horribly misquote science fiction author H. G. Wells for a moment, "minds immeasurably superior to ours" are working on creating just such devices. One day they will succeed, and they tell us the math is sound and that it's just a matter of time before they find ways to make quantum computing viable.

The very first quantum computers will be an order of magnitude faster than the computers we use today, but will still operate like a horse and buggy compared with what they'll eventually become. So what will the first quantum computers be used for?

Very clearly the first quantum computers will be put to use ironing out their own flaws and issues, before being tasked with creating the second generation of quantum computers or at least assisting scientists with their own research. This doesn't mean they'll be able to self-replicate and rise up against us though, as the computers and software we have today can be and have for many years been used to help design what comes next.

Following this, there will be pressing medical and scientific uses for the technology such as finding cures for cancer and other major diseases. The environment will be a pressing issue, including finding practical solutions for climate change. Other uses will then follow such as creating reliable and sustainable nuclear fusion and clean, free energy. Eventually we will use quantum computers to help explore the universe and explain complex physics and the nature of life itself.

I think it's safe to say at this point that none of this will be particularly helpful to your business or organization. Modern computers can already reliably transcribe different languages in live meetings, and many if not most or even all of the tasks required in business and government today can be handled by a single modern PC.

The Security of Quantum Computing

Where quantum computing *will* undeniably affect IT in business and government is on the matter of security. A conventional computer today would need about 300 trillion years to crack the typical 256-bit encryption used by our computer systems. A future quantum computer could potentially crack that in under 10 seconds.

Now, this isn't going to happen any time soon. According to researchers, such a device would require an operational level of more than 4,000 qubits. Google's quantum computer project aims to have a 1,000-qubit operation by the end of 2029. It is possible though that within 15 years, maybe sooner, we'll have to think extremely seriously about data security.

This is even more important when you consider that it's not just companies like IBM, Microsoft, and Google and universities like the Massachusetts Institute of Technology (MIT) developing quantum computers. Nation states are also working to develop the technology and investing heavily in some parts of the world. Imagine then a Chinese quantum computer able to break the encryption used by the Pentagon, the CIA, or the NSA or a quantum computer owned by a rogue billionaire (because we already know these people exist – Ed) who thinks it's time for the people to know about alien life or the dark secrets of the US government.

Today we're focused on data privacy and trying to define what privacy is in a world where hacking is everywhere and it's becoming increasingly tough to secure the data of customers and the general public. A data breach of the magnitude I just detailed could lead to revolution, the fall of entire governments and governmental structures, and even global war.

If we're worried about what an AI can do today to spread misinformation during an election campaign, just imagine what a quantum computer with the equivalent processing potential of a human brain could achieve.

Fortunately for us, the chances of any of this realistically happening in our own lifetimes are incredibly slim. It's far more likely that quantum computing will be used to solve the problems facing the world, and where some actors could use the technology to break encryption, it's also reasonable to assume that the same technology can be used to find new ways to secure that data.

What's important though is that we all understand the different ways new technologies can *potentially* be used, so that we can regulate where appropriate, lobby where appropriate, and prepare where necessary.

The Power of AI

In Chapter 5 I detailed the challenges and benefits of Large Language Model (artificial intelligence) technologies, including the massive power consumption required by these tools, but now these features are being brought down to PC, laptop, and even smartphone level, which hugely helps reduce that consumption.

Later in this chapter I'll also detail how nuclear fusion reactors will, when the technology is properly developed, almost certainly provide limitless clean energy for everybody.

All of this means that these tools aren't going away. In fact already we're seeing some of the software we're using today including Photoshop and AutoCAD getting new tools and features that take advantage of an NPU (Neural Processing Unit) in the latest PCs to allow people to get their work done more quickly, more effectively, and perhaps with a little more flair as well.

This all means that while many people, including myself, can't see a use for this technology in our working and home lives today, in the future we will almost certainly embrace some of what is coming in the same way we embraced online shopping and banking, social media, and cloud computing.

Future Climate Technology

Throughout this book, and especially in Chapter 13, I detailed some of the amazing new technologies being developed that can help us solve climate change or at least clean up some of the damage that's been done to the environment. Clean technology though isn't just about the climate; it's about powering the future of humanity.

Let's take the current experiments taking place around the world to create nuclear fusion reactors. The current generation of nuclear reactors use a process called nuclear fission. Fission is the process of slamming a neutron into a larger atom, forcing it to split into two smaller atoms, and releasing energy in the process. Every time an atom is split a huge amount of energy is released. We use the radioactive isotopes uranium and plutonium for fission reactions, but these produce radioactive waste that can take thousands or even tens of thousands of years to break down.

Fusion works in a different way. In a nuclear fusion reaction two atoms are slammed together so that they combine and form a heavier atom; this uses the elements deuterium and tritium, which are isotopes of hydrogen, and this is the same process that powers the sun. The energy produced is much more than that produced by fission; it's clean, producing no CO_2 and no nuclear waste and with its waste elements able to be recycled in just 100 years. There's no risk of a meltdown as has happened in the past with nuclear fission reactors, and it's almost completely self-sustaining, requiring very little energy to keep the reaction going after it's begun.

This clean energy is as important to battling climate change as anything we could be doing today. Imagine what clean, almost limitless energy could do for the planet. The closure of coal, gas, and nuclear power stations. No further need for oil to power vehicles as electricity would be considerably less costly. New ways to power aircraft and space travel, the power of a small fusion reactor being just what's needed to push a rocket into orbit or a plane around the world. We might also see small personal fusion reactors for communities, business, or individual homes in the same way that companies including Rolls Royce are already producing small fission reactors today.

A world in which the most remote communities have reliable power, cities run on completely clean energy, and there are the resultant benefits to health and well-being that would inevitably come from that, not just for humanity but plants and animals. The future of a green and prosperous planet could very well be made possible by nuclear fusion.

It's All Up in the Air

In December 2022, the Massachusetts Institute of Technology (MIT) announced that a US-based startup called *Make Sunsets* was releasing reflective sulfur particles into the atmosphere in an attempt to ease the effect of global warming by creating cloud (`https://pcs.tv/4dia2Fa`). This is effectively mimicking the effect created by volcanic eruptions.

This process is not without controversy. Called "geoengineering," it's effectively a form of weather control, and we all know that a change in the weather in location A can have a knock-on effect to places B, C, D, and so on, right around the planet.

This isn't actually a new solution. For some years now companies including Mercedes have been spraying different substances into the atmosphere above their plants to reduce clouds and, in the case of Mercedes, help prevent rain from falling on new vehicles in the massive car parks at their factories.

The Chinese government used the same method to help keep the air clear and sunny throughout the 2008 Beijing Olympic games. There are other studies, too, into how this type of activity could help the planet and help reduce the effect of global warming.

It's been found, for example, that some substances, including salt and gold, can, when released into the atmosphere, reflect heat from the sun back into space. Now gold is understandably expensive, but there are already projects around the world testing this with salt and saltwater.

As I've already mentioned, geoengineering (a.k.a. weather control) is highly controversial, given that most of the worst effects of climate change come in the form of extreme weather events (wildfires, flooding, landslips, hurricanes, etc.), and affecting the clouds and the weather above your own country can and will inevitably have knock-on effects with communities in neighboring countries at least. This will be an interesting technology field to watch, however.

Societal Changes

There are major societal changes that in some cases are coming and in other cases might happen in the future that can help reduce the impact of climate change on the planet.

One of these is with the construction industry and building maintenance. Around 11% of global carbon emissions come from the construction industry. This is because of the enormous carbon cost of producing concrete. A study by Princeton University Student Climate Initiative in 2020 found that the creation of one pound of concrete produced 0.93 pounds of carbon dioxide (https://pcs.tv/4ekcGMk). Now, scientists are working on ways to produce cardon-free concrete.

Building maintenance, which includes the heating and running of commercial buildings around the world, accounts for around 28% of global carbon emissions. There are huge amounts of work being put into research on how the emissions from buildings and construction can be reduced. These come both in the form of carbon-capture technologies for the production of concrete and other construction materials like steel and in the form of smarter building and construction techniques, including making buildings sustainable by design and repurposing existing buildings instead of constructing new ones.

Changes will inevitably be implemented to transportation, especially public transport as investment continues into hydrogen-powered vehicles. Currently hydrogen fuel is expensive and difficult to produce, but as one of the most abundant substances in the universe, and where the only emission is water, it's clear we will begin seeing hydrogen charging for vehicles in the coming years.

This also ties into cities and entire nations trying to encourage the public to use public transportation instead of their own vehicles, as currently around 23% of global carbon emissions come from transport. We might sneer at the thought of a hundred delivery vans in our local area every day dropping off everything from groceries to Amazon packages, but this is still a substantial drop from the thousands of vehicles that would be on the road if every household had to travel to collect these things themselves.

Then there are changes to the food we eat and how it's grown and produced. I wrote early in this book how my own dogs eat biscuits made partly from insects. These are high in protein, extremely sustainable as they breed extremely quickly, and very tasty when mixed with some vegetables. Insect-based diets along with other foods such as meats made entirely from plants and vegetable proteins will in time fill more of our own diets, and we may not even realize what we're eating comes from an insect or a plant and not from a cow.

Smart Energy

Research is also well underway into smart energy grids, capable of scaling production up and down quickly to meet demand. Way back at the beginning of this book, I wrote about how the biggest waste of energy from electrical and electronic devices comes in the form of heat and noise. If your PC is getting hot, then that's energy the device isn't using, but that's being created and then being expelled. Conversely if you walk past an electricity substation in your area and hear a low buzzing sound, that is the sound of energy being wasted.

It's very true that there is no single energy production method on the planet that has a 100% conversion rate, so some energy will always be lost until we solve this, but if in addition to working to increase those rates, the energy grid itself can more quickly adapt to the needs of the grid and the country at the time, less energy will be wasted and less carbon will be pumped into the atmosphere as a result.

Let's take the example of a coal-fired or a nuclear power station. These operate in similar ways from the standpoint of energy production in that any changes made to the amount of energy they produce must be slow and changed over a period of hours or days. It's simply not possible currently to have these power stations suddenly reduce their output to 30% at night when less energy is needed. The amount of energy being produced stays the same throughout each full 24-hour period, and it has to be stored somehow or used.

Having an energy grid that is more adaptable can only reduce carbon emissions considerably, but this technology could still be some way off into the future.

Wasn't the Future Supposed to Be Flying Cars?

Think back to the cartoons and movies of the 1950s and 1960s, and flying cars were everywhere – this was the future of humanity, with super-tall gleaming skyscrapers, robots helping with domestic chores and throwing a frisbee for the dog, and everybody happy and enjoying life to the fullest.

At the other end of the scale sits Ridley Scott's depiction of Los Angeles in 2019 (2019? Geez! – Ed) in the movie *Blade Runner* (Warner Bros., 1982) as a smog-filled, constantly rainy, dark, and gloomy place with a foreboding atmosphere.

Flying cars could still be a thing, especially with the current testing of drone passenger vehicles and aircraft powered entirely by hydrogen fuel. It's also possible that the more dystopian world depicted in *Blade Runner* could be in our future to at least some degree. The truth is we simply don't know and can't predict it.

Live in the Moment!

This is why I always say we should be conscious of the future and what the possibilities of living in it might be, not just for us but for future generations, but we shouldn't dwell.

The reason for this goes back to what I said about a computer wasting energy as heat and noise. Humans are very good at wasting energy, too, and this can come in many forms. The one I'm talking about though is worrying about things you can't change, can't predict, or won't happen for a long time anyway.

If we spend our days worrying about what might be, we're not putting that energy into what's happening *now*. This is why, while we are concerned about the future of the planet and the future of humanity, it's great to see that so many scientists and organizations around the world from universities to charities are already well into researching everything from the future of cement to food, transport, weather, flights, shipping, forests, consumption, manufacturing, and more.

The planet will be here long after we are; it was here for billions of years before we got here, remember, and has been teeming with life for most of that time. Our concern, and quite rightly, is for our own survival and prosperity. Humanity won't survive if we make our planet inhospitable to us, but worrying about what the Earth will look like in 100 or 200 years isn't helping.

What does help is concentrating on today, what we can all do, how we can make positive changes, and how we can inspire the people around us. That's where we come in. You and I between us are already doing things. I've detailed in this book what I'm doing, and I'm always striving to do more, and you'll know what you're doing and want to achieve.

Closing Thoughts

The future is now, the future is bright, and the future is what we make it. We achieve all of this by living in the moment, looking at the world and our environment in a positive way, and asking what we can be doing that's better. That, frankly, is all anybody can ever ask of us as it's a healthy and a positive way to live.

If you can take other people with you on the journey, that's even better still. I was very lucky that Apress invited me to write this book and also consider myself very fortunate that they later invited me to update it for a second edition. That's one of my contributions, to try and cut through the noise and the confusion and to help people including yourself see that it's not doom and gloom and that there's actually a hell of a lot already being done and a lot of excitement and positivity about the future and about climate change. I hope I've achieved this.

All I can ask is that you take that positivity; build on it with your own thoughts, words, and actions; don't look back; and don't worry too much about tomorrow. Tomorrow is another day, and the sun is always rising somewhere in the world.

Index

© Mike Halsey 2025
M. Halsey, *The Green IT Guide*, https://doi.org/10.1007/979-8-8688-1233-0